KOHUT'S FREUDIAN VISION

KOHUT'S FREUDIAN VISION

Philip F. D. Rubovits-Seitz

in collaboration with
Heinz Kohut

THE ANALYTIC PRESS

1999   Hillsdale, NJ   London

Published by
The Analytic Press, Inc., Publishers
Editorial Offices:
101 West Street
Hillsdale, New Jersey 07642

www.analyticpress.com

Typeset by CompuDesign, Rego Park, NY

Index by Leonard S. Rosenbaum

Library of Congress Cataloging-in-Publication Data

Rubovits-Seitz, Philip F. D., 1921–
Kohut's Freudian vision / Philip F. D. Rubovits-Seitz in collaboration with Heinz Kohut.
p.   cm.
Includes bibliographical references and index.
ISBN 0-88163-284-8
1. Psychoanalysis. 2. Kohut, Heinz. I. Kohut, Heinz. II. Title.
BF173.R785   1999
150.19'5'092–dc21   98-47795
                                                              CIP

Printed in the United States of America
10 9 8 7 6 5 4 3 2 1

To Randi

Contents

Acknowledgments

I am indebted most of all to Heinz Kohut, M.D., who was second only to Freud in helping me understand the complex theoretical system of psychoanalysis. I am grateful also to Professor Thomas A. Kohut for his encouragement and cooperation regarding the publication of his father's lectures on psychoanalytic theory. Professor Kohut has indicated to me that he is pleased that his father's lectures on psychoanalytic psychology are being published. "I am very familiar with those lectures," he said; "I used my father's copy to prepare for my final exam at the Cincinnati Psychoanalytic Institute. I think those lectures really are impressive, revealing a side of my father that very few people know, and I hope therefore that they will finally be published" (personal communication, 1996). I am grateful to Professor Kohut also for his suggestions regarding the organization and content of Part IV.

My old friend and former editor, Natalie Altman, kindly advised me regarding publication of the present volume. The editorial assistance of John Kerr and Nancy J. Liguori of The Analytic Press has been invaluable in preparing the manuscript for publication.

I am grateful to my son, Franz Seitz, Ph.D., for sharing his expertise with me regarding linguistics, psycholinguistics, and cognitive science, and also for his technical assistance, including the computer graphic reproductions of Kohut's diagrams in the "Lectures on Psychoanalytic Psychology." I extend especially warm thanks to Randi Rubovits-Seitz, M.D., whose help and encouragement have sustained me every step of the way.

Introduction

Long before his development of self psychology, Heinz Kohut was considered by many of his colleagues and students to be the best theoretician and teacher at the Chicago Institute for Psychoanalysis. Kohut took pride in his "intellectual and emotional commitment to classical analysis" (Kohut, 1978b, p. 932):

> I had studied classical theory and knew it well. I knew it well enough to be able to separate the wheat from the chaff. That allowed me, in the metapsychology courses that I taught for many years at the Chicago Institute, to deemphasize those parts of traditional theory that did not seem to be relevant and explanatory and to emphasize those that did [pp. 932–933].

Even the framework that Kohut (1978b) proposed for self psychology stressed his commitment to traditional psychoanalysis. He set himself three criteria for the formulation of this theoretical structure: First, "the new psychology of the self must remain in an unbroken continuum with traditional psychoanalytic theory"; second, it must "not disregard the fact that the classical theories, especially as expanded in the form of modern ego psychology, though applicable in only a restricted area, are neither in error nor irrelevant"; and third, the new theory "must not be dogmatic and definitive, but open to change and capable of further development" (p. 937).

I was a colleague, collaborator, coteacher, and friend of Kohut's for over a decade at the Chicago Institute, prior to his development of self psychology. He was a dedicated Freudian scholar, theorist, clinician, and teacher throughout his psychoanalytic

career. He emphasized the necessary complexity of psychoanalytic psychology and devoted much of his creative energy to explicating and teaching that complexity. He succeeded in making the
intricacies of Freudian theory comprehensible—not by simplify-
ing it, but by means of a unique, nonreductive synthesis.

Because current interest in Kohut's work has focused so completely on self psychology, some of his best thinking—particularly his synthesis of Freudian theory—is in danger of being lost.
Most of his writings have been collected in a series of volumes,
The Search for the Self, edited by Paul Ornstein (1978a,b, 1991a,b),
but many of his pre–self-psychological writings consist of book
reviews, panel discussions, and correspondence that do not
reveal the psychological depth and breadth of Kohut's Freudian
vision. The chapter that Kohut and I coauthored on "Concepts
and Theories of Psychoanalysis" (Kohut and Seitz, 1963) may
come closest to demonstrating his grasp of psychoanalytic theory. Unlike most of us, however, Kohut was at his very best in
explicating psychoanalytic theory when he was lecturing. With
that in mind, it occurred to me that perhaps the most effective
way of presenting Kohut's synthesis of Freudian theory would be
through a previously unpublished compendium of his lectures on
psychoanalytic psychology, which I wrote some years ago in collaboration with Kohut.

During the decade or so preceding his development of self
psychology, Kohut taught a two-year theory course on psychoanalytic psychology to candidates at the Chicago Institute for
Psychoanalysis. Looking back on the experience some years later,
Kohut (1972–1976) described the course in the following way:

> It was a two-year course given in the second and third years of
> the curriculum, and it dealt with psychoanalytic theory using a
> mixture of a chronological and a systematic approach. I gradu-
> ally developed in these courses an approach to the development
> of psychoanalysis from a chronological point of view, from its
> inception with Breuer's Anna O., and the conceptual scientific
> breakthrough by Freud regarding the meaning of Anna O. on
> "chimney sweeping." From those beginnings, I tried to show how
> the subsequent sequence of discoveries and of theoretical for-
> mulations was not just an accidental development, but seemed
> to be, really, an unfolding of a kind of predetermined schedule
> of discovery and formulation, which, on the whole, I think could
> be shown rather nicely. First, there was a crude conceptualiza-
> tion, the penetration to hidden material as if one were opening
> an abscess, disregarding all the intervening structures. This was

an approach in which any means were considered to be all right to reach unconscious material directly. Of course, it all began with hypnosis, as you know. Then, gradually, more and more attention was paid to the intervening structures. Then it was no longer so much a question of what was to be reached in the course of the analytic exploration, but *how* it was to be reached and *what* the intervening structures, the defenses, were and what the development was that took place on the basis of whatever the unknown enclave of the early childhood traumatic experience was. And it became increasingly important, of course, to learn *how* this defensive development took place. In other words, how out of an id psychology an ego psychology gradually developed; how, out of a therapeutic and explorative approach of robbing the unconscious of its contents through hypnosis, there gradually developed the type of analysis we now call resistance analysis, analysis by free association, or character analysis. In brief, the intervening structures became more and more important rather than what was to be penetrated to. So, in general this was the approach I took during those many years [pp. 125–126].

Kohut's mastery of psychoanalytic theory, combined with his expressive use of language and extemporaneous style of lecturing, made the course a memorable experience for students. Paul Ornstein (1978c) described his own response to Kohut's lectures this way:

What struck me most in these lectures was Kohut's precision—he insisted upon nuances of meaning, as if we were dealing with an "exact science"—showing us the logic of the creative leap from the clinical data to clinical theory and to metapsychology, and at the same time invariably showed us the areas of uncertainty, the vagueness and ambiguity of certain concepts and those areas where basic knowledge was still lacking. Equally striking was the ability to move with ease from the clinical to the theoretical and from the theoretical to the clinical, so that we had an immediate sense of the basic clinical data upon which psychoanalytic theory had been built [p. 3].

Ornstein added that Kohut's presentations "appeared unique; an idiosyncratic gift for synthesis" (pp. 3–4)—an observation that corresponds closely with my own conclusion that Kohut's synthesis of Freudian theory, and even the continuities that he constructed between traditional psychoanalysis and his later concepts of narcissism and self psychology, were products of a highly developed capacity for syncretic reasoning.

My collaboration with Kohut began in 1958, three years after I joined the staff of the Chicago Institute. Kohut had not yet begun to teach his course on psychoanalytic psychology when I was a student at the Chicago Institute (from 1950 to 1955), but soon after I became a member of the Institute staff I began hearing from students how excited they were by his lectures. I asked Kohut if I could audit his course, to which he agreed. The lectures were given weekly for two years, on alternate weekends, to second- and third-year candidates. I did not take part actively in the class discussions—that is, questions raised by students and answers by Kohut—but merely listened and took careful notes of the lectures and discussions.

Like the students, I found the lectures both fascinating and highly informative, but I also had many questions about the contents of the lectures that I needed and wanted to discuss with Kohut. He agreed to meet with me after each class to discuss any points that were not clear to me. Those meetings soon led to our collaboration on the extensive notes I was making of the lectures. Evidently he recognized some potential in my notes for a future publication, which materialized subsequently in the chapter we published together in 1963. Our meetings following each class thus came to include not only my questions about that day's lecture, but also a review of the revisions I had made of the previous week's lecture notes, based on Kohut's clarifications and elaborations.

By the end of the two-year course, my distillation and reworking of the lecture notes formed a compendium of 125 pages. All of the wording and phraseology of the compendium were my own, the conceptual content Kohut's. Perhaps because his native tongue was German, he sometimes used rather long and involved sentences, which was less of a problem in listening to his lectures than it was in written form. My writing of the compendium was guided by two goals: to record the substantive content of the lectures accurately and to make the material as clear, readable, and understandable as possible. I made two copies of the compendium, one for Kohut and the other for me. To prepare the compendium for its present publication I revised the text still further to clarify remaining ambiguities, to increase readability, and to eliminate repetitions.

Following our work together on my lecture notes and the compendium, Kohut asked me to become the substitute teacher for his course, taking over for him when he was out of town,

which occurred frequently during those years because of his positions as Secretary and then President of the American Psychoanalytic Association. He suggested also that we collaborate on a
chapter he had been asked to write for a book entitled *Concepts of
Personality* (Wepman and Heine, 1963). I agreed to participate in
both projects, which led to a continuation and expansion of our
collaboration. The compendium proved invaluable for both the
teaching and writing projects: It served as an instructional guide
for me in teaching the course, and I used it as the basis for writing the first draft of the chapter.

Collaboration with Kohut was very satisfying intellectually but
at times could be difficult. He was a stickler for what Ornstein
(1978c, p. 3) called "precision," insisting on just the right word or
phrase for what he was thinking—sometimes at the expense of
the overall sense and sound of a sentence. In his correspondence
with Anna Freud, she had called attention to Kohut's overly frequent use of "insertions" in his sentences—an attempt to be as
accurate and comprehensive as possible but that had a distracting
effect on the reader. Despite her advice, Kohut remained tireless
in his search for the exact wording of concepts. If I suggested that
we move on, he protested that we had to "get it right." I was more
interested in getting the job done; Kohut was intent on precision
of thought and language (see, e.g., Kohut, 1981a, p. 525, in which
he referred to himself as "very persnickety" about the final form
of his writings—which was not the case, however, when he was
lecturing. He was spontaneous and never at a loss for words
when lecturing). In spite of our differences—or perhaps partly
because of them, in the sense of complementarity—we stuck
with the project and completed the chapter entitled "Concepts
and Theories of Psychoanalysis" (Kohut and Seitz, 1963), which is
included as Part II of the present volume.

By the time the chapter was completed, I had done enough
substitute teaching for Kohut that he suggested I teach one year
of the two-year course and he the other. After doing that for a
couple of years, Kohut withdrew from the course completely and
turned it over to me. From my standpoint, taking over the course
was a mixed blessing. There was some satisfaction in being able
to teach the entire course, but at the same time I realized that
Kohut would be a very hard, if not impossible, act to follow. My
style of teaching was much less didactic than Kohut's, and the
students wanted more lecturing. More specifically, of course,
what they wanted was more Kohut.

Before I left the Institute in 1966, Kohut and I had begun collaborating on two further writing projects—one on "Varieties of Psychological Structures" and the other on "Three Sectors of Psychological Functioning" (the sectors of transference, progressive neutralization, and creativity). Both of those projects were based on notes and outlines of various lectures Kohut had presented to psychoanalytic organizations. After I left the Institute neither of us could sustain sufficient interest in the projects, however, so they were never completed.

The compendium of Kohut's lectures on psychoanalytic psychology (1958–1960) is published for the first time as Part I of this volume. I believe that these lectures, in combination with the 1963 chapter based on the compendium, represent the best illustrations so far available of Kohut's mastery and unique synthesis of Freudian theory. To be sure, some aspects of the lectures seem out of date now—for example, some of the metapsychological theorizing and the almost exclusive focus on intrapsychic events—but much of the material is still relevant, not only historically with respect to the development of Freud's theoretical system but also to both ego and self psychology, as well as to the psychoanalytic theory of therapy. The fact that each lecture has been compressed into just a few pages of writing inevitably changes the tone of the presentations from their original extemporaneous lecturing mode to that of a carefully worded summary. Still another difference is that the writing style is my own rather than Kohut's, so that much of Kohut's charisma as a teacher was lost in my transformation of his spoken words into a concise written text. On the other hand, the basic conceptual content of the lectures is faithfully recorded and was checked and rechecked by Kohut.

I hope that present-day psychoanalysts, including self psychologists, will find these lectures as fascinating and informative as I did, and still do. Not only is Kohut's interpretation of Freudian theory still relevant in most respects, but also the Freudian foundations on which he constructed his concepts of narcissism and self psychology are indispensable to an understanding of Kohut's subsequent contributions (see, e.g., Kohut, 1984, p. 221, n.1). As Kohut commented in a later series of lectures on self psychology, "all these insights that we now have could not have been arrived at if we did not already know all these things that Freud discovered" (1972–1976, p. 356).

Part III of the present volume is an attempt to understand Kohut's method of synthesizing Freudian theory. I restudied

Kohut's lectures on psychoanalytic psychology, as well as the essay we wrote on psychoanalytic theory, in an effort to discover how he dealt with the complexities of this "loosely concatenated theoretical system" (Kaplan, 1964, p. 298) without resorting to oversimplification. I found that Kohut appeared to focus frequently on syncretistic concepts in Freud's writings—that is, concepts that combine, unite, or synthesize phenomena that differ from or oppose each other in specific ways. I was struck by the variety of instances in which Kohut seemed to zero in on syncretic concepts in Freud's writings and then use them to integrate and explicate psychoanalytic theory. To illustrate that finding, I present numerous examples in which Kohut appeared to draw on Freud's use of a syncretizing strategy to formulate his concepts and theories.

Part IV extends the findings of Part III to Kohut's later investigations of narcissism and self psychology. By restudying Kohut's writings on the latter subjects as well as related material in Freud's volumes, I have found numerous examples in which the posited syncretic propensity that seemed to characterize Kohut's earlier synthesis of Freudian theory appears to have been operative also in the many continuities that he constructed between traditional psychoanalysis and his developing concepts of narcissism and self psychology. Thus even in the final and most fully developed phases of his work, Kohut's Freudian vision appears to have illuminated his investigations, concepts, and theories.

KOHUT'S FREUDIAN VISION

Part I

Kohut's Lectures on Psychoanalytic Psychology

(1958–1960)

HEINZ KOHUT AND PHILIP F. D. SEITZ

Lecture 1

Three Periods in the Development of Psychoanalysis

This course is an introduction to the theories developed by Freud. Psychoanalytic theory is not a fixed body of knowledge, but has undergone continuous change. The course will not attempt to follow a strict chronological progression from the case of Anna O. to the latest papers in the *International Journal*. Instead, the theory will be discussed in large "chunks," only more or less historically ordered. What is presented from the past will be colored by what we know now.

The first phase (approximately the first year of the course) covers from the beginning with Breuer and Anna O. up to around 1920, when Freud began writing a new set of papers: "Beyond the Pleasure Principle" (1920); "Group Psychology and the Analysis of the Ego" (1921); "The Ego and the Id" (1923); and "Inhibitions, Symptoms and Anxiety" (1926a). The second phase extended from 1920 to 1937, and the third phase, which is not covered by this course, extended from 1937 to the present. This course attempts to provide perspective on your assigned reading—that is, a pulling together and systematizing of what you will read.

The first period might be labelled with catchwords like "The Period of the Id," "the Unconscious," and "Infantile Sexuality," but those terms do not really express what happened then. It is true that the main interest at that time was on the overwhelmingly new experiences of the Unconscious—forces within a person that he or she knows nothing about but which impel the person to behave in certain ways. Very soon, however, Freud came to see the Unconscious as the remnant of infantile psychological life, infantile sexuality, and childhood drives.

3

The second period is the one we think of these days in connection with the structural point of view, characterized by the systems id, ego, superego, and external world. Separation of the first two phases is artificial, however, unless one thinks of the distinction in terms of emphasis at the two times. The concept of ego, for example, was well known to Freud as early as the 1890s but was not given much emphasis at that time. Freud concentrated instead on the more impressive discoveries of infantile strivings and how the latter persist in the adult. The writings in one period are predictive of what will be developed further in the later periods. Even concepts such as the neutralizing capacity of the ego and infantile and childhood experiences were anticipated in Freud's early writings. During the second period, the different aspects of personality were considered more equal in importance.

Until 1920 Freud had focused on only one infantile drive: infantile sexuality. During the second period, drive psychology was expanded and enriched by further studies of infantile aggression and hostility. Freud knew about infantile aggression much earlier, of course; for example, he knew that the child's oedipal strivings were not just sexual–libidinal appetites, but also included hostile–competitive death wishes. In "Beyond the Pleasure Principle," Freud (1920) first stated that remnants of infantile aggression and hostility are equally as important in the formation of adult neuroses as derivatives of infantile sexuality.

There is a logical sequence in Freud's clinical interests and investigations. He started with hysteria, then turned to compulsion neurosis, next to melancholia, and finally to paranoia and schizophrenia. He seems to have worked from the surface downward—from the less to the more severe forms of psychopathology.

The third period might be headlined "The Period Of Ego Autonomy." Originally the ego was thought of as arising from modifications of the id. In the third phase, the ego was (and is) thought of as a structure in its own right. In his 1937a paper, "Analysis Terminable and Interminable," Freud noted that defenses could not be explained entirely on the basis of instinctual vicissitudes and infantile experiences. He concluded that there must be something more to personality development, and he suggested that in addition to the factors of native drive endowment and traumatic frustrations in infancy, the ego must be predisposed innately to certain lines of development.

At about the same time, Heinz Hartmann (1939) proposed his important theories of primary and secondary ego autonomy *(Ego*

Psychology and the Problem of Adaptation). With respect to secondary autonomy, certain acquisitions of the ego are reinforced during specific periods of infantile conflict. For example, how the child's toilet training is managed will influence his later attitudes about orderliness. Through educational pressures, the child will learn to control his desire for immediate infantile pleasure in evacuation. Hartmann pointed out that even though an activity like orderliness may have originated in conflict, it may in the course of further development separate itself from the conflict and become secondarily autonomous—that is, no longer a defense but an "autonomous ego function."

The extreme of orderliness is compulsive orderliness, which suggests considerable distance between the infantile wish and the adult behavior, but some remnant of the infantile drive must still be present and active, making it necessary for the ego to clamp down on itself to avoid any temptation to smear. Clinical observation reveals that the intensity of the compusiveness waxes and wanes with the amount of anal–sadistic drive stimulation.

When Hartmann refers to secondary autonomy he speaks from the further clinical observation that even some of the most effective and adaptive adult activities may be traced to a time when infantile precursors of such behavior were intensely conflicted. Scientific activity in adulthood, for example, may have origins in frustration of childhood curiosity and looking. Freud's scientific genius for mastering puzzling problems may have developed in part from traumatic puzzlement about the very different ages of family members in his childhood environment. No autonomy is irreversible, however. An analyst's infantile sexual curiosity, which may play a part in his wanting to know and understand what goes on in patients, is usually autonomous. At times, however, it can lose its autonomy and become reconnected with infantile conflicts. When that happens, blind spots occur.

Both drive development and the innate maturational capacities of the ego influence what the ego eventually becomes. There are optimal times when the ego is ready for specific maturational advances, which Hartmann conceptualized as primary ego autonomy. Thus the development of the ego may be viewed from the standpoint of the ego itself. Conflicts of traumatic intensity may occur as a result of experiences that are incompatible with the innate maturational timetable of the autonomous ego.

Lecture 2

How It All Began

This year of the course is devoted mainly to the first phase in the development of psychoanalysis, up to the introduction of the structural point of view. Chapter 7 of Freud's (1900) book on dreams will be reviewed, probably in the third quarter. Before then, read thoroughly chapters 1 through 6 of the dream book. The other reading assignment is the best survey of the first period, Freud's "Introductory Lectures on Psychoanalysis" (1915–1916 and 1916–1917)—a difficult and profound book, requiring very close study, especially the third part (1916–1917) on psychopathology.

Psychoanalysis began with a patient who could be considered the true inventor of this method for studying the mind, Anna O. Her contribution was that she wanted to talk about her suffering and wanted someone to listen. She was a social worker, and despite the various attempts to prove that all of the early psychoanalytic patients were seriously disturbed and schizophrenic, there is no evidence of that in the case of Anna O. Her real name was Bertha Pappenheim. Her psychological suffering was mainly hysterical—for example, dissociated states and unreal dream experiences.

Anna O.'s wish to talk about her problems found a willing ear in the Viennese internist Joseph Breuer. She was very literate and spoke English, and so did Breuer, so they conducted the treatment in English. Using a foreign language may have been an important factor in the treatment, by diluting some of the intensity of the experience for both patient and doctor. Anna O. invented the term *chimney sweeping* for her free associations. Her treatment went on for over a year and came to naught, but it was recorded and demonstrated the complication of transference.

A number of years passed before Breuer's experience with Anna O. came to the attention of Sigmund Freud, who used it as the basis for developing psychoanalysis—not only as a method of observation, but as a set of abstractions from those observations. A cornerstone of psychoanalytic theory ever since Anna O.'s notion of chimney sweeping has been the concept of something that could be "swept out"—some "dark, dirty" material which, if removed, would improve matters, unclog them, free them up. This concept in psychoanalysis follows the surgical model for the treatment of abscess: Drain the abscess and gain relief of symptoms. We know now that Anna O. developed a transference neurosis, so that it became more important to her to see Breuer than to get relief of her symptoms. Mrs. Breuer sensed this, became jealous of Breuer's prolonged treatment of Anna O., and insisted that the family take a long holiday in Italy.

Breuer's early theory, based on the surgical model of draining an abscess, was a good theory; in Hartmann's terms, it had optimal distance from the observed facts. It was not so close to the facts that it merely repeated them, and it was not so distant that clinical gusto was lost. A good theory has an optimal degree of generalization from the observed facts.

The notion of chimney sweeping became the concept of "catharsis" in Breuer and Freud's (1893–1895) book, "Studies on Hysteria." At first it was thought that the "abscess" consisted of ideas, but it soon became clear to Freud that the ideas must be charged—or, as we say, "cathected"—in some way. He reached that conclusion from the fact that interpreting ideational content alone did not relieve the symptoms. The "charge" that Freud postulated must "cathect" the ideas was the charge of affect. The main issue in treatment, therefore, was to get at the affective charge and drain it.

Because the patient sometimes did not want to be "drained," the technique was the same as for surgery: force the patient. Almost everyone was using hypnosis at that time—it was very much "in the air"—so Freud tried hypnosis to force the draining of the abscess. It was a big step from using hypnosis to "command" symptoms away, to using it for cathartic purposes—that is, using it to find out what produced the symptoms. Freud's early writings about his use of hypnosis indicate that, as in the case of Anna O. and Breuer, patients tended to come back for more and more hypnotic treatments. Freud did not understand that phenomenon at the time, because he did not yet know about transference.

8 Kohut's Freudian Vision

Freud then developed the theory that there must be some force between the underlying "psychic abscess" and Consciousness that kept the abscess from becoming conscious. That concept led to a change in technique: The patient was allowed to struggle with his or her resistances. The change from catharsis to resistance analysis was not as momentous, however, as the step from hypnosis (for "commanding away" symptoms) to catharsis.

The concepts of this phase were those of the early 1890s—for example, "The Neuro-Psychoses of Defence" (1894). Already at this stage the concepts were remarkably complete: They included the Unconscious, defenses against the Unconscious, split of Consciousness originating in traumatic experiences, and reexperiencing traumatic events and emotions in the treatment. Freud knew also that what had to be changed was not just one side of the conflict; both sides had to be dealt with. Perhaps the main thing Freud did not know at that time was transference.

Originally the concept of trauma was a very simple one—namely, a recent event in which the person had been overwhelmed with emotion. It did not take Freud long to deduce that the recent event was no more than an intermediate trauma. He observed that recent traumata tended to cluster around certain recurrent complexes, usually sexual, which could be traced back to disturbing childhood events. Eventually he traced all traumata back to sexual events of childhood, which he believed were the main source of traumatic experiences in early life. With respect to the treatment of such problems, Freud was always sensitive to the importance of the interplay between clinical observation, theory, and therapy. He considered psychoanalysis the best form of psychotherapy, although the least immediately effective.

There is no "one theory" of the first phase. All one can suggest is a rather general theory that emphasized certain matters at a particular time. Freud wanted to develop a theory that would encompass not only neurotic phenomena but also normal behavior. That is why studying the psychopathology of everyday life (1901) became so important to him. He hoped to prove the validity of his concepts about psychopathology by demonstrating their existence in total mental functioning.

The "Project" (1895) was an attempt to "neurologize," but Freud soon got over the need to do that. The trouble with the Project was that there was no way to find out how such activities took place neurophysiologically. For a long time, however, Freud retained a need to conceptualize in terms of concrete imagery.

Freud used a simple set of "ordering principles" to classify and bring some order into the mass of psychological data that he observed. He developed and used five such ordering principles:

1. The principle involved in the concept of "depth psychology" —that is, levels of mental functioning, a hierarchy of psychological functions.
2. The topographic point of view.
3. The dynamic point of view.
4. The economic point of view.
5. The genetic point of view.

Lecture 3

The Dynamic and Topographic Points of View

The discussions thus far have dealt mainly with psychoanalytic developments during the final decade of the last century. In the middle of that decade, Freud (1900) undertook his own self-analysis, which came to a comparative conclusion with his writing "The Interpretation of Dreams." He continued his self-analysis systematically until the end of his life, however, devoting about half an hour a day to it.

The Dynamic Point of View: that is, ordering the phenomena in terms of interacting forces. Psychological material clearly lends itself to that kind of ordering. Wishes, urges, and strivings can be represented diagrammatically with an arrow having direction, force, intensity, and object. Strivings of that kind can be experienced as driving forces. Similarly, the concept of conflict can be expressed schematically as a clash between opposing forces.

By themselves, however, the preceding concepts were not crucially important in the development of Freud's dynamic psychology. Two other implications of the dynamic viewpoint had a greater effect on Freud's thinking: First, the concept of conflict suggested to Freud that the mind must have a *built-in readiness* for or tendency toward internal conflicts. This aspect of Freud's thinking was highly important, but it is often overlooked. It is overshadowed even further, however, by Freud's concept of Consciousness.

Freud conceived of Consciousness at that time as an "inner sensory organ." The essence of Freudian dynamics is that the important wishes, strivings, or forces of the mind are not conscious. One of Freud's greatest strokes of genius was that, whereas most people tended to think in terms of either neurological activity or conscious mental functioning, Freud was able to conceive of a psychological life consisting of wishes, fantasies, dreams, and other mental activities that exist in the same sense that the external world exists. We assume that the external world exists whether we are looking at it or not. Freud could conceive of the same being true of the psychological life.

This concept is so simple that it is difficult: The discipline of psychoanalytic psychology is based on the principle that the essence of psychological functioning is not conscious. Freud suggested a reason for our tendency to reject unconsciousness—namely, the blow to our self-esteem that our vaunted Consciousness of mental processes is distinctly limited rather than all-important. Just as Copernicus wounded humankind's self-esteem by his discovery that the earth is not the center of the universe and, similarly, as Darwin injured our human pride still further by finding that we do not have a separate and unique creation, Freud's discovery that Consciousness is only a small and relatively insignificant part of mental functioning was yet another blow to our self-esteem.

Freud concluded that the essential quality of the psychological has nothing to do with Consciousness, just as the essential nature of external reality has nothing to do with being seen. It exists whether seen or not and whether conscious or not. The position of Consciousness in psychoanalytic theorizing is that of a fixed point, however, in the same sense that Archimedes meant in his claim that he could move the entire world if given a fixed point in the universe.

The main problem with the concept of the Unconscious is the word *unconscious* itself. The word makes it seem as if unconsciousness is a "quality" of mental functioning, but as indicated previously, the essence of the psychological is independent of whether it is conscious or unconscious, seen or unseen. Consciousness of the psychological is merely a directing of attention to the psychological—a mere momentary perception of the psychological—which goes on whether paid attention to and perceived by Consciousness or not. This concept led Freud to the ordering principle called the topographic point of view.

The Topographic Point of View: With this ordering principle, Freud was able to study and theorize about the psychpathology of everyday life, dreams, and wit. Freud assumed, for example, that

the psychopathology of everyday life must be influenced by
another system that is not seen. His model was:

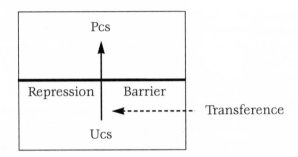

Freud referred to the mechanism by which the unconscious
system influences the preconscious system by the much-misun-
derstood term *transference*.

Freud observed about the psychological that its essence is
dynamic but that to know about it requires looking at it with the
perceiving organ of Consciousness. Fisher's (1954; Fisher and
Paul, 1959) tachistoscopic experiments provided strong support
for that concept: That is, highly complex images projected tachistoscopically, of which the subject is not conscious, appear in
dreams that night in minute detail.

QUESTION: When Freud presented his concept of Consciousness as an inner sense organ, was that a later development of
his ideas about conscious, preconscious, and unconscious
processes?

ANSWER: It belongs early in the development of his ideas. In a
descriptive sense, "unconscious" means not "conscioused"—
that is, not observed by Consciousness.

QUESTION: Is the sensory organ of Consciousness the same as
the ego?

ANSWER: No. Freud conceived of "Pcpt.–Cs." (Perception
–Consciousness) as a perceptual system at the outer rim of the
ego. Turned outward, it functioned as external conscious perception; turned inward, it served as conscious introspection.

QUESTION: Could Consciousness be part of the ego?

ANSWER: Yes, that makes more sense.

Lecture 4

Conflict, Transference, and Infantile Sexuality

The propensity of the mind for conflict was a major concept in Freud's theorizing—that is, a dynamic system with an inherent tendency toward an inner organization of forces that oppose and balance each other. Even external frustrations (of inner drives) could be viewed as having a counterpart within the mental apparatus itself—an inner readiness to take a stand of opposition to the drives. In addition, Freud's earliest topographic model did not consist merely of a Preconscious and an Unconscious with a repressive barrier between them, but also included a biological parallel or analogy between sexual drives and ego drives:

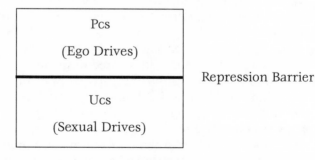

Freud visualized the Unconscious as full of pleasure-seeking (sexual) drives that have a race-preservative function, whereas the Preconscious contains self-preservative (ego) drives that attempt to assure the individual's survival. The two sets of drives were presumed to be in conflict with each other at times. This concept was only an "oddity," however, and Freud did not pursue

13

it. It is not a psychological but a biological theory, although it can be viewed as a precursor of Freud's later theory: oedipal–incestuous wishes *versus* castration fear.

The concept of a readiness of the mind for conflict was not in itself so new. What was revolutionary, however, was the groundwork that it laid for a dynamic psychology with a structural–topographic perspective. The nature and qualities of the processes in the Preconscious and the Unconscious could now be differentiated. Freud called the processes in the Unconscious "primary processes" and those in the Preconscious "secondary processes." He concluded that both sets of processes are independent of Consciousness.

The prototype of secondary processes is rational thinking. We do not really know what the primary processes are like. We know them only from instances in which the primary processes invade the secondary processes. We cannot demonstrate the primary processes directly but can infer some of their qualities and characteristics: For example, they employ condensation and displacement and operate with large amounts of "free, unbound" energy, as opposed to small amounts of "bound" energy with which the Preconscious functions. Thus we can study only secondary processes and can infer actions of the primary processes only when the expected activities of the secondary process are disturbed or distorted in some way.

Invasion of the secondary process by primary processes is called "transference." An example of such a transference is obsessive thought, which intrudes itself insistently, has a driven quality, and disturbs and distracts regular secondary process thinking. The phenomenon of "technical transference" (to the analyst) is only a special form of the basic (intrapsychic) mechanism of transference and was not discovered until later.

Freud formulated slips and dreams as examples of transferences, but he also described neurotic symptoms as transference phenomena resulting from the intrusion of unconscious processes into the Preconscious and attaching themselves to preconscious contents. Writing, for example, is a preconscious activity, but if an old masturbatory complex attaches itself to writing, then the rest of the Preconscious may treat writing as if it were masturbation and not allow such activity, which might lead to the symptom of writing block. Freud called phenomena of that kind the symptoms of a "transference neurosis"—neurosis because the disturbance of writing persists. The transferences involved in slips and dreams are only transient and thus are not considered symptoms.

Transferences from the Unconscious to the Preconscious attach themselves to "day residues," which are memories of recent, often fleeting experiences that have no practical meaning or importance. If a person is shown tachistoscopic pictures, for example, he will use the briefly glimpsed, seemingly irrelevant images as day residues in dream formation that night (Fisher, 1954; Fisher and Paul, 1959). Why? Because they are so insignificant, so lacking in practical value, they are readily available for, and lend themselves to, transferences from the Unconscious. The same mechanism helps to explain why the analyst so readily becomes an object of transference: The analyst does not have much practical significance as a source of immediate gratification in the patient's life. If the analyst were to become the supporter, helper, friend, or gratifier of the patient, he or she would not be as readily available as an object of transference—hence the so-called day residue function of the psychoanalyst.

Another development in Freud's concepts of structural topography was his growing understanding of infantile sexuality—its nature as a very pleasure-seeking set of feelings and drives. He conceived of the ego developing out of the id as a result of external frustrations that prevent immediate satisfaction of the infantile pleasure-seeking drives. He theorized that in the Unconscious the Pleasure Principle prevails—that is, the expectation of immediate gratification. In the Preconscious, by contrast, the Reality Principle holds sway; the pleasure-seeking drives are more subdued, postponed, and delayed. The puzzle that Freud had to solve was why some infantile sexuality remained undifferentiated instead of being transformed into preconscious secondary process activities.

We must keep in mind that infantile sexuality is not exactly the same as sexuality in the adult sense. The closest that adult mental life (or adult experience) comes to the intensity of infantile sexuality may be something like the height of orgasm—which, significantly, is associated with a different kind of Consciousness, a Consciousness perhaps of primary process. Thus for adults, orgasm may be the only remaining experience that approximates the quality and intensity of the primary process.

Freud (1921) wrote in "Group Psychology and the Analysis of the Ego" that he did not want to change the term *sexuality* for these infantile experiences because he had chosen the term *a potiori*—that is, he selected the term that refers to the best known among various experiences of similar kind. When a baby sucks, for example, the pleasurable intensity of the experience is comparable with "sexual" excitement and satisfaction. Freud theorized that every activity was originally highly "sexual" (or "sexualized"): walking, talking, looking, writing—all began as sexually experienced actions. Moreover, all of these experiences can become resexualized: In obsessional neurosis, for example, thinking itself, which was originally a highly pleasurable erotic activity, becomes resexualized, and the patient's ego then treats it as a sexual danger even to think.

When the Preconscious is working properly, desexualization of preconscious processes is so effective that preconscious activities no longer have an erotic quality; as mentioned previously, Freud needed to account also for instances in which infantile sexuality does not become desexualized and is not transformed into smoothly functioning preconscious activities. How he dealt with that problem is discussed in the next lecture.

QUESTION: Is there any connection between the content of a day residue and the content of an infantile wish?

ANSWER: Freud said there may be, but not necessarily. For example, if the infantile wish has to do with ambition—a wish to be as big as one's father—it might attach itself to a day residue about someone having mentioned a full professor. Thus the connection between preconscious content and infantile wish may be only symbolic. Something in the previous day must have stimulated the childhood wish. What specific day residue is chosen to represent the infantile wish seems to be determined by its being just far enough removed from the actual wish, and at the same time just close enough to it, to provide a representation of the wish without doing so too directly.

Lecture 5

Optimal versus Traumatic Frustration, Memory versus Hallucinations, and Daydreaming

Continuing the discussion from last time: Freud had inferred that a variable amount of infantile sexuality is not transformed and desexualized into secondary process preconscious activity, but it remains fixated at an unconscious primary process level dominated by the Pleasure Principle. To account for these differences in the fate of infantile sexuality, he proposed a distinction between two types of frustrating experiences during infancy and childhood: mild to moderate, or "optimal frustrations," which lead to the transformation of infantile sexuality into secondary process, and overly intense, or "traumatic frustrations," that produce repression of and fixation on infantile sexuality. This explanation also included related concepts, which will be discussed today, regarding the development of memory out of hallucinations and the function of daydreaming.

Freud's reasoning included the following hypothetical sequence of experiences in infants:

> When a baby is hungry, it tries to relieve the hunger by random activity. Mother comes and feeds. By the next time the baby is hungry, a structural change has occurred; the baby is able to recall the previous experience and uses whatever engrams were laid down to hallucinate satisfaction. The phantasy does not work for long, however, because hunger increases; random discharge occurs again. Mother comes, and satisfaction ensues; now the baby has its first opportunity to differentiate between reality and hallucination—between the hallucinated memory of a previous real satisfaction and the actual experience of a realistic satisfaction in the present.

Thus a baby learns gradually to differentiate between the hallucinated mother and the real mother. With the hallucinated mother the hunger increases; with the real mother it subsides. The infant learns from these experiences to make memories out of hallucinations. The kinds of experiences that lead to such learning—that is, the ability to distinguish between hallucinations and reality—are experiences of "optimal frustration," in contrast to experiences of trauma. Making the distinction between hallucinated and real satisfaction is much more difficult for the infant or child in the case of traumatic experiences.

Similarly, if a parent does everything for a son, the child retains his infantile, primary process identifications with the parent and thus imagines that he can do everything as well as the parent, rather than learning through optimal frustration that he is not able to do everything himself. In certain narcissistic characters one sees a great deal of omnipotent identification with parents, but no skills.

How much and at what times in a child's development trauma occurs (in relation to the parents) vary a great deal. Trauma goes on at all times. Trauma is a psychoeconomic concept in psychoanalysis, referring not to the content of an experience but to its amount and intensity. The degree of trauma is based in part on the external event, but also on other factors such as when the event occurs in the life of the child. Seduction experiences, for example, are less traumatic at some periods than at others, although they may be traumatic at any time.

Traumatic experiences tend to fixate the child at the developmental level of hallucinated satisfaction. Any unconscious content that is walled off from the Preconscious becomes insusceptible to learning; it follows the primary process Pleasure Principle of immediate, hallucinated wish-fulfillment—For example, the same hysterical symptom occurring repeatedly for 60 years, never achieving real gratification but persistently repeating the hallucinated wish-fulfillment. Conditions of optimal frustration, on the other hand, facilitate the gradual development of secondary processes out of primary processes.

REVIEWING: Optimal frustration leads to discrimination between wish-fulfilling hallucinations and reality. The former involve lack of discrimination between external reality and internal phantasies of hallucinated "reality." This is an important concept to grasp; that is, how the individual experiences events is crucial.

QUESTION: Is it necessary to account for memory growing out of hallucinations? Perhaps memory develops directly out of experiences rather than out of discriminating between hallucinations and external reality?

ANSWER: Grasping the concept I have described is difficult. It is hard for us to conceptualize a mental apparatus in which everything that goes on within it is "reality." What produces that state of affairs is primary process functioning and the associated Pleasure Principle. Only experiences of optimal frustration can change that immature state of psychological functioning to the Reality Principle. Otherwise the child, and later adult, will remain fixated on delusions of omnipotence and hallucinated satisfaction.

QUESTION: But aren't such delusions defensive?

ANSWER: No. In persons who were "spoiled" as children, one finds fixated primary process omnipotence delusions that are not simply defensive overcompensations.

DAYDREAMING

There is also a realm of thinking between primary process–Pleasure Principle thinking and secondary process–Reality Principle thinking: the realm of daydreaming, in which the wish and its fulfillment are one and the same. Once again, the difficulty in grasping this concept is the problem of recognizing that primitive processes exist in which there is no difference between external reality and one's own mental processes. The tremendous narcissistic investment we make in our secondary process thinking contributes to this blind spot. Our original primary process omnipotence phantasies are often transferred to secondary process operations; we then consider the latter to be the alpha and omega of all mental functioning. The pleasure in primary process hallucinations, therefore, is not given up entirely but to some extent is merely transferred to omnipotence fantasies regarding our secondary process thinking.

[Note: These lectures follow a tradition of spelling unconscious phantasies with *ph*, whereas preconscious and conscious fantasies are spelled with *f*. Other traditions that Kohut followed included capitalizing the first letters in the noun forms of Consciousness, the Preconscious, and the Unconscious and capitalizing the first letters of Pleasure Principle and Reality Principle.]

Lecture 6

Psychic Trauma and the Economic Point of View

The Reality Principle includes the realization that when a wish arises there must be some waiting for its fulfillment and some steps taken to satisfy it. The Pleasure Principle does not recognize that reality but assumes satisfaction of a wish as soon as it appears. If one thinks of a continuum from Unconscious to Preconscious, it is possible to conceptualize a gradual change from primary to secondary process and from Pleasure Principle to Reality Principle. One of the most difficult intellectual and emotional feats that one must accomplish to understand the Pleasure Principle is to imagine, as Freud could, that the primitive Unconscious contains nothing but wishes fulfilled. All there is in this primitive layer of the psyche are wish-fulfilling hallucinatory phantasies.

During a later phase of development, the child normally projects its original omnipotence phantasies to the parents. If the child is overly spoiled, however, it retains an unusal amount of narcissism or omnipotence; at the same time, because he or she lacks actual skills, such a child feels inferior. Similarly, as discussed in the previous lecture, overly frustrating experiences make it difficult for the Unconscious to differentiate into Preconscious, so that experiences of the latter kind also lead to the retention of narcissistic omnipotence phantasies.

The question arises whether, during the infant's primitive hallucinatory Pleasure Principle functioning, the baby imagines satisfaction even when he or she cries? The answer is yes. The cry is originally a purely reflex act that often brings the mother, but crying is independent of the baby's primitive mentality, which is hallucinating wish-fulfillment all the time.

What Freud originally called "infantile sexuality" had these Pleasure Principle, primary process, unconscious qualities: intensive pleasure-seeking qualities having urgency and need for fulfillment of wishes in relation to the infant's own body. A certain amount of infantile sexuality having these specific qualities remains as a foreign territory in the mind and can, under certain conditions, invade preconscious–secondary process–Reality Principle functioning. Take, for example, some hostile feelings in the repressed–fixated reservoir of primitive unconscious mental functioning. To the compulsion neurotic, the hostile feeling is tantamount to its immediate fulfillment (destruction). Wish and fulfillment are not differentiated, and the compulsion neurotic can "undo" such an impulse only by use of countermagic. We assume that the intensity and omnipotent quality of the compulsion neurotic's underlying hostile feelings must be considerable because the intensity of his defenses against them is so great.

We have been discussing what Freud called the Topographic Point of View: There are two parts of mental functioning, preconscious and unconscious, which are not directly connected with each other but have a barrier between them; that the Unconscious is characterized by primary process, Pleasure Principle, infantile sexuality and aggression; optimal frustration leads to maximal differentiation of Unconscious into Preconscious, of primary into secondary process, of Pleasure Principle into Reality Principle; and over- or underfrustration leads to fixation on unconscious, omnipotent, Pleasure Principle, infantile sexual and aggressive, hallucinatory wish-fulfilling, primary process functioning.

We proceed now to the Psychoeconomic Point of View. The economic factor par excellence in psychoanalytic theory is the experience of trauma. Trauma cannot be defined objectively apart from the subject but is understood as an experience of such intensity that the child cannot integrate it. Traumatic experiences are those that cannot be dealt with by progressive integration into the Preconscious but must be walled off and kept repressed at the sacrifice of further differentiation. Trauma is overstimulation, whether from overly gratifying or overly frustrating experiences.

Trauma leads to repression of and fixation on infantile sexuality and aggression. Trauma involves not only what occurs externally but the dovetailing of external events and inner psychic organization at the time. One such factor associated with the inner psychic organization is the developmental stage of the libido (and aggression) in the child. Another factor of importance in the psychoeconomic concept of trauma is the issue of time—that is, how suddenly the child is confronted with tasks that demand rapid transitions from Pleasure Principle to Reality Principle functioning, whether such demands are made abruptly or in a gradual and fractionated way over a longer period of time.

During psychoanalysis, traumatic experiences that were repressed rather than integrated into the Preconscious during childhood are mobilized again. Thus, as Rado (1925) noted, psychoanalysis is a process of prolonged, delayed mourning—a gradual giving up of infantile objects and phantasies.

Lecture 7

Primal Repression and "Actual Neurosis"

Reviewing the previous discussion of primary process functioning, the following is an example of the magical–omnipotent, wish-fulfilled nature of primary process thinking: A woman experiences a muscle spasm in connection with a memory of her mother giving birth to a sibling. The muscle spasm in this case is a hysterical enactment of giving birth to a child. The correct interpretation, therefore, would not be simply that the patient wanted to have a baby like mother. The correct interpretation would be that the patient was *having* a baby like her mother. She does not just wish for a baby, but gives birth to a baby in a primitive, symbolic mode of primary process thinking.

The difference between primary and secondary processes is largely an economic or quantitative one. The secondary process deals with relatively small amounts of energy. The primary process deals with large quantities of energy. The secondary process has a controlling function over the primary process. The "Genetic Point of View" is relevant to the origin of this dichotomy: The Unconscious retains residues of infantile sexuality and aggression that, as a result of trauma, were unable to be integrated into the secondary process. Repressive mechanisms had to be employed, so that the unfulfilled wishes were walled off and retained in their original form.

Turning to the concept of Primal Repression: The depths of the Unconscious, which cannot be uncovered, contain the walled-off traumata of early life. It is the intensity of the early infantile primary process, of infantile sexual and aggressive impulses in the presence of an immature, vulnerable, easily overstimulated (and thus traumatizable) ego, that is responsible for the many early wallings-off or primal repressions. Trauma, the conceptual keystone of the economic point of view, is always relative to the degree of (im)maturity at a given time. No more primal repression occurs after the Oedipus complex.

The concept of Actual Neurosis holds that some psychological symptoms have no particular psychological content but are a direct result of sexual overstimulation. Originally the anxiety neurosis was believed to be an example of actual neurosis, in contrast to anxiety–hysteria (phobic neuroses), which are characterized by highly structuralized symptoms having symbolic psychological content. Glover (1939) considered certain kinds of insomnia to be actual neuroses, rather than sleep phobias.

Freud developed the concept of actual neurosis from clinical observations of male patients who complained of "contentless" anxiety, in whom the anxiety symptoms had certain qualities of orgasm and in whom the symptoms disappeared when the man's wife was pregnant. Freud reasoned that chronic use of coitus interruptus (for purposes of birth control) produced the condition and that when the man's wife was pregnant, coitus interruptus was unnecessary. Incomplete discharge of sexual stimulation from coitus interruptus was believed to be the source of overstimulation, to which the ego then reacted with intense, contentless anxiety.

Lecture 8

The Genetic Point of View

Reviewing the Economic Point of View: Freud placed great emphasis on the relative quantity or intensity of experiences. Compare, for example, the difference between actual neurosis and psychoneurosis. Freud postulated that in actual neurosis, undischarged libido from coitus interruptus later intrudes into Consciousness as anxiety, the latter representing a transformation of the dammed-up libido. Later Freud added that actual neuroses could result from the damming up of aggressive as well as sexual tensions.

Freud applied the concept of "libidinal imbalance" not only to anxiety neurosis but also to neurasthenia. Here again he postulated that undischarged quantities of excitation produce symptoms directly, not by structural–topographic conflict. As an example he suggested the neurasthenia of adolescence, in which prolonged masturbatory stimulation with only partial discharge and satisfaction leads to an accumulation of undischarged libido, which may then produce "toxic" changes—for example, symptoms such as nuchal headaches.

Sleep disturbances may represent psychoneurotic disorders, on the one hand, or actual neuroses, on the other. In the former, the insomnia may result from sleep being equated with forbidden fantasies, which can lead to neurotic inhibition of sleep. In the case of actual neurotic insomnia, undischarged tensions disturb sleep directly. The latter condition is closer to psychotic pathology: compare, for example, the schizophrenic's difficulty in going to sleep and the psychotic depressive's early-morning awakening.

Certain concepts of psychosomatic medicine also derive from the theory of actual neurosis. In his paper on psychogenic visual disturbances, for example, Freud (1910) distinguished between hysterical blindness as a psychoneurotic symptom and other conditions of the eye caused by hypererotization or libidinization of the eye, which may actually damage the physiological functioning of that organ. Alexander's (1950) later distinction between conversion reactions and vegetative neuroses employed the same distinction.

QUESTION: What is the relation of the following observation to the concept of actual neurotic insomnia? Following certain types of sports, athletes have difficulty sleeping—for example, after ping-pong, tennis, and squash. After other sports, such as football, athletes sleep well. Could the difference be due to hostile tensions not being as completely discharged in the former sports and thus producing insomnia of the actual neurotic type?

ANSWER: That could be the answer. Fenichel (1945) referred to the "damming up of libido"; but damming up of other tensions also occurs—for example, damming up of aggressive tensions. The specific characteristic of these conditions is that they do not depend on structural conflict, but only on a dammed-up state. Freud delimited the term *psychoneurosis* from *neurosis* on the basis of that distinction: Actual neurosis is based on "psychoeconomic imbalance" produced by undischarged tension; psychoneurosis results from structural conflict.

How does free association fit into these various points of view and approaches? Waelder (1960) suggested that in free association, the ego is supposed to regress in one area (and therefore underwork), but overwork in another—specifically, in observing itself. It is a common misconception that free association is a purely passive or negative process, a giving up of something (controls, self-criticism). Free association is much more than just letting oneself go. It also involves actively allowing even unpleasant mental contents to become conscious so that they can be experienced, perceived, and investigated.

Free association, therefore, is work—work that produces a gradual extension of the ego. It would be an inaccurate caricature of this concept to say, however, that what we strive for in analysis is a personality that is all preconscious in place of unconscious. Freud (1937a) pointed out in "Analysis Terminable and Interminable" that the goal of analysis is different from that. Any walled-off content that is not active, and for which repression is working satisfactorily, is left alone. Even reality testing can become pathological!

The Genetic Point of View: In some ways this viewpoint most accurately characterizes psychoanalysis. Freud approached the genetic question originally from his studies of psychoneurotic symptoms, dreams, and so forth. But what is the difference between dynamic formulations and reconstructions from the genetic point of view? The latter deal with those traumatic situations in which an old (nonpathological) dynamic equilibrium is replaced by a new, permanent (pathological) one. The genetic point of view goes beyond the recognition of certain dynamic patterns that repeat themselves in the patient's life and therapeutic process. A dynamic reconstruction is not complete in the genetic sense, even when traced back to childhood. Similarly, when free association is used and the same pattern occurs in the transference to the analyst, that is "dynamic," not "genetic."

A formulation becomes genetic when the reliving involves not only the repetitive pattern but also the specific inner mental and external environmental events that occurred at the time of the childhood trauma (Hartmann and Kris, 1945). The repetitive pattern is actually a symptom that defends against repetition of the trauma itself. The genetic repetition can occur only in the transference. It is rarely remembered directly as the original event, but it is relived in the transference where it is "reconstructed" and then sometimes may be remembered.

Clinical example: A man described a recent job situation in which his work, which previously had been good, deteriorated after the appearance of a younger coworker in the same department. In the course of the analytic work, it was found that the work setback resulted from jealousy and anxiety produced by competition with the new coworker. The same dynamic could be established in relation to previous job situations. His childhood history suggested the same problem in relation to schoolmates and particularly toward his younger brothers. Thus the dynamic formulation of this pattern was guilt about sibling rivalry leading to work inhibition. The pattern was repeated in his analysis. At first he did good analytic work, with a steady flow of free associations; then came a setback and resistance. Analysis of the resistance revealed that the patient had "noticed" a "new" patient of the analyst's. The same dynamic formulation and interpretation were made as before. Work flowed again. On a later occasion, severe resistance set in. Slow progress in the analysis of the resistance revealed fantasies that the other patient was very ill, that he looked weak and pale—which was not actually the case. Memories of illness in a younger sibling then emerged. Finally, after many such phases of severe resistance, dream material made possible the reconstruction, and later memory, that a younger brother had died in early infancy, during a period of intense hostile jealousy on the part of the patient.

Genetic formulation: Prior to the traumatic event, he had experienced a normal amount of hostility toward rivals. After the traumatic event, inhibitions were imposed against dangerous hostility toward sibling figures. What was the trauma? An insecurely established ego had barely accepted the fact that wishes cannot kill, that thoughts are not omnipotent. Death of his brother, combined with numerous auxiliary factors such as his parents' withdrawal from the patient during the traumatic period, severely threatened his thinly established reality-ego, which then walled itself off permanently from any further integration of hostile competitiveness toward sibling figures.

Lecture 9

Symptom Formation

Reviewing: The economic point of view in psychoanalysis applies particularly to the concept of "psychoeconomic imbalance." In mourning, for example, there is no structural conflict but only the "work" of discharging the tension associated with separation, which is carried out by breaking up the grief into small pieces that can be tolerated more easily. Rado's (1925) theory of "working through" in analysis follows the same psychoeconomic principle of a fractionated, gradual giving up of lost objects from the past. Freud's concept of play is based on the same concept: Compare his description (1920, pp. 14–17) of a child's game called "Gone," in which the boy gave himself fractionated doses of object loss in order to discharge and master his fears of separation.

Freud's early approach focused on three main subjects: (1) the psychoneuroses; (2) the psychopathology of everyday life; and (3) dreams. The concept of symptom formation was central to all three; the theory of symptom formation in the psychoneuroses was the same as Freud's conceptual models of dreams and the psychopathology of everyday life. All three represented "transference" phenomena.

The symptom itself was explained from topographic, economic, and genetic points of view. The psychoneurotic symptom begins with something that occurs in the relations between the "second system" (the Preconscious; later, the ego) and reality. He called this disturbance by the most general name that he could apply: frustration. This factor, by itself, does not cause the psychoneurosis but is an indispensible step in its development.

30

Common examples of such frustrations include being disappointed in love, failing to receive a promotion, and so forth.

The first reaction to such a frustration is an increase in daydreaming, which is an activity of the system Preconscious. Daydreaming represents a "regression in the service of the ego" (Kris, 1952), an adaptive and necessary means of "softening the blow" of reality frustrations. It involves turning away from painful reality in a flexible manner, being restored by daydreams, and then returning to reality, ready to find a promising new goal or object. Freud called this process "Introversion," or "Manifest Regression." The process is under the control of the Preconscious but is closer to the Unconscious and the primary process than to the usual activities of the Preconscious.

Freud called the decisive step in the development of a psychoneurosis "Regression Proper," which differs from Manifest Regression. In persons who have left large amounts of libido fixated at various points in development, there is relatively little libido left for normal, flexible regressions to cope with reality frustrations. When a manifest regression is not sufficient to deal with such frustration, Regression Proper may set in, whereupon the libido rushes back to unconscious positions of libido fixation. A reality frustration has then revived an old libidinal object attachment in the repressed Unconscious.

Prior to Regression Proper, the dynamic system had been characterized by a state of relative balance—that is, a fixated incestuous love had been balanced by an equal or greater repressive force. The balance, or overbalance, gave the second system (Preconscious) a certain amount of freedom. When Regression Proper occurs, however, the cathexes that had been available for attachment to reality objects flow back to old libidinal attachments from the past.

The balance then changes. What was like this, $\downarrow\!\uparrow$, is now like

this: $\uparrow\!\downarrow$. The fourth step in Freud's concept of psychoneurotic symptom

formation is thus an increase in repressed object libido, which is produced by turning away from reality objects to childhood objects. The result is an increase in undischarged (and undischargeable) object libido, which threatens to create an "actual neurosis." Freud considered this endopsychic state of psychoeconomic imbalance the "actual neurotic core" of psychoneurotic symptom formation.

The motivation for still further elaboration of the psychoneurotic symptom was conceptualized by Freud as an attempt to avoid anxiety, which threatens to occur in the system Preconscious in response to any eruption of undischarged libido. The further developments in symptom formation have the function of relieving such anxiety. If the psychoneurotic symptom were removed in some way, the patient would experience intense anxiety attacks. With the symptom intact, the anxiety disappears: Compare la belle indifference of the hysteric. The "primary gain" of psychoneurotic symptom formation is thus to maintain protection against the threat of anxiety produced by the basic psychoeconomic imbalance, the latter resulting from an increase in undischarged libido.

What takes place in these final steps of symptom formation occurs, once again, in the second system, the Preconscious. Freud called this final step a "Compromise Formation" in the form of a symptom. The symptom is made up of both the drive forces and the forces of punishment for it. This conflict produces a state of balance within itself, at the expense of the ego giving up part of its own integrity to the conflict. The symptom is thus a foreign body within the ego, which the ego recognizes as something alien within itself. The ego can do nothing about the symptom, however, except to rationalize it. Some symptoms, like inhibitions and phobias, are easy to rationalize. Compulsions are more difficult to rationalize, although some can be: for example, "just checking."

What gave this theory its real "meat" were all of the clinical findings regarding the emotional life of children that these concepts helped to explain: for example, dependency and separation problems, childhood fears and phobias, sibling rivalry, the Oedipus complex, and others.

Turning now to a *longitudinal perspective*: As a result of repression, the period of infantile sexuality (and aggression) gives way to the period of latency.

QUESTION: "Repression" rather than "resolution"?

ANSWER: Both occur. Unmodified object attachments are repressed. But there is also the actual "transfer," rather than "transference," of libido to other objects.

One can discuss the development of the ego in terms of the drives (oral, anal, phallic), in terms of the object, or in terms of the anxieties (and methods of mastery) involved. There is also an overall development from the Pleasure to the Reality Principle. All of these processes go on together, but we cannot discuss them simultaneously; we have to consider them individually.

Freud conceived of the two systems, Unconscious and Preconscious, as achieving a balance at around the age of five or six, when there is a transition from the infantile period to latency. He postulated that at least a "transitional neurotic" development occurs at that time—fleeting phobias, for example—even in the ideally brought-up child. These (post)oedipal phobias differ from the preoedipal phobias, the former being transference phenomena that follow the model of psychoneurotic symptom formation.

These "transitional symptoms" then disappear and "character" develops instead. Certain personality characteristics may develop at the points of weakness in the structure: for example, hysterical character with frigidity developing as an intense inhibition of sexuality, associated with sexualization of nonsexual activities. Example: giggling, reacting to every medical examination as a flirtation, but frigid during intercourse. Other types of personality characteristics also may develop at this time, for example, compulsive character, phobic (avoiding) character, and others.

Lecture 10

Symptom Formation from a Longitudinal Perspective

Reviewing: Early psychological development can be studied from various standpoints: from the sequence of phases in libidinal development, the sequence of developing ego functions; the different kinds of anxiety experiences; and others. An important concept in Freud's early system was that every activity that later becomes nonlibidinal was originally libidinal. When a baby cries, for example, it does so not because it experiences "hunger"—a more complex, later experience—but because of libidinal oral frustration, which is relieved (discharged) by sucking: Compare the universal use of "pacifiers" for infants. Even locomotion is originally a "sexual" activity and is undertaken primarily for (erotic) pleasure gain.

When we speak of "orality," it is important to keep in mind that the nature of oral libido is not the same in the oral and phallic phases; both the nature and intensity of orality are different in each separate phase. Yet all of these infantile sexual stages have something in common that is not present in later (e.g., latency) phases. By the time of latency, a balance of forces has been reached that was not present before. At the transition from the Oedipus complex to latency, the sexual nature of infantile activities recedes into the background, is repressed.

The various characteristic defenses that develop at the point of transition are not pathological unless the defense impoverishes the child. The characteristic defense is determined largely by the particular aspect of preoedipal sexuality that needs extra protective repression. The crucial theoretical issue is the transition from the Oedipus complex to latency. The importance of that transition is best illustrated by reviewing Freud's classic concepts of compulsion neurosis.

Freud's concepts of compulsion neurosis: To begin with, we postulate a mother during the toilet-training period who both seductively encourages the child's anality and then punishes the child for it. The mother externalizes an inner conflict of her own with the child. The child reacts with alternate rebellion and submission and also with a strong fixation on anal–sadisitic libidinal and aggressive aims. The child does not have a neurosis at this time, however.

The child then proceeds to experience an oedipal period of development, but with what might be called an anal coloring. As a result, certain aspects of the Oedipus situation are reacted to in specific ways: for example, with a sadistic conception of the primal scene and anal theories of impregnation and birth.

Not only are the child's libidinal oedipal phantasies anally colored, but also his or her anxieties are different: for example, fear of being shamed sadistically and of being totally controlled. As a result, the transitional phobias preceding latency tend to be anally influenced and thus have an expecially primitive, archaic quality: for example, phantasies of "anal castration."

The first true regression occurs at this point, at the transition from the Oedipus conflict to latency. The child regresses from the intensely frightening fantasies and feelings of anal–oedipal relationships with his or her parents and reverts back to a more regressive preoccupation with anal fantasies and anal masturbation. The anti-anal character defenses then develop, which give the defenses of compulsion neurotics a double layering: the strong surface defenses directed against the repressed anal–erotic and anal–sadistic phantasies, and the whole system of anality itself, which is a defense against the oedipal phobia.

What develops next are the well-known character traits of orderliness, stinginess, antiemotionality, and hyperrationality. The symptoms of compulsion neurosis not only are expressions of and defenses against anal–erotism and anal–sadism, but also express and defend against anally colored oedipal strivings.

What about cases in which a patient with an apparent compulsion neurosis turns out to be schizophrenic or paranoid? Does that make sense in the context of the preceding theory? To answer that question we must differentiate between an "archaic ego activity" and a symptom. Rituals, for example, are an archaic way of dealing with dangers; but if a person in a primitive culture believes in the efficacy of superstitious rituals, he is not a compulsion neurotic. The compulsion neurotic handles inner tensions by means of compulsive rituals. A ritual, therefore, is sometimes but not always a compulsive ego activity directed against anal–sadistic object relations.

Whether the compulsive ego activity is part of a compulsion neurosis or a compulsive defense against other internal or external dangers depends on the nature of the primitive object relation that is being defended against. In some cases, the crucial difference is whether the unconscious infantile object(-imago) is retained (as in compulsion neurosis) or abandoned (as in schizophrenia and paranoia). Thus a particular ego activity is not necessarily indicative of the underlying psychological structure.

Lecture 11

Freud's Theory of Psychosis

Reviewing: The symptoms of a transference neurosis can develop only after a fairly well-organized barrier has been established between the primary and secondary processes. Only then can a true phobia, which is a transference phenomenon, occur. Example: A patient has an exaggerated fear of the atomic bomb. Analysis leads to recovery of memories from around the age of six, memories of fearing earthquakes. A brief, transitory phobia occurred at that time, then disappeared, and later in life appeared again. It was possible in this case to connect the original phobia of earthquakes with infantile–sexual voyeuristic activities at age six and with discoveries made as a result of the voyeuristic activities.

There are also earlier, preoedipal phobias, but they are a different story with a different structure. It is at the time of the oedipal conflict, with its associated castration anxiety and superego development, that the repression barrier becomes firm enough—with preponderance of the system Preconscious over the system Unconscious—that transference phenomena such as (oedipal) phobias are able to develop. One cannot speak of "transference" without the existence of two stable and separate systems, because "transference" means transfer of qualities from the system Unconscious to a carrier in the system Preconscious.

In dreams, the preconscious carrier is a day residue that tends to be a relatively unimportant, inconsequential event. The analyst is a day residue par excellence, because he remains so quiet, neutral, and unobtrusive in the patient's life (see Part III of Freud's [1916–1917] "Introductory Lectures" for more about these concepts).

37

Freud's Theory of Psychosis

First, according to Freud (1915b; see also Fenichel, 1945, pp. 415–452), there is a similarity to transference neuroses:

1. A disappointment in reality, a frustration. How the patient reacts to such frustrations is influenced by the "complementary series."

2. Manifest regression: an increase in daydreaming, the same as in transference neuroses.

3. Regression proper: The difference between transference neuroses and psychosis lies here. In transference neuroses, the pull regressively comes from old childhood fixations on incestuous or otherwise forbidden objects. The regression in schizophrenia is toward preobject levels or fixation points. In schizophrenia, the core of the personality contains no (or markedly reduced) libidinal attachments to objects. In psychosis the regression is to an objectless fixation point that is threatening, not as an old highly cathected position of object attachments that might lead to punishment as in the transference neuroses, but because in these objectless regressive states large quantities of nonobject libido flood the person's own body and thus become traumatic, leading to:

4. Psychotic (in contrast to neurotic) hypochondria. According to an astute observation by Glover (1947), this type of hypochondria is the psychotic's effort to "theorize" about the strange bodily experiences produced by the objectless libido that attaches itself to his body organs. He attempts to relieve the condition by talking about it, complaining about it; he complains, for example, that the world seems to be slipping away. It is not the external world, however, but the inner unconscious core of objects that is losing cathexes.

Unlike the schizophrenic, even a Robinson Crusoe can have the feeling of object experiences all about him, because the experience of objects is fundamentally an inner experience based, for example, on memories and daydreams about objects. The experience of objects depends on the intactness of libidinal object cathexes in the deep layers of the psyche. Loneliness is not schizophrenia. In the psychoses, the cathexes withdrawn from object-imagoes become attached to body organs and produce disturbing organ tensions, an "actual neurosis."

Thus psychotic hypochondria is the actual neurotic core of psychosis, corresponding with the traumatic (anxiety) neurosis as the "actual neurotic core" of the psychoneuroses. When psychotic hypochondria occurs, the body organs lose their meaning of I–You; they cease to be instruments of object relations. An experience of preobject, autoerotic, narcissistic tension sets in, a state that is painful to the psychotic because the healthy residue of his ego observes itself losing its equilibrium, its organization, its inner objects. Experienced schizoid characters protect themselves from that pain by walling themselves off from the world. They know their sensitivity, and know that if they make contact with people and get hurt they will regress to the objectless–narcissistic–autoerotic state that is so painful to the remaining ego. Another common and frightening regressive symptom is the delusion that the world is coming to an end, the basis of which is that due to the narcissistic regression the psychotic is the world, his inner object world is collapsing; the object cathexes in his Unconscious are "coming to an end."

5. The pain of narcissistic regression motivates the psychotic's attempts to make restitution—that is, to regain contact with (inner) objects in order to "cure" the psychotic state. An example of such restitution, according to Freud (1915b), is the psychotic's use of neologisms. Although the psychotic's nuclear (childhood) objects are decathected in the Unconscious, the verbal representations of objects in the Preconscious remain cathected. In his restitutive efforts to heal himself, the psychotic hypercathects the preconscious word-symbols of objects. As a result, words take on greater meaning; they become "objects," and the patient creates new "objects" out of his words. He "loves" words and "plays" with them as if they were not just the symbols of objects but objects themselves, which produces the neologisms of the schizophrenic patient.

Additional restitutive efforts include the development of delusions and hallucinations. In his seminal paper on the "influencing machine" in schizophrenia, Viktor Tausk (1933) was able to fathom the essentially objectless narcissistic state of a psychotic patient who at the same time tried to express and explain the strangeness of that state. It was a stroke of genius on Tausk's part when he recognized that the patient's delusion of an "influencing machine" was an attempt to regain some kind of contact with objects: "At least they are after me, trying to get me." Who is? Not objects, because they are decathected. Then what is that behind the patient, chasing him? A narcissistically hypercathected experience of his own buttocks and feces, which have been projected (restitutively) as external "objects"—a desperate attempt to regain some kind of contact with objects. Like neologisms, therefore, delusions and hallucinations provide a restitutive pretense of object relations.

From a longitudinal perspective, the traumatic fixation in psychotic pathology occurs very early—for example, in connection with experiences of not being able to trust reality. As a result, an "*as if*" adjustment is made. Psychotic regressions begin occurring in early adulthood, when frustrations associated with adult object relations are frequent. So much cathexis has been fixated at an early objectless state that not much is left over for later development, most later development being merely an attempt to defend against the traumatic core.

The frustration for schizoid persons in early adulthood is often an experience such as marriage, which interferes with the defense of keeping distance from emotional involvements: Compare the danger for these patients of too much closeness. In therapy these patients need to learn that they are different from other people; they must accept and live with that fact. They may have to learn that marriage and having children are not for them. They need to respect themselves with their differences, rather than attempting to imitate others by getting married and having children.

Lecture 12

Freud's Theory of Depression, and Preoedipal Phobias

Reviewing: In his early formulations, Freud considered symptom formation in both the neuroses and psychoses to be "compromises"—between ego and id in the transference neuroses and between lost reality and attempts to regain it in psychoses. In some respects, both neuroses and psychoses represent retreats from reality. In the neurotic, the interpersonal conflict that produces frustration and introversion sets in motion a regressive reactivation of feelings and memories associated with old object relationships, which when revived produce conflict with preconscious strivings—a structural conflict. The transference neurosis is a prototype of such internal, endogenous pathology.

The psychotic regression, on the other hand, is to early narcissistic positions that also resulted from traumatic experiences, but in this case of a particularly early and severe kind. In the process of psychotic regression, internal objects are lost, and as the narcissistic positions regressed to are preobject, they are experienced as strange and frightening kinds of pleasures—dangers that may destroy the person. Restitutive symptoms in the psychotic, such as hallucinations, delusions, and neologisms, are comparatively healthy attempts to regain contact with objects. In psychiatric hospitals, ward personnel often assume that the development of delusions or hallucinations in a psychotic patient indicates that the condition is getting worse, whereas in fact the opposite may be the case.

FREUD'S THEORY OF DEPRESSION

The fixation point in depression is midway between an objectless narcissistic state and the beginnings of object strivings. The repressed rage in these patients is toward a vague object that is not entirely clear or defined (e.g., the breast) and is still confused with the self, hence Freud's concept that the object loss in depressives is specifically that of a love object chosen on the basis of identification—that is, a narcissistic object choice. What is lost is thus very close to the self, like losing a part of one's self. These concepts help to explain the "self-devouring" nature of the rage in depressive patients: The object toward which the rage is directed is not fully differentiated from the self, so the rage, which should be an outwardly directed object rage, is still too much identified with the self and thus has the qualities of a self-directed rage.

Why is the superego in such patients always more punitive than the parents were? Because the superego results not only from the parents' actual punitiveness, but also from the parents' unconscious hostilities, and still further from the child's hostile projections to the parents.

PREOEDIPAL PHOBIAS

We have discussed the oedipal phobias as the nucleus of the transference neuroses. The preoedipal phobia is the nucleus of psychosis.

Clinical example: A two-year-old child is frightened by the buzz of a fly in the room. In a child that young we are dealing with an unstable psychological system in which drive control is not yet certain or secure. The child goes through periods of oscillation between newly acquired drive control resulting from the skills he develops—which are not yet firmly established, however—and unmastered drives, which can still break through and be perceived as something frightening. The latter perception and anxiety may be projected into the external world, as in the buzz of the fly. At such times the child needs his parents nearby to calm him and to help him feel reassured that his drive control is secure.

Every new skill that is learned has drive control significance—see, for example, Freud's (1932) paper "The Acquisition and the

Control of Fire." He developed the interesting theory that every major advance in human progress is due to success in drive control. The "taming of fire" may have come about, for example, when primitive man developed the capacity to control his drive to extinguish the feared fire, the urge to urinate on it. According to this concept, the fire had been feared largely because inner drives had been externalized or projected onto it.

It is important to distinguish, however, between projections through a repression barrier, as in the case of Little Hans (Freud, 1909a), and projections from an insecure, crumbling ego with release of id drives. "There are projections and there are projections," and one must specify which kind he or she means: Compare, for example, the difference between a projection of id contents and the projection involved in empathy as an attempt to understand another person.

Just as schizophrenic delusions are the schizophrenic's theories about his narcissistic experiences and hypochondriacal symptoms are the hypochondriac's theories about his narcissistic body experiences, so are the preoedipal phobias the young child's theories about his disturbing drives—drives that newly acquired skills have not yet firmly and securely mastered.

Even sleep is a skill and, as such, has drive control significance. Some people have never learned it—have never learned how to give up the pleasure of one more story, or one more pleasure of any kind, and go to sleep. Fear of sleep can also be a fear of losing drive control, a form of insomnia that must be seen in the context of psychotic personality structure. There are other forms of insomnia—true sleep phobias, for example, which are transference neuroses— in which sleep is feared because it takes on the transference meaning of a forbidden sexual activity.

Lecture 13

Chapter 7 in "The Interpretation of Dreams"

Freud (1900) wrote that his work on dreams might stand or fall on one small detail: The reporting of dreams is so faulty. He suggested that forgetting itself is part of the dream censorship. The determinism of psychic events demands that distortions and differences in the telling of dreams must have reasons, too. In fact, distortions and differences in the retelling of dreams are the most important parts of the dream to analyze.

The question then arises: Why in the greatest 100 pages of Freud's entire writings did he introduce the subject with such a seemingly minor point—the forgetting of dreams? The answer is that by approaching the matter in this way, his major discoveries do not seem like oddities but appear built-in to our everyday mental functioning. That is, the same forces that are operative in the "strange" activity of dreaming, during the sleep state, also operate in our more familiar waking state. Hence, there are forces and counterforces operating and interacting during both sleep and waking states.

Memory functions, too, have a dynamic basis: We remember what we can afford to remember—what we dare to allow ourselves to remember. Memory has both structure and dynamics. One remembers against resistances, just as one dreams against resistances. Freud (1925) made a similar point in his paper "Negation": The Unconscious (actually, the id) knows only wishes—no negations or even partials. Thus the infantile psyche can only hallucinate wishes as fulfilled. If a patient dreamed of a "vague woman," Freud would ask who she was. If the patient replied that it was not his mother, Freud concluded that it was his mother. The concept "no" must come from the other system (the secondary process). True free association has the same characteristic: It includes only positives. By contrast, the forgetting of dreams exemplifies the inhibiting, negating influence of one system (preconscious, or Pcs) on the other (unconscious, or Ucs).

QUESTION: If the forgetting of dreams occurs during the waking state, and if these are the same forces of censorship that are operative in the dream work, then the dream must still be going on when the person is awake, and dreams may not be confined to sleep. Is it possible that dreaming goes on all the time, regardless of whether awake or sleeping?

ANSWER: Id contents attach themselves to day residues constantly. What we usually call a dream, however, is the "manifest dream." A "dream," for example, is not the same as Silberer's (1909, 1912, 1919) anagogic imagery. The transferences that go on all the time between the id and the deeper layers of the ego are not usually conscious to the person. Why? Because the conscious and preconscious ego heavily overlays these deeper ego processes and tends to cover them by their sheer mass. Highly creative, especially artistically creative persons, can suspend these higher layers by a "contraction of the ego" and observe what is going on in the deeper ego layers where transferences take place from the id to day residues. Herbert Silberer was very good at doing that: For example, in a reverie about smoothing out an essay he was writing, an image of a carpenter's plane smoothing a piece of wood came to his mind.

That kind of thinking in concrete images lends itself most readily to transferences from id contents. In the uppermost layers of the ego, mental functioning occurs mainly in the form of words and concepts—in deeper layers as imagery. Freud (1914c) accepted Silberer's (1919) concept of "threshold symbolism," which is applicable in this connection: For example, a person dreams that he sees two people quarreling, which represents symbolically a transference of primal scene id content. The dreamer (in the dream) then moves from room to room—a pictorialization of the dreamer observing himself waking up. The latter imagery lacks the structure, however, of an id transference to the ego; it is an anagogic image of the type called "threshold symbolism," which occurs at the threshold between sleeping and awakening.

There is a continuum in the ego from surface words and concepts to more primitive, concrete, imagistic ego functioning. The deeper, more primitive ego activities more nearly approach the primary process mode of thought; thus a continuum exists between primary and secondary processes. The deeper ego activities are more primary, less secondary processes. With contraction of the ego, regression can occur to the level of a more primitive, concrete, imagistic type of thinking, as in daydreaming, hypnogogic, hypnopompic, and anagogic phenomena. Images of that kind are the material out of which a dream may be made, but they are not the dream or the dream work itself.

There are resistances against such regressions. Artists are least afraid of and most skilled at experiencing such regressions. Sense of humor is also based on resilient regressions of that kind, as in punning—regressing quickly to primary process and just as quickly returning to secondary process functioning. Absence of a sense of humor is an inhibition based on fear of such regression, as in fear of sleep. In the voluntary regression of sleep, the "border traffic" between id and ego, which goes on all the time anyway, may become observable. There are also resistances against such observations, but "working over" of such observations (i.e., of dreams and their secondary elaborations) renders them less ego-dystonic so that the dream can be remembered and can become more or less "at home" in the ego. In the Rorschach test, the participant is presented with relatively formless visual materials that serve as day residues on which transferences may be made.

The interpretation of dreams is the most important aspect of psychoanalytic psychology, dreams being the paradigm of this discipline. Freud (1900) suggested that from one remembered fragment of a dream it may be possible to reconstruct the entire dream. That observation places memory and recall in the total framework or context of emotional dynamics.

Example: At the end of an interview, the analyst tells a patient that his appointment will be changed from 9:00 to 10:00 A.M. the next day. The patient accepts the change. The next day the patient recalls that he had a dream, but he cannot remember the content of the dream. Later in the session, after material that seemed to suggest sibling rivalry, the analyst asks how the patient reacted to the appointment change. The patient replies that he had no particular reaction to the change. The analyst then asks, "But didn't you feel again that you were being replaced by your brother?" The patient agrees somewhat sheepishly that such a thought had occurred to him; and then suddenly he remembers his dream, which dealt with sibling rivalry.

Freud pointed out that not only may the dream itself be forgotten, but the interpretive work done on a dream also may be "sucked away" by the resistances. Another example is inhibition of introspection and psychological-mindedness, which may be due to fear of the regression involved. Compulsive inhibition of introspection is often based on a fear of reviving the temptations and anxieties of masturbation.

Lecture 14

Chapter 7, Section A: The Forgetting of Dreams

Reviewing: By beginning chapter 7 with the subject of forgetting dreams, Freud built his dream theory into the psychology of the total personality and its functioning. With that approach he undercut the prevalent resistance of isolation—the attitude that dreaming is an isolated, esoteric phenomenon that is beyond the person's control.

The importance of mental forces called *resistances* can hardly be overemphasized. The resistances are the most important aspects of analytic work. Analysis without resistance is not really analyzing. Analysis that changes the balance of forces in the mind is always analysis that struggles against resistances.

There are certain parallels between dreaming and what we do in analysis—for example, regression in the service of the ego for an adaptive purpose. In analysis the patient lies down and part of the patient's ego regresses while another part remains alertly awake, observing the regressive part. Sterba (1934) referred to this phenomenon as a "splitting of the ego" in analysis. The analyst's presence is very important in this regard. At times the analyst insists that the patient "wake up" completely and see what maladaptive processes have occurred in the regressed part of his ego. All of this depends on a certain kind of relationship with the analyst: a trusting, loving attitude. The analysis is not merely a sleeping-regressive activity, therefore, but is a partially regressive, partially wakeful process. All comes to naught unless eventually the transferences to the analyst have been resolved by complete "wakefulness" about them.

QUESTION: What did Freud mean by his statement (in section A, chapter 7) about the "navel" of the dream—that is, the point at which there is such a condensed tangle of dream thoughts that they cannot be unravelled?

ANSWER: That concept refers, among other things, to the process of analysis—tracing connections from current events to their unconscious ramifications. Take the example of Freud hearing that someone was appointed to the rank of full professor. Why couldn't he dream straightforwardly of wanting to be a professor? Where is the resistance located? He could recognize fairly easily his not wanting to be the kind of person who would be superficially ambitious. But the wish to be a full professor also had connections with infantile phantasies of greatness, associated with oedipal rivalry toward his father. It was the unconscious infantile connections that produced both the intensity and the persistence of his wishes for greatness, and also the resistances against those wishes. Because the infantile wishes have many ramifications, which are condensed as overdeterminants in the images of a dream, we can never trace all of the connections and branches of the infantile complex.

Free association follows a path that is opposite to that of the dream work. It need not follow a direct or straight path, however, or even the same path that was followed by the dream work. Although dream work goes on all night, what Freud called "the dream" was its manifest content, which is perceived by the "eye of Consciousness" as an external event. With respect to both inner and outer perception, Freud concluded that Consciousness is partially, but never completely, asleep during the sleep state. A selective amount of wakefulness continues during sleep, both toward the outer world and toward dreaming. Unless the dream content is perceived it is not called a dream, but "dream work." Kleitman's (1963) studies confirm this: Dreams (according to the preceding definition in which the dream content is perceived by Consciousness) occur mainly when a person is waking up.

Lecture 15

Chapter 7, Section B: Regression

Reviewing: Freud emphasized that wishes are not represented in dreams as possibilities, probabilities, or with any "perhaps," but in the present tense as wishes fulfilled.

QUESTION: Isn't all thinking, not just dreaming, based on fulfilled wishes?

ANSWER: The dream is a regression to a primitive psychological state in which there is no differentiation between wishing, thinking, and acting. In this primitive mode of mental functioning, wishes are simply thought of as fulfilled. This concept is not just a logical tour de force but is a fundamental quality of primitive mental functioning. Thus, "a person dying of thirst dies 'drinking'" (i.e., hallucinating satisfaction).

The question whether all thinking is wish-fulfillment must be answered also in terms of Freud's (1911b) two principles of mental functioning. The Reality Principle is not entirely different from the Pleasure Principle, but is a specialized form, a refinement, of the Pleasure Principle. The Reality Principle involves a detour on the way to pleasure, but its purpose is still to obtain a maximal amount of pleasure.

For the baby—psychologically, not biologically—the experience of hunger and feeding is registered only in terms of sensory impressions, not in terms of biological phenomena. Later, when discrimination occurs between hallucinatory and real satisfaction, the detours in reaching a goal (e.g., thinking about it) still have a slightly sensory quality that reveals itself, for example, in one's choice of words or imagery.

Thinking processes follow the same course of development as the development from the Pleasure Principle to the Reality Principle—that is, becoming more able to wait, putting aside immediate pleasure for eventual satisfaction. Even when parts of the thinking process become autonomous, they still do not occur without some kind of pleasure gradient. It would be a genetic fallacy, however, to say that "all thinking is wish-fulfillment"; for even though adult thinking processes (following the Reality Principle) develop out of the original Pleasure Principle, that is not to say that adult thinking processes are the same as the original, primitive, infantile, hallucinatory, Pleasure Principle, wish-fulfilling type of thinking.

CHAPTER 7, SECTION B

In this section Freud discusses the "agencies"—a poor translation of his term *Instanzen*, which means "hierarchies," like "going through channels" in a bureaucracy. Freud pointed out that the processes he was describing must have a direction; they aim toward reestablishing a state of balance that has been disturbed. As long as the baby is in a state of primary narcissistic balance, one cannot speak of psychological processes; the latter occur only after the primary narcissistic state has been disturbed. When psychological processes begin, their original form is the primary process type of thinking: immediate hallucinatory wish-fulfillment. Freud stressed that the positive memories laid down must be differentiated from the organ that perceives and registers the experiences.

Freud employed two analogies for the relationship between the Preconscious and Consciousness:

1. *Nontopographic analogy:* an "eye" or "searchlight" focused on some of the processes going on in the Preconscious. The "Eye of Consciousness" has to exert some effort to make the preconscious mental activity perceivable (i.e., conscious). That effort is the "attention cathexis" that hypercathects selected preconscious mental activities:

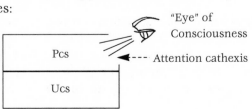

2. *Topographic analogy:* A barrier exists between the system Consciousness and the system Preconscious, which a preconscious content must overcome by being charged with attention hypercathexis in order to become conscious:

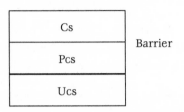

Perception, however, cannot be examined in isolation from the drives. We turn toward and perceive that which the drives impel us to search for and perceive. Perception-consciousness (Pcpt.-Cs.) is driven to scan the world because hallucinatory wish-fulfillment fails. At first the baby scans internally for sensory impressions (memory traces) of mother–breast–satisfaction, which the infant finds, but these memories do not relieve the imbalance produced by hunger for very long. The moment those memories fail to satisfy, the internal sensory impressions of mother–breast–satisfaction ("hallucination") are separated from realistic impressions of satisfaction and become the first memory. These early memory systems are returned to regressively under the stress of drive wishes in dreams and daydreams (cf. "manifest regression" or "introversion" as the first step in the process of symptom formation).

QUESTION: If in the dream there is a regression to those early memory traces, why doesn't the dreamer dream directly of satisfaction—for example, in the form of early memory traces of satisfaction?

ANSWER: Because dreams are not merely primitive mental processes but are "compromise formations" between disturbing primitive wishes and the reduced but still active defensive functions of the (partially) sleeping ego.

QUESTION: How do these concepts apply to those first dreams in analysis in which the analyst appears in an undisguised form?

ANSWER: That is due to the fact that either the analyst actually resembles an important childhood imago or the patient's defensive ego mechanisms are very weak and allow the formation of an immediate deep transference. Normally in analysis, a realistic bond is formed initially between the analyst as a reality figure and the realistic ego of the patient. On the basis and background of that realistic bond, a gradual regression, against resistances, then occurs, which results in the development of the transference. The transference is then analyzed— that is, realistic and unrealistic aspects are differentiated by the reality ego, which is supported by the reality of the analyst. First dreams that express an immediate deep transference without sufficient resistance are an indication that the patient's reality perception (of the analyst) is weak—a warning signal prognostically.

QUESTION: What is memory?

ANSWER: It is a permanent alteration on the basis of experience. "Remembering" is making a memory conscious. Memory itself has nothing to do with Consciousness. A memory becomes a memory by virtue of an experience losing some of its sensory quality, so that it can be differentiated from real perceptions but is recognizable as having been perceived in the past.

Lecture 16

Chapter 7, Section B: Regression (continued)

Reviewing: Freud postulated that in dreams the excitation travels backward from its usual direction. It usually travels from perception to motor activity, but in dreams it travels backward, toward perception—hence the concept of "topic regression" in dreams. What Freud was trying to explain with this concept was why dreams "look" the way they do, full of primitive pictures and lacking the logic of thinking processes in the waking state.

QUESTION: "The motor end is progressive, the sensory end regressive." What is the meaning of that? How does it apply to patients?

ANSWER: The concept refers to the relationship between the perceptive and motor ends of the mental apparatus. When a libidinal or aggressive impulse arises "from the depths," it must be guided by (perceptual) memories from the past in its choice of and path to motor discharge. If the flow is from the perceptive-memory end to the motor end, the flow is "progressive," the usual direction of the reflex arc. If recathexis of memories is accepted as sufficient satisfaction in itself, however, that would be "regressive."

QUESTION: What about "acting out"? Doesn't it follow the opposite pattern—that is, less "regressive" than being able to allow some (sensory) fantasies about the impulse?

ANSWER: Acting out is not true action. That is, it does not involve integrated patterns of behavior based on memory traces. It is a transference from the unconscious part of the ego to some situation in reality and then doing something that is related more to a direct satisfaction of the infantile wish via hallucinatory fulfillment. Acting out, therefore, is more regressive.

QUESTION: Would sleep-walking be homologous to acting out?

ANSWER: Sleep-walking has more to do with the mimicry of hysterical attacks. The small child often observes by attempting to be like what he observes: For example, in watching a bird, the child may flap his arms. Hence perception and body motion are closer together in the primitive, undeveloped psyche. Somnambulism is often a walking toward the room where the parents have intercourse, which is more akin to hallucinatory satisfaction of infantile wishes than it is to action. In somnambulism, as in acting out, we are not dealing with integrated voluntary action but with an instance of "the horse running away with the rider." In somnambulism the rider is passive and apparently asleep; in acting out the rider pretends to be in control of where the horse is going, although in reality he has to accept the direction of the horse. To make these distinctions about the psychological nature of different kinds of actions, one must study the underlying psychological structures of the actions involved—that is, the relation between Unconscious and Preconscious (or, better, between id and ego), how it was laid down, and the mechanisms of its occurrence.

Dreams have a propensity for regressive sensory-perceptive reactivation of memory images instead of following the normal channel toward Consciousness and action. That tendency is facilitated by resistances that continue to operate against the "normal channel," even during sleep. A part of the inclination toward hallucinatory processes results from the fact that external reality is (largely) shut out when we sleep (cf. the correlation between progressive deafness and the incidence of auditory hallucinations; and the related finding that the lower the amount and accuracy of mental imagery in a particular sensory modality, the higher the incidence of hallucinations in that modality [Seitz and Molholm, 1947]).

Freud proposed three ways of describing the single phenomenon of regression: topographic, temporal (i.e., regression to older behavior patterns), and formal (i.e., regression in form; e.g., to more primitive forms of mental activity). Usually all three varieties of regression are involved together. Freud emphasized also the similarity of regression in dreams and in symptom formation.

The regressive context in which day residues are woven into dreams poses a special problem. At times, the day residue seems to have been perceived in a waking context within the realm of secondary process mentation. Its appearance in the dream results from dynamic connections with unconscious contents and thus is related to regressive strivings. At other times, an immediate perception that is used later in a dream was already regressive when it was perceived.

Example: A patient noticed (unconsciously) the analyst's new eyeglasses. That night he dreamed of them in a context of projected infantile voyeurism as big, searching, dark-rimmed eyes. In this case, the new eyeglasses were perceived originally in the regressive voyeuristic context with which the patient was preoccupied at the time. It is likely that most perceptions that become day residues are perceived simultaneously in both realistic and (formally) regressive ways.

Lecture 17

Chapter 7, Section C: Wish-Fulfillment

A preconscious wish by itself cannot produce a dream. For dream formation to occur, the preconscious wish must activate an unconscious connection with an infantile complex. The same is true not only of dreams but of any influence from the Unconscious. Wanting to become a professor, for example, was a preconscious wish in Freud, but by itself that wish could not produce a dream. His preconscious wish was fed constantly by transferences, however, which can and do produce dreams. Even then Freud did not dream manifestly of being a professor.

Freud's original model was:

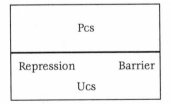

Note complete separation of the two systems by a repression barrier.

His later model became:

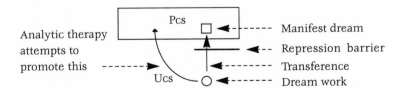

Thus movement of unconscious contents into the Preconscious may occur not only by transferences across or through the repression barrier, but also more directly (as shown in the second model) as a result of therapeutically induced reduction in defensive activities. Freud's concept that unsatisfied wishes and unsolved problems of the day give rise to dreams gained indirect support from later experiments by Zeigarnik (1927), who found that unfinished tasks are remembered longer and more clearly.

QUESTION: How can the dramatic acting out of the severe hysteric and of the psychotic be differentiated?

ANSWER: The hysteric acts out memories of fantasies dealing with object relationships; the schizophrenic acts out inner objectless narcissistic experiences. Psychoanalytic theory helps to distinguish between these two types of "breaks" with reality. The neurotic break is a regression from a frustrating current object relationship to a libidinal (incestuous) object of childhood. The psychotic regresses farther, breaks with the infantile objects, and reverts to narcissistic substitutes for the lost infantile objects. The break with reality in the neurotic is a break with current objects. The break with reality in psychotic patients is more serious, a break with the original infantile object ties that underlie and provide the foundations for all later object relationships.

Lecture 18

Chapter 7, Section C: Wish-Fulfillment (continued)

Dreams may be divided into those with open wish-fulfillment and those in which the wish-fulfillment is disguised by the censorship. The wishes in dreams arise from the Unconscious. Dreams are instigated by day residues, but an imperceptible preconscious wish during the day may succeed in giving rise to a dream only if it allies itself with an unconscious wish. Freud theorized that the day residues become attached to "energies" of the Unconscious and that transferences to the Preconscious then occur in the production of dreams. Psychoanalysis approaches the unconscious depths from the surface downward, one layer at a time.

With respect to the formal aspects of unconscious activity (i.e., the form it takes), the part of a dream that has a peculiar sensory intensity is the point of direct wish-fulfillment in the dream. Preconscious wishes do not have the same form, "color," or characteristics as unconscious wishes. Preconscious wishes do not seem as foreign or alien to the ego. Unconscious wishes have a quality of foreignness, a more concrete quality, and quantitatively are more powerful. In the unconscious portion of the superego, the form of punishment is also more archaic: for example, "If you do that you'll get your penis cut off!"

The two systems, Unconscious and Preconscious, are incompatible. In the Unconscious, the more intensely one wishes something, the greater the sensory impression that it registers in the Preconscious. The Unconsicous consists only of drives seeking wish-fulfillment. The attitude of the Preconscious toward the dream is "Go ahead and have the dream. After all, you are only dreaming."

QUESTION: At what stage of development can we begin to think of a baby in psychological terms?

ANSWER: Much depends on the definition of *psychological*. It might be better to rephrase the question and ask at what stage we can imagine the existence of some kind of self-awareness in the baby—some precursor of introspection. To review a previous discussion: The undisturbed organism in primary narcissistic balance need not be aware of itself. The paradigm of the first really serious and repeated disturbance of this balance is the biological imbalance that produces the experience of hunger. The biological imbalance leads reflexly to crying. The cry brings the mother, who feeds the baby, and the hunger subsides. This sequence of events, which can be described satisfactorily in biological and social terms, leaves the organism structurally different than it was before. A biological alteration corresponding with the psychological concept of "memory trace" is now present. Schematically:

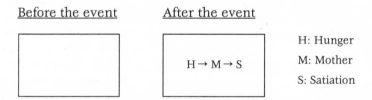

Before the event   After the event

$$H \rightarrow M \rightarrow S$$

H: Hunger
M: Mother
S: Satiation

It is questionable, however, whether one can assume a self-awareness, a budding introspection, at the stage of the preceding diagrams. A second episode of the biological changes associated with hunger then occurs. The infant cathects (biologically) those structural alterations in its organization that correspond with the sequence $H \rightarrow M \rightarrow S$, which (from the standpoint of the observer) may be called a primal hallucination. Cathecting the $H \rightarrow M \rightarrow S$ sequence, however, does not prevent the hunger tension from increasing. The reflex cry recurs, the real mother comes and feeds, the hunger subsides; now there are two parallel experiences that the baby begins to differentiate:

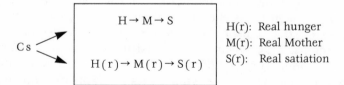

Cs

$$H \rightarrow M \rightarrow S$$

$$H(r) \rightarrow M(r) \rightarrow S(r)$$

H(r): Real hunger
M(r): Real Mother
S(r): Real satiation

A beginning introspective awareness gradually develops as a differentiation between:

1. The hallucinatory experience of recathecting (psychologically) the structural change produced by a formerly real event.

2. The experience of the real event itself. As a result of this differentiation, the hallucination becomes a memory. At this stage we can assume a rudimentary awareness and can think in "psychological" terms.

Further developments can be grasped more clearly in psychological terms: repeated hunger experiences, repeated recathecting of the memory trace, and repeated reexperiencing of the real feeding. Each time that sequence occurs, recathexis of the structural change becomes less a goal in itself and more of a way station on the path to real satisfaction. The cry becomes less of a passive reflexive experience and more of a psychological act—"calling"—directed by the underlying memory of the feeding mother. The later psychological sequence then becomes

Hunger → Topographic regression to memory function → Action

The memory becomes less and less vivid, and finally in the adult contains only traces of the original sensory cathexis. Thus the secondary process develops out of the primary process under the influence of "optimal frustration." In the adult, if the regressive memory cathexis becomes the real goal again (topographic regression), with its original sensory vividness and a conviction of its reality, we speak of such a state as "hallucinations." Dreams are examples of such topic regressions.

Lecture 19

Chapter 7, Section D: The Function of Dreams

In the sleep state the Preconscious is focused on the wish to sleep. Unconscious wishes excited by events of the day produce disturbances of sleep. In addition to being stimulated by day residues, unconscious wishes may also be transferred to day residues. Section D of chapter 7 deals with the model of mental functioning that Freud attempted to develop at that time—how the various activities of the mind affect and are balanced by each other. He employed the following very simple model in 1900:

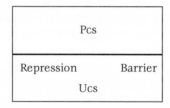

Freud postulated a wish for sleep in the Preconscious, which is relative however; what actually occurs is partial wakefulness. The ability to sleep in an ego activity—not just a biological given, but a learned activity (cf. Kris's [1952] concept of controlled regression, "regression in the service of the ego"). The child has conflict about going to sleep; he would like to stay awake and play longer. The parents must help the child learn how to give up higher functions and go to sleep.

Decathexis of the system ego in sleep involves more than the exclusion of external stimuli. Inner stimulation—for example, unconscious drives—also need to be excluded. It is the Preconscious that goes to sleep. Sleep, therefore, is not merely an id function but also an ego activity in which the person learns to decathect his or her own ego system. The child is aided in learning this process by parents providing protective wakefulness for the child, so that he can give up his own wakefulness and feel secure enough to fall asleep. The child also learns this by identification with what the parents do to prepare for and bring on the state of sleep.

One of the reasons that Freud was intent on developing a model of sleep was because it provided a model for psychoanalytic therapy. For example, the analyst takes over the function of protective-supportive wakefulness while the patient lies down as if asleep and undergoes a controlled ego regression. The parallel between the therapeutic situation and sleeping was worked out further by Lewin (1954). Some of the most severe resistances in psychoanalysis are those of absolute silence, in which a patient with a relatively weak ego is unable to allow any regression or give up any control but avoids both by saying nothing.

Patients with extreme insomnia tend to have weak egos that cannot afford to give up wakefulness and undergo regression. On the other hand, the condition may be a sleep phobia—that is, fear that some barely checked sexual fantasy may emerge during sleep. More severe sleep disturbances in potentially schizophrenic patients may involve fear of the sleep regression becoming a terrifying narcissistic regression. In the insomnia of depressive patients, the sleeping ego may be awakened by the emergence of frightening oral-sadistic impulses.

Complete repression is neither necessary nor even possible during sleep. The process of dream formation makes it possible for intrusions from the Unconscious to be handled by dreaming while the rest of the ego continues to sleep. By the process of dreaming, the ego renders the dangerous id impulses harmless. When an unconscious wish becomes active during sleep, however, its intrusion into the Preconscious produces conflict with the preconscious wish to sleep.

During sleep the system Preconscious has shrunk and the mode of thinking regresses, becoming more like that of the primary process—experiencing rather than remembering. The wish and its fulfillment are close together during sleep, and the intrusion of a wish has strong sensory qualities. The wish stimulates primitive defensive maneuvers in whatever portion of the ego it enters. The defensive activities circumscribe the disturbance, the ego observing and treating it as a foreign body—a process that allows the rest of the ego to go on sleeping.

QUESTION: If the Preconscious were not sleeping when an unconscious wish intruded, would that produce a symptom rather than a dream?

ANSWER: Yes. The dynamics of dream formation and symptom formation are very similar—dreams occurring in the sleep state, symptoms in the waking state.

QUESTION: Freud said that the function of the dream is to protect sleep, but he stated also that much of the dream work goes on even before the person goes to sleep. Is that consistent?

ANSWER: Yes, because the most crucial part of the dream work, so far as the protection of sleep is concerned, occurs during sleep at the very point when the balances in the mind are disturbed and the disguised manifest dream is produced.

QUESTION: Are there states in which the cathexis of Consciousness itself is altered?

ANSWER: Yes. Increase of cathexis produces attention, focused attention, vigilance, and the like. A decrease of cathexis occurs, and may be marked, in the case of drug intoxication, concussion, and other such conditions. The decrease of cathexis during sleep, by contrast, is only moderate. During sleep a decathexis of Consciousness, the Preconscious, and the Unconscious occurs, but the decathesis is relatively greater in the systems Conscious and Preconscious. The imbalance of cathexis between the Unconscious and Preconscious during sleep necessitates dream formation to contain and neutralize unconscious intrusions. Registration of dreams occurs during periods of both falling asleep and awakening, when Consciousness is only partially decathected. An emergency recathexis of Consciousness is also available during sleep in case outer or inner stimuli call for greater activity by the ego and Consciousness. One cannot sleep well unless he can trust his capacity to wake up in case something unusual happens.

QUESTION: What did Freud mean by the "pleasure premium" of ideational processes?

ANSWER: He meant that one cannot think, have thoughts, without at least some residue of sensory experience that gives the ideation a small but still definite tone of pleasure.

Lecture 20

Chapter 7, Section D:
The Function of Dreams (continued)

There is no connection between the experience of time passage in dreams and the passage of time that an observer might ascribe to a dream. Time passage is part of the language of dreams, just as a snake, or vagueness, or rapidity of movement may express something in a dream. If time seems to pass slowly in a dream, it does not mean that the dream was actually long and drawn out, but it is a way of expressing some content in the dream. Freud explained that the mind is able to do that because the Preconscious has an enormous storehouse of memories that can be used in making a dream. Every book we have ever read, for example, is remembered in the storehouse of memory and can be brought forward for use in expressing whatever conflict and defenses are involved in a given dream. The actual process in the dream work of calling up such a story is quite rapid—like pressing a button and the number 3 being called up (cf. the post-Freudian, cognitive science "computer model" of mind).

QUESTION: What is the mechanism in the dream work that produces a sense of long time passage in a dream?

ANSWER: The storehouse of memory contains many memories of time passing slowly. Memories of that kind are called upon to represent slow time passage in dreams.

QUESTION: Are "traumatic memories" readily available for use in dream work?

ANSWER: No. Trauma produces sudden "wallings off" of infantile impulses. Thus traumatic memories cannot be remembered directly because they are not in a state that permits remembering. They can come out only in the form of transferences to the Preconscious.

QUESTION: It sounds as though the process by which walled-off traumatic events are brought out by analysis is the same as the process of normal development.

ANSWER: Yes, it is. The psychoanalytic process makes possible a reliving of missed phases of development. The most time-consuming part of analysis, however, consists of work with the many encrustations that have developed to keep the traumata walled off. Toward the end of this protracted, painstaking therapeutic work, one may then see a sort of reenactment of the original walled-off impulses and defenses.

QUESTION: Is the Preconscious inactive during sleep or is it actively working on problem solving?

ANSWER: A certain amount of problem-solving activity goes on, but at a reduced rate. Most problems are not solved during sleep or by dreams.

QUESTION: When Freud spoke of an unconscious idea intruding into the Preconscious, did he mean an "idea" or an "impulse"?

ANSWER: Strictly speaking, an impulse—actually, its cathexis. It is only when an unconscious impulse has transferred itself to a preconscious idea that the ego reacts with an "archaic hysterical attack" of anxiety and treats the intrusion as a threat because it is now in the realm of possible motor action (the realm of the Preconscious). As long as the impulse stays in the Unconscious behind the repression barrier, it is not a threat.

In a similar vein, one should not speak of unconscious emotions, because in Freud's early model emotions were part of the preconscious motor discharge reactions to the intrusions of drive-laden unconscious impulses. Using Freud's later model, however, in which much of the ego is unconscious, one may speak of unconscious emotion, because in that context it would refer to the unconscious part of the ego. The question is not really one between impulse and no impulse, but between impulse and modified impulse—the latter having the form of preconscious secondary process ideas and activities. The question is thus one between the highly erotic (and aggressive) drives of infancy and the "more rarified" activities of the secondary process. Even in these more "rarified" activities, however, there is still some libido left—for example, when we are "interested" in something.

It is worth noting also that the dream Freud presented in chapter 7, section D, illustrating libido being converted into anxiety, is the first time he discussed the concept of "primal scene."

Lecture 21

Chapter 7, Section E:
Primary and Secondary Processes

Why does Freud begin this section by equating the somatic and external sensory perceptions that occur during sleep (e.g., church bells ringing or the pain of a furuncle) with the day residues that contribute to dream formation? They are both located in the Preconscious. The day residues are retained in the Preconscious. Similarly, the external ringing of bells or pain of a furuncle enter the Preconscious via the system Perception–Conscious and thus lend themselves to transferences from the Unconscious. The somatic pain or external perception, like a day residue, may or may not disturb sleep. If a sensory stimulus is highly significant, it will awaken the sleeper—for example, if someone yells, "Fire!" If the emotional intensity of the stimulus is low, however, it becomes available for use as a preconscious carrier of transferences from the Unconscious. Thus Freud's equating sensory impressions during sleep with day residues was based on their similarity of location in the structures of the mind and their potential functions as day residues.

QUESTION: Does the day residue have to have some resonance with the unconscious wish that it activates and for which it becomes the preconscious carrier?

ANSWER: That depends on what one means by "resonance." Freud would say that the day residue "must lend itself to" transference from the unconscious wish. But the day residue must also be recent, trivial, and ambiguous in content. Thus transference objects are not chosen primarily because their content is similar to the content of unconscious wishes, but mainly because they are recent, trivial, and ambiguous (cf. Fisher's [1954] and Fisher and Paul's [1959] investigations of tachistoscopic images in dreams. Some investigators report, on the other hand, that day residues themselves are not ambiguous but that the person's way of perceiving when transferences are made to day residues may be characterized by ambiguity).

Dream thoughts can be formed during the day and be well developed before the dream is actually dreamed that night. Structurally, this suggests that certain preconscious thoughts and memories that occur during the day preceding the dream already begin to make connections with specific unconscious complexes that are active at the time. That night an intrusion of the unconscious complex into the Preconscious may occur, in which case the preconscious thoughts that were formed and organized during the day are already available for use as carriers of the transference from the Unconscious.

Dreaming occurs when the equilibrium between the Unconscious and the Preconscious is unequal, when the Unconscious is "stronger" than the Preconscious. In deep sleep (and in unconscious states following head trauma), the Unconscious goes to sleep too. Intrusions into the Preconscious do not occur under those conditions. Dreams occur when the Preconscious is relatively weaker than the Unconscious, for example, when falling asleep or waking up. In falling asleep, the Preconscious starts going to sleep rapidly, more rapidly than the Unconscious, making the Unconscious relatively stronger. It is then that intrusions from the unconscious are most likely to occur.

The role of Consciousness in these relationships is another factor, but one about which less is known because it is so difficult to study. The contributing factor in this connection is the extent to which the system Conscious is cathected or decathected.

Dream thoughts go on all the time—all day, for example. But they do not necessarily give rise to a dream unless (1) an unconscious wish is activated, (2) the unconscious wish has an opportunity (when the Preconscious is relatively weaker than the Unconscious) to transfer across the repression barrier to a preconscious day residue, and (3) the unconscious wish that is transferred to a preconscious carrier is then observed by Consciousness.

Although the system Conscious may turn actively toward the manifest dream (e.g., during psychoanalysis), Consciousness is passive vis-à-vis the dream thoughts. The dream work, with its often remarkable imagery, goes on altogether independently of Consciousness, which only "looks on," often with surprise, at the results of this foreign dream activity. "Right of entry" into Consciousness is not guaranteed simply by the transference of an unconscious wish to a preconscious day residue. Such dream thoughts may be denied Consciousness by their being repressed again—"drawn or sucked away into the Unconscious," as Freud (1915b) put it; but see also his later (1926a) essay, "Inhibitions, Symptoms and Anxiety," in which he discarded the earlier theory of an "attraction by the Unconscious." Similarly, just as there are resistances to remembering the dream, there are also resistances to remembering the day residues.

The dream work proper begins when the day residue makes a connection with an unconscious wish. The psychological structure formed in that way is quite similar to the structure of the psychoneurotic symptom. Up to a certain point in both dream and symptom formation, "manifest regression" can take place without being pathological. Similarly, day residues can be carried over into preconscious thoughts and memories without yet leading to a dream. But if the "manifest regression" proceeds to the further stage of "regression proper," with flowing back of libido from current objects to childhood objects, pathological symptom formation has begun. By the same token, when day residues make a connection with an unconscious wish during dream formation, a psychological structure is formed that proceeds to elaborate itself in a way that is foreign to the system Preconscious.

Lecture 22

Chapter 7, Section F: The Unconscious, Consciousness, and Reality

QUESTION: Does the Pleasure Principle apply only to the first system or to both the first and second systems?

ANSWER: When we speak of the Preconscious and Unconscious topographically, separated by a repression barrier, we may say that the Pleasure Principle applies to the functioning of the Unconscious, whereas the Reality Principle applies to the Preconscious. We must remember, however, that such a topography is the result of a long and gradual process of development, and in the latter sense the Reality Principle may be considered to have grown out of the Pleasure Principle (see Freud's [1911b] essay, "Formulations on the Two Principles of Mental Functioning"). The Reality Principle still retains the central feature of the Pleasure Principle—namely, seeking maximal pleasure and a minimum of necessary discomfort.

The Reality Principle is only a detour on the way to fulfillment of the Pleasure Principle. If the detour is too long, the delay itself may then be libidinized by various mechanisms. Even the most highly sublimated, aim-inhibited activities still retain some degree of sensory pleasure. The essence of repression is also to transform unpleasure into pleasure. Some pleasure-seeking impulses in the id would produce unpleasure in the form of anxiety and thus are repressed to avoid the anxiety.

The ability to foresee unpleasure in the future is a highly significant and useful development in improving adaptation to reality, but its ultimate aim is still to secure pleasure and to avoid pain. Thus the relationship between the Pleasure and Reality

Principles may be thought of as a continuum. At one end of the continuum, the wish and its satisfaction are very close together—ideally, immediate satisfaction, as soon as the wish arises. At the other end of the continuum, the wish and its satisfaction may be far apart or much delayed. Between these extremes are all gradations of postponement between the wish and its satisfaction.

Summing up this point: In the scheme of the topographically divided psyche, we think of the Pleasure Principle and the Reality Principle as different methods of functioning. From a developmental perspective, however, we must be able to conceive of the Pleasure Principle and the Reality Principle as a single continuum.

QUESTION: What is the "Purified Pleasure Ego"?

ANSWER: It is one of the devices or "tricks" that the developing psyche employs to protect itself from disturbances in its pleasurable narcissistic state. Anything unpleasant is attributed to the outside; everything pleasurable is attributed to the self. To employ this device, the psyche must be able to differentiate between self and not-self. The ego attempts to claim everything pleasurable as part of the self and attempts to differentiate the unpleasant as the not-self or the outside. Controlling and owning are not yet differentiated from being. Later, when the narcissistic state is disturbed still further, the parents will be invested with qualities of omnipotence. Still later, some of the narcissism projected to the parents will be reintrojected by the child to form that part of the superego called the ego-ideal.

QUESTION: But isn't the "essence" of repression a counter-cathexis?

ANSWER: No, a decathexis. The countercathexis comes afterward, like a "flying buttress" on a Gothic cathedral, to bolster and support the main wall, which is decathexis. Repression underlies all of the various other defenses.

QUESTION: What is the distinction between repression and denial?

ANSWER: Denial is a "turning away" from an external perception. Repression is an internal "turning away" from inner perceptions of disturbing impulses and wishes. We must remember, however, that mixtures of denial and repression are common, as denial is used to ward off external perceptions that might arouse disturbing inner impulses or wishes.

QUESTION: In a sense, isn't all ego energy countercathectic energy?

ANSWER: That question will be answered when we come to the structural point of view and discuss the ego in detail.

Chapter 7, Section F: The Unconscious, Consciousness, and Reality

Freud compared Consciousness with an eye, or a photographic plate, placed at the ocular of a telescope. The "virtual image" in the telescope may then be registered. What we see through the organ of Consciousness is not the same as what actually goes on in the mental processes themselves, but is changed through the operation of being observed by Consciousness.

The Unconscious is the true psychic reality. The essential nature of unconscious reality is as unknowable as the essential nature of external reality. External reality can be known only to the extent that we perceive it with our sensory organs, and the inner reality of the Unconscious can be known only insofar as we are able to perceive it through Consciousness.

Just as the eye has no memory, Consciousness also has no memory. There are no memory traces in Consciousness. We are prone to overestimate the role of Consciousness in intellectual activity and artistic creativity. Even in these higher forms of psychic functioning, most of the important mental activity goes on preconsciously.

QUESTION: What is meant by there being two ways of viewing or considering Consciousness?

ANSWER: In one context, Consciousness is a perceptual organ for observing "psychical qualities." The schematic model of that concept would be:

Pcpt.–Cs. (with two
surfaces, one
turned outward,
the other inward)

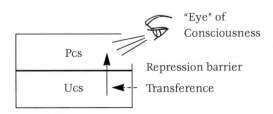

The contents of the Preconscious are changed by the process of becoming Conscious. Thus to differentiate conscious preconscious processes from preconscious processes that are not conscious, a different model is needed:

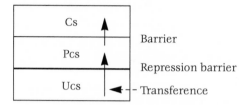

Psychoanalytic therapy enlarges the area of the Preconscious in certain sectors over that of the Unconscious. Consciousness is always at the frontier of learning, a temporary attention hypercathexis in the service of learning. The essential nature of analysis, however, is not in making things conscious but in expanding the area of the Preconscious at the expense of the Unconscious. The process of analysis, in which expansion of the Preconscious is opposed by emotional resistances, can occur only at the cost of some suffering in the form of anxiety. Similarly, the process of learning something consciously by means of attention hypercathexes also entails some "pain": For example, focused concentration on what is to be learned can be maintained only if other, potentially more pleasurable matters are ignored and made to suffer delay.

This completes our review of chapter 7 and of the first phase in the development of psychoanalytic theory.

Lecture 23

The Second Phase in the Development of Psychoanalytic Theory

The first period in the development of psychoanalytic theory was characterized by the topographic point of view. The second period emphasized the structural differentiation of mind into id, ego, and superego. The third period, which began around 1937 with the publication of Anna Freud's (1936) *The Ego and the Mechanisms of Defense* and Heinz Hartmann's (1939) *Ego Psychology and the Problem of Adaptation*, stressed the autonomy and dominance of the ego.

The second period of theory became necessary because certain clinical observations could not be accounted for on the basis of the earlier, simpler theoretical model, which led Freud to write his important paper, "On Narcissism" (1914c) and his papers on paranoid and depressive psychoses, "The Schreber Case" (1911a) and "Mourning and Melancholia" (1917c).

It was specifically the phenomena of narcissism and the psychoses that could not be fitted into the earlier, simpler model of the "transference neuroses." In the Schreber case, Freud recognized that the essence of the pathology was regression to a narcissistic state, with abandonment of object relations or cathexes. He also described certain mechanisms associated with such pathology—namely, defensive regression to narcissism and a restitutive attempt to regain contact with objects. With respect to the question of homosexuality in paranoia, Freud theorized that the regression from object relations occurs via homosexuality to narcissism and that the attempt to reestablish object cathexes retraces the same path, beginning with homosexual objects.

In mature object love the object is completely differentiated as "other," but it is loved. In the continuum from narcissism to object love, heterosexual relationships and homosexual relationships may involve more or less narcissism and more or less object love. Some varieties of homosexual relationships are closer to mature object love than some heterosexual relationships. Schematically:

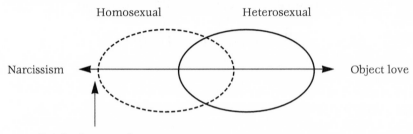

In pathological regressions to narcissism, psychosis occurs at the point when regression has proceeded beyond homosexual relationships to an essentially objectless narcissistic state. In restitutive attempts to regain relationships with objects, homosexual objects are recathected first because they are easier to establish; they are more like one's self and thus are closer to narcissism.

In his essay "The Unconscious," Freud (1915c) proposed his important theory about the psychological structure of neologisms. He postulated that the psychotic break with reality takes place in the depths of the Unconscious. The concrete "things" in the Unconscious—that is, the memories of actual object relationships in the depths of the Unconscious—are decathected. In an attempt to regain a semblance of object relations after the loss of the primary objects, the psychotic's psyche hypercathects the secondary process. The word symbols of objects are then treated by the schizophrenic as if they were actual objects themselves. The schizophrenic plays with words, combines them to form neologisms, but disregards their symbolic function because what is symbolized (the object) no longer has significance for him.

Lecture 24

Melancholia

Reviewing: We have been tracing the further development of psychoanalytic theory after the original id-oriented period but prior to the structural point of view. The first period in the development of psychoanalysis was devoted to the study of the "transference neuroses": the conversion hysterias, phobias, and obsessive-compulsive neurosis. Dreams, too, being transference phenomena, were studied during the early period of psychoanalysis. Before the advent of the structural viewpoint, a transitional period occurred in which new discoveries were made about narcissism and the psychoses. Freud became interested in a group of clinical phenomena that could not be explained in terms of transference. This is not to say that transference plays no part in these conditions, but only that transference is not at the center of symptom formation in narcissistic pathology.

In the case of melancholia, Freud theorized that the fixation point is intermediate between objectless narcissistic strivings and object interests. The rage in the depressive is toward a vague, ill-defined object that is not entirely clear (e.g., the breast), and that is still confused with the self. Hence Freud's concept that the object loss in depressions is specifically the loss of a love object chosen on the basis of identification—a narcissistic object choice. What is lost in the depressive is very close to the self. This concept helps to explain the "self-devouring" nature of the rage in such patients: That is, because the object whom the rage is directed toward is not fully differentiated from the self, the rage is not so much an outwardly directed object rage as a rage directed inward against the self.

QUESTION: Are the clinical syndromes of "anxiety reaction" and "hypochondriacal reaction" synonymous with what has been described here as the "anxiety neurotic nucleus" of the psychoneurosis and the "nuclear hypochondria" of the psychosis?

ANSWER: No. The "actual neurotic core" of the neurosis and psychosis—"anxiety neurotic core" in the case of psychoneurosis and "hypochondriacal core" in the case of psychosis—is a theoretical construct. Clinical symptoms of anxiety or hypochondria may occur in either a neurotic or psychotic structure.

QUESTION: How can the observation be explained that, on deeper study, obsessive–compulsive neurosis sometimes turns out to have an underlying schizophrenic core?

ANSWER: Although true phenomenologically, a structural distinction must be made. We must differentiate between archaic modes of mastery through magic, the modes of functioning of an early phase of ego development; and the total structure in which these forms of mastery through magic are embedded. The archaic ego attempts to ward off dangers by magical means—for example, by isolation, undoing, and ritual. Magical devices of that kind may be used also to influence an animistically interpreted external environment through religious rituals, which correspond with the mechanisms employed in psychopathology (cf. Freud's [1913b] "Totem and Taboo" and Ferenczi's [1913] "Stages in the Development of the Sense of Reality"). Thus the archaic ego uses such magical mechanisms in its fight against internal threats, both in neurosis and psychosis.

What determines whether pathology is neurotic or psychotic does not depend, therefore, on what the symptoms themselves are, but what they protect against. If a compulsive symptom protects against libidinal and aggressive object-strivings (usually of a regressive anal-sadistic nature), it is a neurotic symptom. But if the compulsive symptom protects against the danger of regression to a threatening objectless state, then it is a psychotic symptom. This distinction, once again, has useful clinical implications: It facilitates the clinician's understanding of the inner danger that the magical maneuvers attempt to ward off, and thus provides clues to therapeutic management.

Lecture 25

The Structural Model and Neutralization

Reviewing: Freud's investigations of psychopathology began with the more "mature" forms of pathology—the hysterias, for example—and deepened gradually to the more severe disorders: compulsion neurosis, and eventually the narcissistic disorders.

QUESTION: Is the anxiety in schizophrenic patients due entirely to the strangeness of the narcissistically regressed state, or is some of the anxiety due to loss of object relations?

ANSWER: It is both, and the two are related. Basically, it is a fear of being unable to discharge libidinal and aggressive tensions—a fear of such tension accumulating, with insufficient outlets (objects) for discharging and thus reducing the tensions.

In the case of depressions, Freud theorized that the original relationship with the mother had been disturbed, leading to fixation on a type of relationship in which the object is not well differentiated from the self. In "Inhibitions, Symptoms and Anxiety," Freud (1926a) described how the normal mother helps the child learn gradually to tolerate and master the frustration and pain of separation from her. If that kind of "optimal frustration" is not provided, and if instead traumatic separations prevent the gradual mastery of such frustration, then the child may become fixated, as a primitive security measure, on object choice of the identification type. The latter type of object choice predisposes to depressive pathology.

This brings us to the concept of "neutralization." Freud proposed that what characterizes the depressive is (1) narcissism, that is, regression to a narcissistic type of object choice in which the self is fused with the object; (2) aggression, specifically the self-devouring rage; and (3) oral-fixation, which is intimately associated with the narcissism of the "object relation" and with the specifically oral–sadistic nature of the rage. In addition, we can define the oral–sadistic impulses of the depressive as primitive, "nonneutralized" drives.

The "headlines" of this period in the development of psychoanalytic theory are Narcissism, Aggression, Neutralization, Structure, and the Superego. In making the transition from the original topographic model,

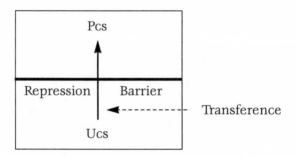

to the newer "structural" model,

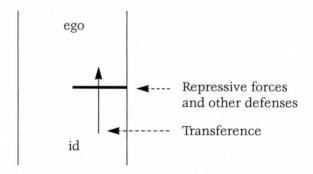

Freud now recognized that the repressing forces of the ego, which oppose the libidinal and aggressive drives, are themselves quite unconscious and cannot be made conscious without analytic work. That concept led to the conclusion (more explicitly than before) that interpretations should be directed first at the unconscious defenses, calling the attention of the rational, cooperating, preconscious ego to the unconscious defensive activities.

QUESTION: Why did Freud now refer to the defensive activities as unconscious? Why not continue to consider them preconscious?

ANSWER: Because defensive activities are not available to awareness, cannot be made conscious simply by the application of attention cathexis, but require analytic work—the overcoming of various resistances—to make them conscious. Freud no longer spoke of the "Preconscious" but of "the ego," one part of which is preconscious and another part unconscious. The forces opposing infantile drives were no longer considered merely a process of decathexis (repression), but also included a fairly elaborate set of additional "defenses," which themselves were unconscious.

The foregoing theoretical changes applied to the "transference side" of the new model in which, as in the earlier model, infantile primary process tendencies could transfer across the repression barrier to preconscious "carriers" (now, transfer across a barrier of unconscious repressive and other defensive ego forces to the preconscious part of the ego). But the new model also included a "nontransference side," regarding which Freud now theorized that experiences of optimal frustration allowed the gradual building up of "neutralized" experience, structure, and skills. An example would be a parent's handling of smearing in the child. If the smearing is handled in a loving way that provides substitutes for the original smearing drive, rather than by an unloving, angry attempt by the parent to stamp out the infantile tendency completely, the child experiences optimal frustration of the drive. As a result, the child builds up the structure and capacity for "neutralizing" such drives—a process quite different from repression, reaction formation, and other defenses.

What makes it possible for a parent to teach a child in this way? The parent uses his or her own libidinal and aggressive forces to deal with the child's pressing infantile drives. If the child exhibits an upsurge of aggression, for example, the parent counters it with some libidinal force; that is, the parent soothes the child lovingly, which opposes and tends to neutralize the aggression. Later, the child identifies with the parent's handling of aggression in that way. When he feels himself becoming very angry, his identification with the parent's loving firmness toward his infantile rages reminds him that "You don't need to get so angry; you are loved." If the child has an upsurge of libidinal drive, the parent counters it with a small amount of aggression:

"No, no," or shaking the index finger as a warning signal—that is, a small, symbolic amount of aggression on the part of the parent that helps the child to stop what he is doing.

The memories of many such experiences with one's parents contribute gradually to the development of healthy ego structure having the function of neutralizing drives—a type of structure that makes up that portion of the ego not separated by a barrier of repression and other defenses (cf. Hartmann, Kris, and Loewenstein, 1946).

Lecture 26

Aggression

QUESTION: In the development of neutralized structure, is the child's aggression countered only by libidinal forces from the parents, or is it sometimes opposed also by parental aggression?

ANSWER: The issue is not so much what is opposed by what, but the intensity of the controlling or prohibiting forces at any given time. This is an economic question. Optimally, aggression in the child is best handled by the mobilization of libidinal forces in the parents. A child's tantrum, for example, is best handled by a calming, soothing, loving attitude rather than by counteraggression. Later, as a result of having introjected many such experiences, the child will act the same way toward himself when angry. The end result is not an absence of structure but the development of neutralizing structure, which is under the control of the ego and available for use in attitudes and behavior such as characterologic firmness.

In persons who have developed such structure, the old "murderous" aggressions are hardly discernible any more. If the situation demands it, a person with healthy, neutralized structure is capable of free, effective aggression. By contrast, in a person who lacks such neutralized structure—the person, for example, whose childhood aggressions were often countered by tantrums or severe threats from the adults responsible for his care—the outcome might well be a tendency toward outbreaks of primitive, unneutralized aggression, alternating with periods of totally inhibited aggression. The latter pattern is not as "free" aggression as that which occurs in the person with neutralized structure, as both the angry outbursts and the periods of inhibited aggression are beyond the person's control, and there is always the danger of unneutralized, "murderous" aggressions breaking out. As a result, such a person may need to maintain an intense inhibition of all aggression, even necessary and indicated aggression, by equally primitive, archaic counterforces.

> QUESTION: Would it be correct to say that the neutralized structure that is built up in the child comes about by or from a process of "fusion"?
>
> ANSWER: No, the process is called "neutralization." It makes a great deal of difference whether the love and training methods of the educator are themselves neutralized or unneutralized. The most effective educational measures for building up neutralized structure in the child are counterforces in the parents, which are themselves neutralized. If the parents' behavior toward the child contains primitive, unneutralized, libidinal, and aggressive impulses, the result is not smoothly functioning neutralized structure in the child but structure on the transference side of the psyche.

We shall speak more about wholesale introjection of traumatic frustrations when we discuss the genesis of the superego. Let us note at this point, however, that it was Freud's discovery of these phenomena and relationships that led to his introducing the concept of superego during this period. One way that unneutralized superego structure might come about is by a parent trying to get the child to behave by "seducing" him to behave. What may develop in such a child is a pattern in which his ego attempts to make peace with his superego by wheedling, bribing, or paying some price—that is, "negotiating a sexual peace by sweetening it up," so to speak. In such a case we may speak of the superego as having been "sexualized."

> QUESTION: So far we have discussed two main reasons for Freud's changing the original topographic model: evidence of unconscious ego activity, and evidence suggesting progressive neutralization of drive energies. Were there any other reasons for adopting the newer structural model?
>
> ANSWER: Yes, but at first is was Freud's preoccupation with ego functioning, which had resulted from studying the deeper forms of pathology. The latter clinical experiences led to new

theoretical concepts. Freud observed how one part of the ego often developed in opposition to the other parts of the ego, much as he had assumed originally that the ego developed in opposition to the id. Freud called such conflicts within the ego "intrasystemic conflicts."

Even when he studied the obsessional neurosis, Freud had been confronted with the phenomenon of a psyche divided against itself. In "Totem and Taboo" (1913b), and in his report of the "Rat Man" (1909b), he described certain archaic aspects of the ego—for example, omnipotence of thought, or equating thoughts and acts. The compulsion neurotic develops certain reaction formations within the ego that oppose the ego phantasies that his thoughts are omnipotent. The reaction formations may produce, among other things, the well-known "unpsychological attitude" of the compulsion neurotic—that is, an inability to tolerate anything irrational or to accept even the reality of emotions. Everything must be filtered through a sieve of rationality to guard against the dangers of latent thoughts that are considered omnipotent.

From this discussion we can see that two principal types of conflicts are possible: "intersystemic" conflicts between ego and id, or between ego and superego, on the transference side of the psyche; and "intrasystemic" conflicts between opposing parts of the ego itself—for example, between the cooperating, analyzing, observing ego and the rest of the ego.

QUESTION: How is "instinctual aggression" defined?

ANSWER: More will be said about that later, when we discuss the new theory of drive dualism. At this point, we might review a brief historical point about the development of this concept in psychoanalytic theory. Originally Freud dealt mainly with infantile sexuality. As he studied the more regressive forms of psychopathology, which are concerned with earlier periods of development, it became evident that infantile aggression is equally as important as infantile sexuality in these conditions. As early as his studies of compulsion neurosis, for example, Freud had observed the importance of aggression.

QUESTION: Is neutralization the same process as sublimation, displacement, and aim-inhibition?

ANSWER: No. Neutralization refers specifically to the nature and intensity of drives, the extent to which drives are neutralized in contrast to retaining their original primitiveness and infantile intensity. Defining drives in terms of their aims is a somewhat different matter; it has to do with conflicts about object relations rather than with the nature and intensity of drives themselves, independent of their relation to objects.

QUESTION: How does the distinction between intra- and intersystemic conflict apply to therapy?

ANSWER: Earlier in treatment, and much of the time throughout analysis, one deals primarily with intrasystemic conflicts (within the ego). The latter conflicts often involve narcissistic injuries and resistances, which are reactions to the ego's inablility to control part of itself.

QUESTION: Ultimately, however, doesn't conflict—even intrasystemic conflict within the ego—always involve clashes between more and less "mature" (or primitive) forces?

ANSWER: No, although that is often the case, for example, with conflicts between archaic and more rational parts of the ego. In other cases, however, conflicts may occur between incompatible motives on the same level of the ego.

Lecture 27

Aggression (continued): The "Childhood Object" and the Superego

QUESTION: What do we mean by "aggression"?

ANSWER: Originally Freud was preoccupied mainly with the vicissitudes of the libidinal drives; but as he came to investigate the more regressive forms of pathology, he encountered more and more hostile and destructive impulses, urges, or drives. The aggressive impulses had some of the qualities of the sexual drives: a similar urgency or intensity, their being directed at objects, their producing conflicts, and being defended against. As we discuss more about the gradual acquisition of structure and the neutralization of drives, we shall find that the nature of this other kind of drive (aggression) and the degree of its neutralization are crucial issues.

QUESTION: What is introjected in the process of introjection, an object or an experience?

ANSWER: The object as it is experienced. When we speak of the baby introjecting the breast as a "part object," we must remember that from the baby's standpoint the breast is not a "part object" but the whole world. It is a "part object" only to us, as adult observers. Furthermore, if the wish for gratification from an object (e.g., the breast) is frustrated, what is introjected is not the whole object (as seen by an observer) but only that part of the mother which is experienced as frustrating.

Introjection is intimately associated with object loss. If object losses are gradual, as in the case of optimal frustration, the result is small introjections—memories of only mildly frustrating objects. In the case of traumatic frustrations, on the other hand, the result is massive introjection of intensely frustrating experiences with objects. Many small object losses (frustrations) produce correspondingly small introjections, which exert their effects through neutralized energy. Major object losses (frustrations) produce massive introjections that exert their effects through nonneutralized energy. Massive introjections tend to be phase-specific: That is, during certain periods of childhood, when particular drive demands are especially strong, the frustrations experienced during those periods are correspondingly intense and the resulting introjections are inevitably more massive.

QUESTION: What is the difference between introjection and identification?

ANSWER: There is no uniform, accepted definition of those terms. One way of differentiating them is to define introjection as a process and identification as the result of that process.

THE "CHILDHOOD OBJECT"

The concept of "childhood object" has given rise to much confusion. Underlying a neurotic object choice is always a libidinal object of childhood. Such a structure occurs in that part of the psychic apparatus which is separated by a barrier of repression and defensive mechanisms. But what about object choices in the sphere of the psyche that lies outside of structural conflicts, the sphere of conflict-free, neutralizing structure? If a man marries a woman who resembles the loved mother of his childhood, for example, is that necessarily a transference phenomenon? The answer is no; it may represent an object choice determined by neutralized structure from the past.

As a matter of fact, in the case of neurotic object choices based on transference from the past, the man is more likely to marry a woman who is not like his mother. The transference would tend to inhibit his choice of a woman who reminded him of his mother. The person whose object choice is influenced only minimally by such a transference, but is based mainly on conflict-free, neutralized experiences, tends naturally to choose love objects who resemble the person(s) with whom he had gratifying experiences in the past.

The same distinction applies to a patient's feelings toward his analyst. Not all such feelings are necessarily transference feelings. Some such feelings come from the conflict-free part of the ego and therefore are not transferences, which is one of the reasons that analysis tends to be facilitated by the therapist and patient having at least some similarities of background. The therapeutic alliance depends largely on the patient and analyst being able to have a conflict-free, nontransference type of relationship within which transferences can occur and be analyzed. Either extreme of too much transference, overwhelming the whole relationship, or too much friendly alliance which does not allow transferences to develop, can interfere with the analytic process.

QUESTION: Why does it take transferences so long to develop in analysis?

ANSWER: It doesn't. They begin to develop very soon, but initially are so veiled (i.e., defended against) that they cannot be observed clearly or worked with interpretively until later in the analysis.

THE SUPEREGO

Freud described the superego as an integral part of the ego, having to do with wholesale introjections of frustrating experiences with objects. Why did he call it superego, "above the ego"? Because that term expresses the childhood reality of the parents being bigger than the child—above the child. The superego contains images of the introjected, prohibiting (frustrating), commanding parents, and the "voice of conscience" (as in dreams) always seems to come from above the ego.

The superego contains several major components: prohibitions and censures, the ego ideal, and approval. In addition, it has several layers. According to the structural model, only a small part of the superego is preconscious—the part that people call their "conscience." The superego dips deeply into the Unconscious, however, because it is based on introjections from various developmental levels.

Let us consider the development of the part of the superego that contains the ego ideal. Freud conceived of the infant beginning in a state of objectless, omnipotent narcissism: "Whatever I want, I get." The next phase of development attempts to preserve that state in the face of realistic contradictions. In the phase called the "Purified Pleasure Ego," anything unpleasant is attributed to the outside. Some narcissism of that kind always remains in us, some tendency to see the best in ourselves and the worst in others. This can be a difficult therapeutic problem in the analysis of character, and it is especially important in the analysis of future psychoanalysts, who otherwise might tend to see their own "bad" impulses and feelings in their patients.

The next phase is one in which the omnipotence is projected to the parents: idealization of the parents, which the child then participates in, or shares, as a recipient of the parents' fantasied omnipotence. This stage comes about because eventually the reality of the child's actual weakness can no longer be denied. To save what he can of his phantasied omnipotence, the child projects the narcissism to his parents, looks upon them as godlike, and attempts to "regain" his earlier feeling of narcissistic perfection by closeness to his parents. Some people never get over that stage of narcissism, but must always remain close to some "omnipotent" parent figure. Because the parents during this phase are believed to have magical powers, the child imagines that they must be dealt with by magical devices—for example, by "charming" the parent-gods with "magical" words and gestures like smiling (see Ferenczi's [1913] "Stages in the Development of the Sense of Reality").

The narcissism projected to the parents is then lost, which is brought about once again by reality—for example, by the child's surprised discovery that he can lie successfully, that his parents cannot actually read his thoughts. As the wish to have omnipotent and omniscient parents is frustrated, the images of the lost perfect parents are reintrojected, becoming that part of the superego which is called the ego ideal. From then on, if the person does not live up to his superego standards (ego ideal), he experiences some degree of narcissistic injury (a feeling of inferiority), because the ego ideal derives from the original narcissism.

It is important to note that the seemingly positive contents of the ego ideal, our positive aspirations and goals, are derived fundamentally, and somewhat paradoxically, from (negative) prohibitions—against gratifying infantile sexuality and aggression. The original narcissism was associated with the phantasied omnipotence of the child's wishes. In the later phase, the drive-prohibiting parents are seen as omnipotent. The narcissistic balance then depends not on successful wish-fulfillment, but on the successful curbing of the drives in compliance with the parents' demands. If the child lives up to the parents' demands by controlling the drives, he remains in their good graces, shares in their all-powerfulness, and thereby regains a positive narcissistic balance.

Following reintrojection of the morally "perfect" parents, the same tensions continue in the relationship between the ego and ego ideal. If one does not live up to the standards of the ideal, the narcissistic balance is disturbed. If one lives up to the ideal, the narcissistic balance is positive and the person feels morally as big and superior as the parents. Variations in the content of the ego ideal result from individual and cultural differences in parents and parent figures. The powerfulness of the ideal, however, its moral "perfection," is an expression of the projected and then reintrojected narcissism. The ego ideal is thus one's own narcissism, which has been modified in specific ways by its "passage through the parents."

Lecture 28

The Ego Ideal: Censuring and Approving Parts of the Superego

Reviewing: We have been discussing concepts associated with the newly introduced structure, the superego. This structure is part of the ego, but an "upper" part because it is based on introjection of the censuring and idealized parents, who are bigger than the child, above the child. Thus the "voice of conscience" seems to come from above, and one lives "up" to one's ideals. The superego contains the ideals, censuring forces, and approval.

THE EGO IDEAL

One of the basic psychological concepts that Freud applied to his new theory of superego development—as he did to all of his theories—was that development is determined not only by external forces but also by a certain readiness of the psychic apparatus for specific new developments. An example is the child's readiness and willingness at a certain period of development to attribute omnipotence to the parents rather than to himself—a phase of increased "educability" in the child.

In both the earlier period of self-omnipotence (the "ideal ego") and the later period of omnipotence projected to the parents (the "ideal parents"), the main issue for the child is how to deal with his libidinal and aggressive drives. During the earlier period the omnipotence is oriented toward immediate and complete satisfaction of drives, whereas later the emphasis is on controlling the drives—each presumably having survival value for children during those differing periods of development. The child projects omnipotence to his parents as the ones who are able to control drives.

Still later, when his idealized image of the "perfect parents" is lost, the child adapts to this further frustration by the mechanism of reintrojecting his previously projected omnipotence in the form of an ego ideal. The ego ideal's qualities of powerfulness and moral "perfection" retain and reflect the omnipotent aspect of the individual's original infantile narcissism.

The development of neutralized superego structure is dependent on the passage of the child's narcissism through the parents. If the parents' demands are reasonable, the child's reintrojected narcissism will return in a more neutralized and reasonable form than it had before. If a parent's own ego ideal is made up largely of unneutralized structure, however, then the passage of the child's narcissism through that parent will not produce as much neutralization. The child's narcissism will be reintrojected in a relatively unmodified form, betraying its infantile character by its impatience and by an uncompromising attitude of self-righteous perfection.

The Censuring Part of the Superego

Development of the censuring part of the superego exhibits certain parallels with the aforementioned phases of ego ideal development. The three phases in the development of the ego ideal are primary narcissism and omnipotence (the "ideal ego"), projected narcissism (the "ideal parents"), and reintrojected narcissism (the "ego ideal," a structure that retains some features of the preceding two phases). The corresponding phases in the development of the censuring superego are:

1. "Primary masochism"—the initial disposition of potentially hostile–aggressive impulses, prior to their being focused on an object. As the child begins to recognize the role of the "outside" in maintaining drive balance (wish-fulfillment), the primary masochism is transformed into "primary hostility" toward the outside (the phase of the "Purified Pleasure Ego," in which the psyche attempts to project everything unpleasant to the outer world).

2. As the role of the "outside" becomes more distinct, and as the maintenance of narcissistic balance becomes increasingly dependent on being at peace with the now omnipotent parents, the hostility directed toward them becomes untenable. When

projected to them, the child's hostility reinforces his perception and experience of parental anger, which greatly intensifies his fear of committing transgressions.

3. At the height of the drive-retaliation conflict during the oedipal period, the projectively intensified image of the threatening parents is reintrojected and becomes the censuring part of the superego. The censuring part of the superego thus contains residues of the primary masochism, the hostility that was projected to the parents, and the actual hostile behavior of the parents toward the child.

As in the case of the ego ideal, the self-directed hostility of the superego is more or less neutralized, depending on the fate of the projected and reintrojected hostility in its passage through the parents. Latent, unneutralized hostility in the parents appears to intensify the hostile force of the child's censuring superego. Open hostility by the parents, on the other hand, allows at least some rebellion by the child's ego, so that not all of the child's hostile feelings are turned inward. Neutralized firmness in the parents' attitudes towards the child's drives leads to the development of a neutralized and firm superego.

The Approving Part of the Superego

Even parental approval toward the child occurs largely in the service of curbing drives and, as such, produces frustration. In this case, however, what is reintrojected from the "parental passage" is a positive, approving structure for controlling drives, in contrast to a negative, punitive structure. Not all approval by parents leads to smoothly functioning, conflict-free, neutralized structure, however. Approval by parents can run the gamut from poorly neutralized to effectively neutralized response. An example of relatively unneutralized approval by a parent would be an erotically seductive attitude toward the child.

The superego, although part of the ego, is actually closer to the id in its primitiveness, intensity, and emphasis on narcissism and omnipotence. Just as the ego sets up defensive barriers against id drives, it also erects defenses against superego demands. The latter are often important issues in analysis—for example, the patient who defends himself against experiencing guilt by denying any connection between a transgression and "accidentally" injuring himself afterward.

QUESTION: Where among these structures does therapeutic work in psychoanalysis take place? And if the superego is permanent and unchangeable, how can treatment be effective?

ANSWER: The changes brought about by psychoananlysis are minute but may be decisive. What is free association, after all, but the ideal of a "smoothly functioning psyche," free of repressive and other defensive barriers? The "training" or "ego exercise" aspect of psychoanalysis helps the ego to develop more capacity for allowing both drive demands and superego demands to be experienced—but without necessarily giving in to the drives or letting the superego demands "get one down" too much.

The deeper, archaic superego structure may not be modified (or modifiable) by psychoanalysis, but some new structure nearer the surface probably can be added. Healthier new structure may be decisive in modifying the intrapsychic psychoeconomic balance—which, by the way, is one of the reasons that we need an energy concept in psychoanalysis to account for such changes in psychoeconomic balance.

Lecture 29

Narcissism

QUESTION: If narcissism refers to libido directed toward the self, is there any similar or parallel concept that applies to aggression?

ANSWER: Yes, masochism. The explanatory power of this concept is illustrated by our discussion last time about the development of the censuring part of the superego.

QUESTION: Do the concepts of primary narcissism and primary masochism refer to a stage in which libido and aggression are directed towards the self?

ANSWER: No, because the concept of "self" implies a differentiation between self and other objects that has not yet developed at the time of primary narcissism and primary masochism. Actually, these are not psychological but prepsychological concepts. They are hypothetical, prepsychological, objectless phases that we assume may precede psychological development. They are useful theoretical concepts, however, that apply to the earliest end of the developmental continuum.

Within the area of psychologically observable data, the preceding concepts provide an intrapsychic etiologic dimension that we assume interacts with the external factor of childhood experience. Interference with object love, for example, results in heightened narcissism, and interference with object-directed anger increases masochism. The assumption that clinical (secondary) narcissism and masochism are in part a return to a prior state allows for the conceptualization of variations in the "internal pull" of such states—in addition to and interacting with the "external push" of frustrating experiences.

In other words, children with high endowments of primary narcissism and masochism do not reach out as lustily to their environments in love and anger as other children do, and they react to minor frustrations with more extreme degrees of clinical narcissism and masochism. (Compare in this connection Anna Freud's aphorism that it is the mother's job to "win the libido"—that is, to draw the infant out of its narcissistic state by encouraging interest in the mother.)

QUESTION: What is the difference between introjections that result in superego formation and defensive ego introjections such as "identification with the aggressor"?

ANSWER: The difference is that superego introjection occurs at the end and at the height of the period of infantile sexuality and aggression, and therefore represents a reaction to loss—in this case of the "omnipotent parents"—and psychoeconomically, it is a massive introjection in adaptation to that loss, which leads to the establishment of a whole, cohesive, internal "personality": the superego. Ego introjections, on the other hand, are not reactions to massive loss but to frustrating and frightening behavior (e.g., aggression) on the part of the parents; psychoeconomically, they are smaller, part identifications with particular aspects of the frustrating parents' personalities.

QUESTION: What is the difference between primary and secondary narcissism?

ANSWER: Primary narcissism is an objectless, totally undifferentiated state of immediate and complete wish-fulfillment in which libido is not even invested in the "self," as the latter has not yet been differentiated as an object. Secondary narcissism, on the other hand, represents a reflux of narcissistic libido from objects to the self, when objects in the external world have disappointed us.

QUESTION: Why did Freud feel it necessary to postulate a primary masochism?

ANSWER: Because he observed so many clinical phenomena that appear to involve a tendency toward self-destruction—a widespread propensity of that kind. By postulating a primary masochism, he could account better for the readiness with which destructive feelings flow back to become self-destructive.

QUESTION: Which is more pathogenic to a child, a parent who responds to the child's aggression with counteraggression or a parent who flees from the child and avoids him when he is aggressive?

ANSWER: The latter. If the parent stays away from the child to avoid aggression, the child has no neutralizing parental "filter" through which to "pass" his aggression, leaving him fixated on destructive feelings directed against himself. Parents who respond to the child's aggression with counteraggression mobilize the child's aggressions outward, at least.

Lecture 30

The Dual Instinct Theory

We have almost completed our review of the second period in the development of psychoanalytic theory. What remains to be discussed are the Dual Instinct Theory ("Beyond the Pleasure Principle," 1920) and the Problem of Anxiety ("Inhibitions, Symptoms and Anxiety," 1926a). The former can be understood only in relation to the development of Freud's theories in general. That is, originally Freud conceived of conflict between libidinal (race-preservative) and "ego" (self-preservative) drives. He conjectured that in the phylogenesis of the human race, there must have been some survival advantage in curbing the libidinal drives—for example, when those drives involve competition with a larger, stronger rival. That concept led to Freud's notion of an inherited tendency toward castration anxiety. Stated in another way, Freud's first theory was essentially a biological one: sexual (race-preservative) drives in conflict with ego (self-preservative) drives, as in the central argument of the Oedipus conflict. This early theory became untenable for two main reasons:

1. The need to account for aggression, which has some qualities in common with the sexual drives—for example, the tendency to ignore reality.

2. After his studies of narcissism, Freud concluded that narcissism (self-preservation) must be subsumed under the libidinal (rather than the "ego") drives, with the self as object. Narcissistic love of the self, like libidinal drives toward other objects, can undergo all gradations of neutralization—all the way from realistic self-concern to becoming passionately, intensely, erotically in love with oneself.

99

As his concepts about the drives evolved, Freud postulated the existence of both libidinal and aggressive drives. He recognized that these drives were directed toward objects but that they could be turned from the object to the self under the influence of disappointment and fear. Schematically:

Libido → Objects (Object love) → Disappointment → Self (Narcissism)

Aggression → Objects (Object hate) → Fear → Self (Masochism)

Freud characteristically assumed that if, in reaction to external frustration, the drives tended to turn away from an object toward the self, the readiness for such a response could be explained better if one postulated a prior stage in which the drives had once been organized in that way. That concept, he felt, would help to explain the propensity of the mind toward self-love when object love is frustrated and toward masochism when hostility toward objects is blocked. Freud concluded, therefore, that originally there must have been phases of not-yet-outwardly-directed libido and aggression: the hypothetical stages of primary narcissism and primary masochism.

One finds evidence of primary narcissism and primary masochism in the variations of children's reactions to experiences with the environment. If primary narcissism and masochism are thought of as resistances to reaching out toward the external world, a clinging of variable intensity to the original state, one may then sense how such a predilection might influence the readiness for and the extent of a child's retreat to secondary narcissism and secondary masochism in response to environmental traumata.

Freud went still further and attempted to extend his psychological theories into a much broader framework—namely, the general characteristics of biological and physical systems. He subordinated his theories to such broad, general concepts as the "Stability Principle," that all systems tend toward the simplest, most random forms of distribution (Second Law of Thermodynamics). According to that concept, the organic world is a highly differentiated system within the more general inorganic world. As such it is unstable, tending toward a more stable, inorganic state. Freud called that tendency of organic matter to return to the simpler inorganic state the "death instinct" (cf. entropy).

Freud conceived of the psychological as a still more specialized realm within the organic sphere. In contrast to the organic sphere, in which the "Death Principle" prevails, the "Pleasure

Principle" applies to the subordinate psychological realm. The Death Principle is thus the broader concept and hence is "Beyond the Pleasure Principle" (1920). According to this scheme, the Pleasure Principle subserves the death instinct. The Pleasure Principle might do that, for example, by protecting the organic system from accidental death, so that the Death Principle can run its natural course and lead to death in its own time and in its own way.

This is not a psychological concept. Freud never spoke of the death instinct as a death "wish." The wish to commit suicide, for example, is explainable within the realm of the Pleasure Principle. Similarly, the phenomenon of masochism is always explainable within the realm of the Pleasure Principle.

Summarizing the discussion of the dual instinct theory: The Pleasure Principle (and its modification, the Reality Principle) refer to the tendency of the mind in disequilibrium (tension) to strive for return to a previous equilibrium characterized by an absence of tension. The psychological experience of the differential between the current state of disequilibrium and the former state of equilibrium is called a "wish." The process or activity of returning to the original state is called wish-fulfillment. The general tendency to return to previous states of equilibrium is called the "repetition compulsion." The Pleasure–Reality Principle, as well as the death instinct, are instances of the repetition compulsion—that is, tendencies toward return to a former, simpler state. The same tendency applies to the Stability Principle of physical systems. The Pleasure Principle is a special manifestation of the broader Death Principle, which is Beyond the Pleasure Principle. The Death Principle, in turn, is a special case within the still broader Stability Principle. Schematically:

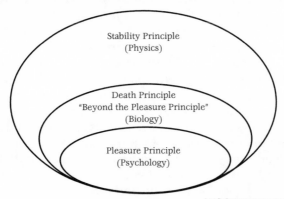

Stability Principle
(Physics)

Death Principle
"Beyond the Pleasure Principle"
(Biology)

Pleasure Principle
(Psychology)

Lecture 31

Changes in the Concept of Anxiety

An important additional development in Freud's theories during the period we have been discussing dealt with changes in the concept of anxiety. Some psychoanalysts considered these changes revolutionary, but from another standpoint the changes, although necessary, were not really drastic. Today's discussion attempts to explain these changes.

In his theory of symptom formation, Freud considered the "actual neurosis" to be the core (psychoeconomically) of the psychoneuroses. A libidinal imbalance in the Unconscious produced by regressive recathecting of childhood objects gives rise to a transference intrusion into the Preconscious. At the moment that the intrusion occurs, the unprepared ego reacts with an economic imbalance and thus with an "anxiety hysteria" (an "actual neurosis"). Secondary defenses are erected by the ego—for example, phobias and compulsions—to buffer itself from the "actual neurotic core" of anxiety. If these symptomatic defenses are interfered with, a psychoneurotic patient will experience the "nameless anxiety" of the "actual neurotic" core.

In his first theory of anxiety, Freud postulated that anxiety is a transformation of libido. In his later theory, Freud proposed that anxiety is produced by the ego. This does not mean that the older theory has to be given up completely. The subtle change in the theory that is revolutionary concerns the sudden intrusion of a drive demand on a vulnerable and unprepared ego. In the first theory, Freud said that the sudden intrusion of libido is "turned into" anxiety. In the later theory, Freud said that the ego "responds to" the sudden intrusion of drive demands with anxiety. According to the newer theory, it is factors such as the suddenness and unpreparedness of the ego to such demands that determine the ego's response of anxiety when its organization is threatened by internal dangers—inner dangers that come not only from the drives but also from the superego.

Just as all other ego activities have a developmental history, anxiety, being an ego function, also has its history and development. Originally anxiety is diffuse, a panic reaction. As the ego develops and the capacity for discrimination grows, however, the anxiety response becomes more and more "tamed," until eventually it evolves into a mere "signal" of anxiety whenever danger threatens.

The change from the earlier to the later theory of anxiety occurred largely because the ego had been given a central place in the functioning and economy of mental life. The whole subject of affect theory in psychoanalysis has tended to develop along the same lines as the theory of anxiety—a gradual "taming" of earlier, more diffuse affects into later, more differentiated "signal" affects. How this taming process comes about is not something that can be reduced to a simplified statement. It is a product of all the factors involved in the growth and development of the ego and its various activities.

QUESTION: How do these concepts apply to the theory of psychoanalytic treatment? Can psychoanalysis correct a faulty ego development so that the patient's ego can learn to experience a more "tamed" loneliness, for example, rather than total desolation?

ANSWER: Viewed in the light of these concepts, all of psychoanalysis is an "ego exercise." The patient begins to feel an unpleasant affect and immediately flees from it, defends himself from it. The analyst encourages the patient to let himself experience the affect. The patient fears that he cannot tolerate it. The analytic situation provides a certain security that helps the patient to let himself experience the affects and gradually "tame" them.

Many clinical phenomena can be explained by the newer concept of anxiety as a reponse of and by the ego to threats endangering its own organization. In some patients, for example, even the relatively slight amount of regression involved in the enjoyment of music or theatre is intolerable, because the ego responds to the regression with too much anxiety (Kohut and Levarie, 1950).

Freud considered the sudden change of birth, from a primary narcissistic balance to the imbalance produced by exposure to external stimulation, which occurs at a time when the ego has relatively little protection from stimulation, to be a significant early traumatic experience of anxiety—in some respects the prototype, or at least the principal original instance, of intense diffuse anxiety.

Freud suggested that whole classes of experiences are predestined to activate specific types of affects in the ego: anxiety, shame, and grief, for example. Freud used some Lamarckian concepts about the inheritance of acquired characteristics to explain such a tendency—that over the aeons of human history affective reponses somehow influenced the germ plasm, eventually being transmitted to offspring. In Darwinian terms, we would say that those infants and adults who happened to have certain affective tendencies tended to survive, because for some reason affective responses of that kind (anxiety, grief, shame, and others) appear to have promoted survival.

Freud (1926a) pointed out also, however (in "Inhibitions, Symptoms and Anxiety"), that although whole classes of experiences are predestined to be responded to with certain types of affects, it appears also that diverse affective responses represent later differentiations of a single, earlier, primitive emotion.

QUESTION: Is there such a thing as unconscious affect?

ANSWER: It would be a contradiction in terms to speak of affects in the Unconscious because, as we have just discussed, affect is considered a response of the (preconscious) ego. It is entirely possible, on the other hand, to conceptualize affects of which one is not aware in the Preconscious. Thus we may speak of preconscious but not of unconscious affects.

QUESTION: Is anxiety always a response to libidinal demands, or are there some instances in which the old theory still applies, of libido being transformed into and discharged as anxiety?

ANSWER: The concept of the "actual (anxiety) neurosis" as the core (psychoeconomically) of the psychoneurosis is still applicable. Transference intrusions of libido from the Unconscious into the preconscious produce an economic imbalance, which in turn gives rise to an "actual neurotic core" of anxiety. The anxiety is a response of the ego to the libidinal invasion, however, not a transformation of the libido into anxiety.

QUESTION: Would it be correct to say that in Freud's later (structural) model, the ego was no longer considered entirely a closed system, but was considered partially independent (or autonomous) and partially not?

ANSWER: Yes, that is correct. One part of the ego forms an unbroken continuum with the id. Another part is sharply demarcated from the id by a wall of defenses. Still another part appears to function more or less autonomously, more or less independently of the drives and from the defenses.

One is tempted to define mental health or psychological normality in simplified terms as an undisturbed separate functioning of the three aforementioned areas. One might consider mental health only from the point of view of the autonomous ego functions, for example, in which case the normal or healthy personality would appear to be a smoothly operating, problem-solving machine. Strong drive intrusions from the two other areas would then be viewed as disturbances. To define mental health in that way has some justification when one focuses on one or the other activity of the ego: For example, passionate interests may interfere with a need for dispassionate assessment of details, and transference intrusions may lead to sexualization and, secondarily, to inhibition of autonomous functions.

Although specific functions can be evaluated in that way, the total personality cannot. Mental health, normalcy, successful relationship to tasks and especially to the human environment, require not only cognitive functions but also access to all areas and aspects of the mind. There are times, for example, when we need access to the forces of the id, when survival or success depends more on our capacity to respond passionately rather than relying on the refinement of dispassionate cognitive functions. There are even times when the ego must make use of transference intrusions, either as an incentive for adaptive behavior or in the service of interpersonal communication in situations that call for a response or an appeal to irrational motivations in the human environment.

In other words, the healthy personality cannot be defined simply by the intactness or firmness of the barriers between its structural components or in terms of undisturbed functions within any one of its systems. There are various types of mental health or normality, some resting more on the functioning of one area, some on the functioning of another. The capacity to make use of various structures is of great adaptive value, and yet there are also successful adaptations in some personality types that relate more to the functioning of one system than to another.

Lecture 32

Inhibitions, Symptoms and Anxiety: Chapters 1 and 2

In chapter 1 of "Inhibitions, Symptoms and Anxiety" (1926a), Freud differentiated between inhibitions and symptoms. *Inhibitions* refer to simple limitations or restrictions of functions, either precautionary or due to energy impoverishment, whereas *symptoms* refer to a more extensive and severe impairment of function. Freud described here in structural terms what he had described previously in nonstructural terms. He discussed writing, for example, as an autonomous ego function. An inhibition of writing is essentially the negative of this ego function. A symptom, on the other hand, cannot be described in such simple ego terms. Symptoms involve other, more complex processes and structures, especially transferences.

To illustrate: An earlier "writing" existed (i.e., smearing), from which the later writing split itself off and became secondarily autonomous (Hartmann, 1939). The old "writing" may under certain circumstances be transferred to the later autonomous ego function, resexualizing and reaggressivizing it with infantile sexuality and aggression, thereby setting up the conditions for a symptomatic inhibition of this ego function.

Chapter 2 takes up the more complex structure of symptoms. Symptoms represent or consist of undischarged, unsatisfied instinctual impulses that have been repressed by the ego at the behest of the superego because the instinctual drive causes disturbances and thus unpleasure to the ego. The anxiety signal of distress by the ego is activated. Like other affects, anxiety is a precipitate of primal traumatic experiences—that is, "memory symbols" that have come to be used as signals, warning against the danger that a traumatic state might be repeated. The symptom develops when repression of the instinctual impulse fails, which allows the repressed to "return" in a disguised, distorted, substitute form.

QUESTION: What did Freud mean by "primal," in contrast to "subsequential," repression? Doesn't primal repression refer simply to repressions that were never conscious in the first place?

ANSWER: Our nomenclature is confused on that point. The simplest form of repression is merely nonperception of the danger. Primal repression refers to the early "wallings off" of psychoeconomic imbalances—that is, traumatic states, "wiping them out," so to speak—by an archaic mechanism of "refusing to acknowledge" that the traumatic state exists. These original primal repressions are wallings-off of (specifically) infantile sexual and aggressive drives prior to the establishment of the superego. After the superego is established, all repressions are "secondary" or "subsequential" repressions (also called "repression proper" or "after-expulsion").

Lecture 33

Inhibitions, Symptoms and Anxiety: Chapters 3 and 4

In chapter 3 of "Inhibitions, Symptoms and Anxiety," Freud (1926a) made the point that weaknesses of the ego give rise to splits between the id, ego, and superego. In more stable ego states, the various parts of the mental apparatus are continuous and inseparable. This point becomes clearer if one recalls the structural diagram of the mental apparatus:

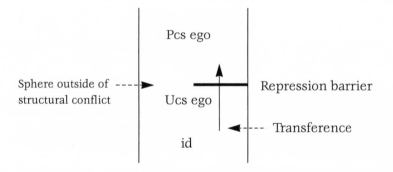

The "strength" of the ego refers primarily to the conflict-free portion with its smoothly functioning organization. The weaknesses of the ego refer mainly to that portion of the ego that is separated by a repression barrier.

Chapter 3 takes up further the manner in which the ego reacts to symptoms. Sometimes the ego merely "observes" the symptom as a sort of foreign body:

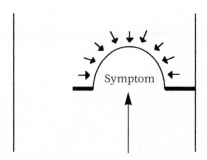

At other times the ego attempts to include the symptom as part of its own organization—that is, to incorporate and make use of the symptom:

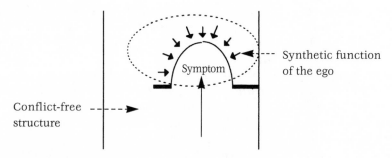

Freud emphasized that the ego operates with neutralized, desexualized (and deaggressivized) energy. That is, the ego contains neutralizing structure, which makes a continual supply of neutralized energy available for the ego's work. Freud proposed that even the ego's tendency to unify all of its parts, including symptoms that intrude into its organization—the so-called synthetic function of the ego—shows traces of the original, cruder sexual drives that strive to bring self and object closer together.

QUESTION: Is the latter concept related to the concept of "stimulus hunger"?

ANSWER: "Stimulus hunger" might be considered the "object-seeking" component or aspect of drives.

"Secondary gain" is the simplest example of the ego's attempt to weave the symptom into its own organization and use it for its own purposes. Freud cautioned, however, that one should not overestimate the role of secondary gain—a caution that he considered necessary because some clinicians attempted to explain the entire basis of symptom formation in terms of secondary gain. Freud emphasized that secondary gains are not the principal basis of symptom formation, but only a secondary exploitation of symptoms by the ego. The ego even invests the symptom narcissistically—for example, the obsessional's pride in his cleanliness.

In chapter 4, Freud presents clinical illustrations of his concepts regarding the psychological structure of symptoms, the examples being taken mainly from the cases of Little Hans and the Wolf Man. Freud emphasized particularly at this point that the neurosis consists of structural conflict. If a servant falls in love with the mistress of a house, for example, he may be in trouble but he does not necessarily have a neurosis. Even unreasonable fears are not phobias—that is, are not a neurosis. Only after structuralization has taken place does a neurosis exist: That is, only after an impulse has been repressed, and the repression has failed, with transference of the impulse to preconscious carriers, may we speak of neurosis.

It is important to realize in this connection that impulses take on a different, more primitive, character when repressed. When repression fails and repressed impulses return, their form is more primitive than it was before they were repressed. The alteration of impulses when they have been repressed is due to associative connections with more primitive, infantile impulses in the Unconscious.

The capacity to form endopsychic structures called symptoms is part of the normal equipment of the mind, and the absence of this capacity is more pathological than symptom formation itself. Comparing the symptom formations in Little Hans (1909a) and the Wolf Man (1918), both cases involved structuralized conflicts about the father. In Little Hans, the repressed oedipal–competitive impulses toward his father formed a complex of feelings in the Unconscious that, after they "returned," had developed an altered, more primitive form—for example, the fantasy and fear that a part of himself might be bitten off by a horse. In the case of the Wolf Man, the regressive web of phantasies in the Unconscious had gone even farther and had become still more primitive, so that when they "returned" from repression his (preconscious) fantasies had taken the form of being totally devoured by a wolf (cf. also Freud's [1926a, pp. 104–105] report of still another patient who as a child had identified with a "ginger-bread man" who in a children's story was eaten up by an Arab chief). Thus the Wolf Man must have been more seriously ill than Little Hans—on the borderline between the neurotic and the psychotic (paranoid) type of symptom formation.

Lecture 34

Inhibitions, Symptoms and Anxiety: Chapter 5

When one first reads "Inhibitions, Symptoms and Anxiety" (1926a), one notices that it seems to wander over various seemingly unrelated concepts and thoughts. On rereading and closer study, however, one finds a remarkable inner consistency in the work. In this essay Freud took the further significant step of freeing himself from the previous, more mechanistic concept that anxiety is a transformation of libido. At the end of chapter 4, he was able to pose the problem of anxiety in a new way, though still with the acknowledgment that more work would be needed to solve the problem.

Chapter 5 reviews the characteristics of obsessional neurosis. Whereas in hysteria the principal defensive mechanism is repression, in obsessional neurosis the major defenses are regression, repression, and reaction formation (in that order). Early in the disease, the penance and asceticism (reaction formations against libidinal temptations) stand out; as time goes on, the symptoms express increasingly the libidinal strivings themselves.

Chapter 5 also discusses "isolation" as a defense mechanism peculiar to obsessional neurosis. Freud concluded that isolation is related to the activity of concentration. In concentration, isolation functions in the service of rational comprehension. In obsessional neurosis, however, isolation operates in the service of the Pleasure Principle; that is, under the influence of an archaic ego, it wards off comprehension by keeping ideas and affects apart—an illustration of a mental function acting as an asset to rational behavior, on the one hand, and as a neurotic defense, on the other.

QUESTION: How are isolation, undoing, and reaction formation related? Aren't reaction formation and undoing similar?

ANSWER: They are alike in that all three are used as defenses against impulses, but from the standpoint of mechanism they are different. Reaction formation does not allow the forbidden impulses into action; undoing does. In addition, reaction formation involves doing the opposite in a single act, whereas doing and undoing are diphasic actions.

This completes our review of the second period in the development of psychoanalytic theory. The third period, from 1937 to the present, is concerned mainly with post-Freudian elaborations and the further ascendency of ego psychology—topics that are covered in other courses. While studying ego psychology, try to keep its origins in mind—the steady advances in Freud's clinical investigations and theorizing which led to his conclusions regarding the importance, even dominance, of the ego in mental functioning.

Good luck in your further studies!

Part II

Concepts and Theories of Psychoanalysis

(1963)

HEINZ KOHUT AND PHILIP F. D. SEITZ

Preface

The following essay was published originally as a chapter in *Concepts of Personality* (Wepman and Heine, 1963, pp. 113–141). It was reprinted in *The Search for the Self: Selected Writings of Heinz Kohut: 1950–1978, Vol. 1* (Ornstein, 1978a, pp. 337–374).

The essay was based on Kohut's (1958–1960) "Lectures on Psychoanalytic Psychology," as summarized in the compendium of those lectures that I prepared in collaboration with Kohut. I wrote the first draft of the essay, which was then modified and expanded by Kohut. The diagrams, which we considered an important part of the work, were designed by Kohut and were rendered by a member of my research staff.

After Kohut finished his work on the second draft, we met regularly to complete the final revisions of the text. The latter process took much longer than either of us had anticipated. Kohut's penchant for "precision" (Ornstein, 1978c, p. 3) led to a prolonged, word-by-word, sentence-by-sentence examination of everything we had written. The sticking point in those discussions was a question of final wording rather than substantive content. We knew and agreed on what we wanted to say but often differed on how to say it. Kohut's persistence usually won out, so that the style as well as content of the essay became distinctly Kohutian in tone. Those who knew Kohut will have no difficulty in recognizing his way of expressing himself as they read this final published version of the essay.

Concepts and Theories of Psychoanalysis

Heinz Kohut and Philip F. D. Seitz

RELATION OF METHOD AND THEORY

Psychoanalysis began with the famous case of Miss Anna 0., who insisted that her doctor, the Viennese internist Josef Breuer, listen to what she had to say. Freud discerned the potential fruitfulness of this novel approach to treatment and he based his own method on Anna O.'s invention—"chimney sweeping," as she had called her talks with Doctor Breuer.

Psychoanalysis began, therefore, in a therapeutic setting. It was characterized from the beginning by a specific method of observing human behavior (i.e., the physician listens to the verbal expression of the patient's flow of thought, and attempts to comprehend empathically what the patient wishes to communicate about his psychic state) and by a specific mode of theory formation (i.e., the physician attempts to bring order into the data which he has obtained about the inner life of his patient). The science of psychoanalysis has developed far beyond the limitations of the therapeutic situation; yet the fact that its principal method of observation was discovered in a therapeutic relationship, and that its predominant usefulness lies still in its therapeutic application, accounts for some of the specific assets as well as for some of the characteristic difficulties of the psychoanalytic method and theory. There can be no doubt, however, that, in spite of the confining influence of its intimate relationship with the goals of therapy, psychoanalysis has become vastly more than a theory of psychopathology; the continuum that it postulates between health and disease has made it a general theory of personality.

Psychoanalysis is a science based predominantly upon a method of clinical observation. It interprets empirical data, and thus its starting point is always observation of behavior and observation of people: of things people say, things people say they feel, and things people say they do not feel. The person to be observed, the patient, is asked to follow the basic rule of psychoanalysis: that is, he is to disclose everything that occurs to him, and he must try not to suppress anything that is embarrassing to him, or leave out anything that he believes to be irrelevant. The analyst does more, however, than simply listen to everything the patient says; his observations are made from the standpoint of certain theoretic concepts with which he orients his mind toward the observed. Psychoanalysis is not a method of "pure" observation—if such a thing actually exists in science—but observation and theory are closely interwoven: observation forming the basis of theories, and theories influencing the direction and focus of observation.

As an example of the relationship between method and theory in psychoanalysis, let us consider the investigation of the psychological significance of nursing activities. "Pure" observation tells us little about the psychology of the infant; all we can see is that the baby nurses and that it then goes to sleep. Although this sequence of events has been watched by countless generations, no scientific psychologic understanding was acquired. Psychological comprehension of the significance of the infant's oral strivings was greatly enhanced, however, by the ever increasing understanding of certain states in adult life, which while not directly applicable to earlier phases, has nevertheless given us valuable leads. Equipped with the knowledge derived from our observations of the intense reactions to object loss in the depressions of adults; of the intensity of oral wishes in addictions; or —in even more direct connection—of the exquisite sensitivity to rejection of those who have suffered intense early oral frustrations, we reexamine the nursing scene and can begin to make certain hypotheses. We are now able to grasp the intensity of the infant's oral strivings; we see the relative defenselessness of the infantile psyche when it is frustrated (its lack of buffering structure); we can comprehend dimly the special status of the object which the baby does not yet experience as separate from himself; and we appreciate the importance of the fact that the baby has no recognition that there is a choice of objects or that they are replaceable. While it is true that some of these hypotheses may not seem to stand on very firm ground when contemplated in isolation, they must support each other by their internal consistency and cohesion when we form our tentative constructions of early psychological states, and they must be checked against the empirical data obtained from the direct observation of children and from the childhood memories of adults. They are, therefore, open to correction or rejection as the evidence demands.

Neither the most ingenious and empathic interpretations of adult psychological states, however, nor the most "pure" observation of children is sufficient in psychoanalysis. As we observe adult behavior, we discern the remnants of childhood experiences; and as we observe childhood behavior, we recognize the seeds for adult functions and experiences. The interplay between present and past, between direct observation and interpretation, is among the most characteristic features of psychoanalysis as a method and as a theory.

In actual (clinical) practice, however, the theoretic knowledge of the experienced psychoanalyst has become so fully integrated into his total observational attitude that he is usually no longer aware of a dichotomy between theory and observation; and, although the psychoanalytic method of observation includes a background of theoretic concepts, the analyst's attitude, in his practice, is characterized by an openendedness of expectation. To be able to listen with suspended judgment and to resist the urge to come to quick conclusions; to accept the possibility of the emergence of an unforeseen message in a communication which may seem clearly intelligible to everyone else: that is the essence of the psychoanalyst's attitude. His attention is directed not only toward the content and form of the patient's communications or to the slow emergence of his conflict patterns, but also is open to the recognition of his own reactions to the patient. Yet neither his attention to the patient's associations nor his attention to his own reactions is focused sharply at first; premature attempts to arrange the data of observation into impeccably logical dynamic patterns interfere with analytic observation. The scrutiny of an isolated section of psychological material (e.g., the interpretation of a single dream) is not a characteristic sample of the work of the psychoanalyst; the psychoanalytically oriented, dynamic psychiatrist, however, is often expected to deduce a dynamic formulation of psychopathological symptoms or of specific character patterns from a limited number of data. While circumstances thus force the analyst (when he functions as a dynamic psychiatrist) to make inferences about the arrangement of psychological forces on the basis of relatively inert and isolated sources of information (through a limited number of interviews, for example), in his major field of competence the analyst's strength lies in his capacity to postpone closures and to observe the living ebb and flow of the thoughts and feelings of the analysand for prolonged periods until the closures are forced upon him.

The analyst validates his concepts, formulations, and theories by applying them to a variety of clinical experiences; he matches them, so to speak, with large numbers of clinical observations, testing again and again whether they lead to comprehension. If the theory, the formulation, or the concept is helpful in the understanding of a large number of clinical observations of similar type—better still if it can be intelligibly varied and then applied to related instances—then the analyst's impression of its validity grows; it is his premise, in other words, that the trustworthiness of a theory increases with each additional observation that it renders intelligible.

The theories of the psychoanalyst should be viewed predominantly, therefore, as attempts to bring order into the nearly endless variety of phenomena that he observes in his patients. Observation without implicit or explicit theory formation, without a hierarchy of the relative importance of the data, is unimaginable. How the analyst orders his data, on what he focuses his attention, and how he tries to understand the patient's communications, are questions that take us to those fundamental concepts upon which both the method and theory of psychoanalysis are based.

The Concept of the Unconscious; the Limited Role of Consciousness

The tenet of the essential unconsciousness of mental activities is the cornerstone of psychoanalytic theory; it exerts a decisive influence upon the observational attitude of the psychoanalyst. Although a vaguely formed notion about the existence of an unconscious mind has found wide acceptance and has achieved a shallow popularity, Freud's revolutionary theoretic innovation is not usually understood.

Freud recognized that Consciousness is not a necessary attribute of psychic activities; he postulated that it should be defined as the sensory organ of the mind. Consciousness, then, according to Freud, is a sense organ for the perception of psychic contents and qualities. One might say that, just as it is the function of the eye to see the objects and events in the external world, so it is the function of Consciousness to perceive endopsychic processes.[1]

Freud had to overcome an ingrained prejudice about the mind in order to define Consciousness as merely a sensory organ and to recognize not only that mental processes may occur outside of Consciousness but that Consciousness is not, at any time, an essential quality of mental activities. Attention to endopsychic activities may bring them to Consciousness; they take their course, however, whether observed by the "eye of Consciousness" or not. The clinical evidence for the relevance and validity of these concepts is overwhelming; experimental support has recently been provided by Charles Fisher (1954) who confirmed Poetzl's (1917) discovery that the unconscious perception of tachistoscopically projected images can be proved through the examination of dreams which occur subsequent to the tachistoscopic exposure.

The psychoanalytic discovery that the domain of Consciousness is limited and that psychic processes may, in essence, run their regular course outside of awareness, led to the recognition of the motivational cohesiveness of unconscious psychic activities.

---

1. Freud's concept of the relationship between Consciousness and the contents and qualities of the mind can be clarified further by the use of an analogy: the psychic contents may be compared with objects and activities present in a landscape which lies in darkness. Consciousness may be conceived as analogous to an observer who has the use of a searchlight which can illuminate the landscape. The focusing of the searchlight (and the variable intensity of its light) would be analogous to what is called "attention cathexis"; the ensuing illumination would be analogous to the process by which psychic contents become conscious. To become aware of psychic contents by focusing attention cathexes on them is thus an active process. The analogy also permits the integration of the following relevant details: extensive activities in the landscape may by themselves enter into the focus of the searchlight and are thus noticed by the observer; and the processes that are already under observation may arouse specific expectations in the observer and may thus determine the direction toward which the observer turns the instrument of illumination.

This conception exerted a far-reaching influence upon the observation of mental phenomena. Through the acceptance and utilization of the concept of unconscious psychic determinism, a host of seemingly fortuitous and purposeless psychological occurrences turned into potentially meaningful data and, thus, an area which previously had been open only to the intuitive grasp of the artist became accessible to the investigation of the scientist. Freud reflected about the motive of mankind's tendency to overestimate Consciousness and to deny the Unconscious[2]; he came to the conclusion that it is our inflated self-esteem which refuses to acknowledge the possibility that we might not be undisputed master in the household of our own minds. Just as Copernicus wounded man's self-esteem with his discovery that man is not the center of the universe, and as Darwin wounded our pride still further by finding that man cannot boast of having been separately or uniquely created, so Freud inflicted yet another blow to mankind's self esteem by the discovery that man's Consciousness illuminates only a narrow and limited part of his own mental activities.

Having shed the prejudice of assigning to Consciousness the position of all-inclusive sovereignty in psychic life, and having thus reduced it to the rank of an instrument of internal observation, we must not go too far and underrate its importance. Consciousness is not all that we would like it to be; many psychological processes take place in our minds which we may not happen to observe or which we are not capable of observing directly. Consciousness is the only light, however, that penetrates into the inner life of man; it illuminates enough of the surface of mental phenomena to permit convincing inferences about some important activities in the depths. Consciousness, as the instrument of psychological perception, is limited in its scope—yet it is all that we possess. It occupies the position of a fixed point of reference in psychoanalytic theory; it is the firm basis from which we must set out, and to which we must return, when we undertake the expanding explorations of unknown psychological territory. "Give me a firm spot on which to stand and I will move the earth," Archimedes is reported to have said in order to illustrate the potentialities inherent in the action of levers. Psychoanalysis has no hope of being able to move the psychological universe—yet

---

2. When used as nouns, denoting the various topographic areas of mental functioning, the terms Conscious, Preconscious, and Unconscious are traditionally capitalized.

what progress it is able to make will be derived or extrapolated through the careful scrutiny of information about psychic phenomena which are accessible to Consciousness; and conscious experience will remain the testing ground for the validity of new theoretic constructions. The essence of psychic life is dynamic, Freud stated; the investigation of the interplay of mental forces, however, requires the perception of their psychological manifestations with the sense organ of Consciousness.

INNATE PREDISPOSITION TO ENDOPSYCHIC CONCEPT

Another important hypothesis which influences the way in which the analyst orders the data of psychological observation is Freud's assumption that man has an inherent propensity for the development of endopsychic conflict. The psyche is conceived of as a dynamic system with an innate tendency toward an organization of forces that oppose and balance each other. The central position of endopsychic conflict is a characteristic, but by no means a specific feature of psychoanalytic psychology. What distinguishes psychoanalysis from other conflict psychologies, however, is the theory of an orderly and stable arrangement of groups of opposing forces which are potentially in conflict with each other. These more or less cohesive groups of forces are often referred to as being located in areas of the mind, and the diagrammatic representations of these localities are the psychoanalytic models of the mind. The first diagram of the arrangement of psychic forces was proposed by Freud around the turn of the century, during his most creative period; it usually goes by the name of the Topographic Model of the mind. The opposing areas (or systems) of the psyche are called the Unconscious and the Preconscious; the modes of functioning of the forces active in these psychic locations are referred to as the Primary and the Secondary Process. The primary processes are characteristic for the Unconscious, the secondary processes belong to the Preconscious. The sense organ of Consciousness may illuminate the otherwise unconsciously proceeding activities in the Preconscious and render them conscious.[3] The processes which take place in

---

3. The totality of the preconscious processes which have become conscious through the work (the focusing of attention) of the psychic sensory organ, Consciousness, is sometimes referred to as a separate system, the Conscious.

the Unconscious cannot, under normal circumstances, be reached directly by Consciousness.

While we probably cannot experience or demonstrate the unalloyed primary process directly, we have become familiar with some of its most important qualities and characteristics, especially through the study of dreams and of certain neurotic symptoms. Its activities are infantile, pre-logical, and unrestrained. It coalesces logically incompatible thought contents (condensation), shifts the intensity of its forces upon objects to which they do not logically belong (displacement), and it is intolerant of delay in the discharge of its tensions (it works with free, unbound energies). The main activity of the mature psyche follows the laws of the secondary process; it is adult, logical, and capable of tolerating delay. Its energies do not shift freely but they remain sharply focused on well-circumscribed objects and contents (it works with concentrated, bound energies).

THE CONCEPT OF TRANSFERENCE

Only secondary processes can be observed directly. The properties of the primary process must be inferred from the study of the characteristic disturbances and distortions which the secondary process undergoes when it is under the influence of the primary process. The influence of the primary process on the secondary process (the penetration of unconscious psychic contents and forces into preconscious thoughts, feelings, or wishes) was originally designated by the term "transference" by Freud (1900). It is important to note that transference, in the original meaning of the term, referred essentially to an endopsychic, not an interpersonal process. An obsessive thought, for example, is a transference phenomenon: the content of the thought ("Have I turned off the gas in the kitchen?") conforms to the secondary process; the unrelenting insistence with which it intrudes, however, betrays the fact it does not belong entirely to rational thinking but that it stems partly from the deeper layers of the mind, and that some of the forces which maintain it have the qualities of an untamed drive.

In current practice (derived largely from Freud's own later, metapsychologically less precise usage), the term transference refers customarily to the patient's revival of feelings and attitudes from childhood in his relationship with the analyst during psychoanalytic treatment. In the present essay, however, the term transference designates a metapsychological concept within the framework of the topographic point of view, in accordance with Freud's original definition. It should be noted that the later, clinically oriented use of the term transference (the misinterpretation of the analyst by the analysand due to the intrusion of feelings and attitudes that are associated with important figures from the analysand's childhood) is not superseded by the emphasis on the original, metapsychological definition which the present writers advocate: transference toward the analyst is simply one specific manifestation of a more general psychological mechanism.[4]

As a matter of fact, the discovery by Freud of transferences toward the analyst occurred relatively late, after he had recognized that dreams, slips of the tongue, and the symptoms of psychoneurosis are transference phenomena: that is, they are amalgamations of primary and secondary processes which are formed as a result of the intrusion of unconscious contents into the Preconscious. Writing, for example, is an activity of the ego.[5] If repressed masturbatory impulses from early childhood are reactivated, they may attach themselves (by transference) to the activity of writing, which consequently arouses guilt and becomes inhibited. The symptom (a hysterical writer's cramp, for example) contains an amalgamation of primary and secondary processes (masturbation-writing) and is called, therefore, the symptom of a transference neurosis.

In dreams the transferences from the Unconscious to the Preconscious attach themselves to "day residues," that is, to impressions of the preceding day which are, in themselves, either insignificant or of little practical importance. In Fisher's experiments, for example, the subjects tended to use the tachistoscopic

---

4. For a more extensive discussion of the advantages which accrue to psychoanalytic theory through an adherence to Freud's original, precise, metapsychological definition of transference, see Kohut (1959, pp. 471–472).

5. The term ego is not synonymous with the term Preconscious. The area of the mind (or the set of functions) to which the term ego is applied includes, in addition to the Preconscious, also a deeper layer which is inaccessible to consciousness. Foremost among the functions of the unconscious layers of the ego are the unconscious defenses. It follows from the preceding statement that the term id is not synonymous with the term Unconscious: the Unconscious is composed of the id and the unconscious layer of the ego (these distinctions are discussed further in a later section of this essay, "The Structural Model of the Mind").

pictures that had been flashed to them as day residues for their dreams. Why? Partly because the tachistoscopic images were isolated from the subjects' life experiences and thus without practical importance to them. Their very isolation (i.e., their lack of significant connections with other preconscious impressions) made them especially susceptible to influences from the Unconscious and, therefore, available for transferences. For the same reason, the psychoanalyst readily becomes a transference object: he has comparatively little significance for the patient as a source of realistic gratification. Conversely, if the analyst were to become the patient's supporter, helper, or friend, his availability as a transference object would be diminished.

The foregoing considerations are relevant to the clinical method of psychoanalysis and elucidate several features of the technical setting. The analyst is usually out of sight for the patient; he reveals little about his own personality, is generally sparing in how much he talks to the patient, and does not provide realistic gratifications of the patient's wishes as they become activated in the treatment (the "rule of abstinence"). The psychoanalytic setting is thus designed to facilitate, initially, what might be called the "day-residue function" of the analyst; it promotes the formation of transferences from the patient's Unconscious (usually pertaining to the patient's unresolved conflicts with the important figures of his early childhood) to the patient's preconscious images of the analyst. The analyst, in turn, as he observes the patient, keeps in mind that the patient's thoughts, feelings, and actions may be influenced via the mechanism of transference by the activities of another psychic system of which the patient himself remains unaware.

The following diagram illustrates the relationship of transferences to the psychic systems:

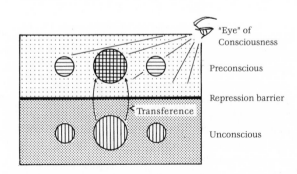

Under normal circumstances, the repression barrier effectively separates the repressed contents in the Unconscious from the Preconscious, and the activities in the Preconscious are therefore not influenced by those in the Unconscious. Under certain conditions, however, the repression barrier is weakened (e.g., during sleep) and permits the intrusion of some unconscious strivings into the Preconscious, where an amalgamation with suitable preconscious contents, i.e., the formation of transferences, takes place. If these intrusions are not excessive, they are tolerated by the Preconscious; if they become too extensive, however, the Preconscious mobilizes its forces and reestablishes the original impermeable barrier. This sequence (moderate intrusions, formation of transferences, intensification of the breakthrough, and reestablishment of firm repression) can be observed when the unconscious components in a dream transference become intensified to the point at which the dreamer experiences anxiety, awakens, and thus interrupts the dream and reestablishes full repression. The mode of operation and the genesis of the barrier which wards off the repressed portion of the psyche from contact with other psychic activities will be discussed later (see Psychic Trauma and the Repression of Infantile Drives and the discussion of the defense mechanisms in The Structural Model of the Mind).

HALLUCINATORY WISH-FULFILLMENT; THE INFANTILE SEXUAL AND AGGRESSIVE DRIVES

As set forth in the preceding section, the analyst's mind is receptive to the discovery of transferences from the first system, the Unconscious, to the second system, the Preconscious. Psychoanalytic conceptualizations and descriptions of unconscious mental processes are largely a result of extrapolations from consciously observed transference changes in the secondary process. In addition—to facilitate communication and understanding—psychoanalytic statements about the characteristics of unfamiliar, unconscious psychological processes have had to utilize descriptive terms and concepts from the familiar reference frame of Consciousness. (See the preceding remarks on page 122 about the role of conscious experience in psychoanalytic theory formation.)

Psychoanalysts describe the qualities of unconscious processes, therefore, in terms of characteristics associated with psychic processes which are accessible to Consciousness, by indicating either how the Unconscious differs from or how it is similar to consciously experienced mental contents. Certain qualities of the primary process (for example its form, intensity, and speed) came to be conceptualized and described by pointing out how they differ from (familiar) qualities of the secondary process. The characteristic wish-fulfilling nature of unconscious strivings, on the other hand, came to be described largely as a result of recognizing similarities with consciously observable phenomena such as wish-fulfilling day dreams. We can extrapolate, therefore (e.g., from observations of night dreams and psychoneurotic symptoms), that unconscious mental activity is similar to conscious day dreams in its striving to construct wish-fulfilling images of its desires. In contrast to our usual secondary process functioning, however, which seeks the real, external objects of its desires through attempts at mastery of the environment by realistic means, unconscious strivings are confined to the creation of hallucinatory images (as in the wish-fulfilling hallucinations of certain psychoses) or to symbolic enactments of wish-fulfillments (as in hysterical attacks).

Psychoanalytic conceptualizations regarding the nature of unconscious mental processes, mechanisms, and contents have been derived largely, therefore, from the study and description of contrasts and similarities between unconscious and preconscious mental activities. More direct observations of mental functions in small children and in psychotic patients have provided important additional data—supporting, refining, and revising the indirect reconstructions of unconscious (primary) mental processes.

The psychoanalytic concept that the dynamic processes in the id (the drives) are characterized by qualities of (infantile) sexuality and aggression was also formulated as a result of studying the contrasts and similarities between unconscious and preconscious mental activities. What the psychoanalyst understands by infantile sexuality and aggression, however, is not exactly the same as sexuality and aggression in the adult. Infantile drives have a characteristic intensity and urgency, and a pleasurable quality, that is virtually unknown to the adult, whose dominant secondary process functioning serves as a screen or buffer and usually protects him against the impact of unmodified drives. Only the height of sexual orgasm (and perhaps, under special circumstances, a paroxysm of maximal rage) can be said to be experienced with a minimum of buffering by the secondary process. The mature psyche is thus able to have intense sexual and aggressive experiences; this capacity, however, appears to be based upon the ability of the mature psyche to suspend temporarily some of its most highly developed functions. It is significant, therefore, that the experience at the height of orgasm and the experience of a paroxysm of intense rage can hardly be described through the use of language, the most important instrument of the secondary process, and that even Consciousness itself appears to be altered at such times.

Freud recognized the meaningful equivalence between the processes in the Unconscious (the infantile psyche) and the sexual experiences of adults, and said that he did not want to change the term "sexuality" to characterize infantile drives and experiences because he had chosen it "a potiori": that is, he had used the term which referred to the best known of the various experiences of a similar kind. Freud found a great deal of evidence for the fact that every activity was originally sexual, with regard to the intensity of its motivation and the quality of its experience: when the baby nurses, the intensity of its pleasure is similar to sexual sensations in adults; and walking, looking, talking, writing were begun at least partially as sexual activities. Seen from the standpoint of biology, and in harmony with the tenets of the theory of evolution, we may also stress the great survival value of the intense erotic pleasure that is associated with the infantile drives and activities: the more intensely and urgently pleasurable these activities are (e.g., the baby's sucking), the more the infant is motivated to perform the survival-promoting functions.

As a result of endogenous maturational tendencies (which, however, are decisively influenced by environmental circumstances) a segment of the Unconscious is transformed into the Preconscious. (As pointed out before, the terms id and ego are now used for the groups of psychic functions which constitute the polarities in this development.) The environmental circumstances which further the differentiation of the Preconscious can be described as optimal frustrations, that is, frustrations which prevent the immediate satisfaction of the pleasure-seeking infantile drives, yet are not of such severity (that is, not traumatic) that they obstruct development. (This topic will be pursued further in the next section.)

Every mature activity that developed from infantile drives can, however, under certain circumstances, return to its primitive form: either openly (in perversions) or covertly (in the psychoneuroses). In obsessional neurosis, for example, thinking itself, which was originally a highly pleasurable sexual and aggressive activity, may again take on the qualities and aims of infantile sexuality and aggression. In consequence of such regression, thinking becomes dangerous and is defended against by the compulsion neurotic (e.g., by the use of magical repetitions, and by other means). When the (preconscious) ego is working properly, however, a neutralization of its activities has occurred (i.e., a progression from primary to secondary process functioning), and the infantile erotic and aggressive quality of its experience disappears.

Optimal Frustration and the Establishment of the Secondary Process

Although the capacity to achieve the use of mature psychic functions must be considered a part of the innate potentialities of human psychological equipment, it is only through a long series of interactions with the environment that the archaic mode of mental functioning (the primary process) becomes gradually converted into the adult form of thinking (the secondary process). Since memories constitute the basic units of the secondary process, it is profitable to examine the psychological forerunners of the memory function, and to study the circumstances which promote the development of the memory trace. To this end we turn to Freud's hypothesis about the establishment of the earliest psychological structures in the infant.

It is impossible for us to define the infant's first experience of hunger in psychological terms. We can state only that physiological processes (later to be experienced as hunger) produce a tension to which the infant responds reflexly with a series of activities. The cry, which is foremost among the infant's reflex responses, alerts the mother; the baby receives its feeding, and the physiological tension state subsides. After this sequence (hunger tension—cry—mother—feeding—satiation) has taken place, however, the infant's psyche has undergone a change; some engram of the hunger-satiation sequence has been deposited; and, when the tension reasserts itself and reaches a certain intensity, the baby's hunger-drive-wishes turn toward the engram of the previous satisfaction to achieve a repetition of the experience of satiation. It is a moot question whether we should call this first attempt to reach satisfaction a hallucination; it is obvious, at any rate, that the turning toward the engram of previous satisfaction does nothing to decrease the hunger: the tension mounts, the reflex cry occurs and real feeding leads again to satiation. The baby now has had its first opportunity to distinguish the experience of the hallucination of a previous (real) satisfaction from the experience of a (real) satisfaction in the present. Innumerable repetitions of this sequence of events lead, little by little, to a lessening of the intensity with which the psyche turns toward the engram; instead of expecting satisfaction from the engram itself, the infant learns to consider the engram as an intermediate station on the way toward satisfaction. As the excessive interest in the engram decreases, it is also experienced less vividly: it takes on a quality that is distinct from the experience of reality. A differentiation of psychic reality and external reality is thus acquired; hallucinations have become memories.

The development of the memory function from hallucinations is enhanced by experiences of optimal frustration. Overindulgence results in less incentive to learn the distinction between fantasy and reality, since feeding occurs so quickly that it coalesces with the turning toward the fantasy-image. Severe frustrations (or inconsistency of maternal response), on the other hand, create a reality that supplies hardly more gratification than the fantasy-image; thus, again, there is less opportunity (and incentive) for the firm establishment of the differentiation. By contrast, optimal frustrations involve sufficient delay in satisfaction to induce tension-increase and disappointment in the attempt to obtain wish-fulfillment through fantasy; the real satisfaction occurs quickly enough, however, to prevent a despairing and disillusioned turning away from reality.

Psychic Trauma and the Repression of Infantile Drives

A certain portion of the infantile sexual and aggressive drives neither develops into adult sexuality or aggression nor becomes transformed into drive-distant preconscious secondary processes, but remains unchanged—walled off (repressed) in the Unconscious. Study of preconscious transference intrusions from the

Unconscious reveals that the repressed drives have retained their original primitiveness and intensity. Having explained earlier how primary processes are converted into secondary processes under the influence of experiences of optimal frustration, we must now account for the fact that a part of the primary processes does not participate in this development.

As indicated in the preceding section, the ability of the infantile psyche to learn to distinguish reality from hallucination (and thus to transform hallucinations into memories) is hampered if the infant is either excessively indulged, or if it is exposed to frustrations of traumatic intensity. Traumatic frustrations of infantile needs ensue when the waiting period exceeds the tolerance of the infantile psyche, or when the gratifications offered by the environment are unpredictable, for example, when feedings are dispensed inconsistently. In either case the infantile psyche turns away from reality and retains self-soothing gratification through fantasy. True overindulgence is unlikely to be encountered during the early phase of psychological development; if it does occur it may stunt development (fixation) through lack of incentive for learning to grasp reality. More important, however, is the fact that overindulgence is not maintained forever by the environment, and that a sudden switch in maternal attitude from overindulgence to frustration is experienced as traumatic by the unprepared psyche of the child.

Traumatic experiences, like experiences of optimal frustration, lay down memory traces; but in the case of traumatic frustrations the infantile drives and associated traumatic memories are walled off (primal repression) under the influence of primitive despair and anxiety. Since the psyche strives to prevent the recurrence of the former state of anxiety and despair, the repression is permanently retained, at the sacrifice of further differentiation of the repressed wishes. Traumatic frustration of drives thus produces a psychologic enclave of primary process functioning and psychic fixation upon direct wish-fulfillment, for example by means of hallucinations. Unconscious contents that are sealed off from the preconscious ego are not exposed to the influence of new experiences and, therefore, are incapable of change (learning); instead, following the laws of the primary process and of the pleasure principle, endlessly repeated attempts occur to achieve immediate wish-fulfillment through hallucinations or through other similar means. A symbolically wish-fulfilling version of an infantile experience may be reenacted over and over again throughout a lifetime by the same recurring hysterical symptom.

Since the original infantile strivings, and the context in which they arose, remain unconscious, however, the wish can neither be gratified realistically nor relinquished.

What constitutes a childhood trauma can hardly be defined objectively; it is a psychological task that the child's psyche cannot integrate into the more differentiated preconscious system either because of the intensity of the demand, or because of the immaturity of the psychological organization, or because of a transient sensitivity of the psyche at the time when the task is imposed on it, or by any combination of these factors. Trauma is thus an economic concept in psychoanalysis, referring not principally to the content of the experience but to its intensity. Trauma is overstimulation, whether from overgratifying or overfrustrating experiences; it involves not just what occurs externally but the dovetailing of external events and inner psychic organization. Although there are certain periods in childhood (most often corresponding with an as yet insecurely established new balance of psychological forces after a spurt of development) during which the psyche is especially susceptible to traumatization, we can safely say that the young child is exposed to traumata at all times.

The time factor constitutes an especially important, and frequently neglected, consideration in the economic concept of trauma. Not only is the age and the developmental stage of the child often crucial in determining the severity of a psychological task, but it may be equally decisive whether the child is expected to perform the feat of a sudden major transition from primary to secondary process functioning, or whether he is permitted to acquire the new functions in a fractionated way over a longer period of time.

Experiences that had not been integrated into the Preconscious during childhood are mobilized again during psychoanalytic treatment; but now, in their therapeutic reactivation, the patient has ample time for their gradual assimilation. The stepwise process, during which traumatic memories are faced again and infantile wishes are reexperienced and slowly relinquished, is called "working-through." This process has been compared with the work that the psyche performs in mourning—except that the bereaved has to give up a love object of the present while the patient learns that he must forego the hope of fulfilling unmodified infantile wishes, and that he must relinquish the objects of the past.

The interrelationship between theory and practice, and specifically the influence of the aforementioned psychoeconomic considerations on the therapeutic procedures of psychoanalysis, can be illuminated further by focusing on the method of free association. Free association is commonly described in negative terms, as a giving up of controls, a disregard of self-criticism and the like. Free association, however, involves more than relaxation; at the crucial junctures it summons the ability to tolerate the admission of unpleasant mental contents to Consciousness, to be perceived and experienced. Free association, therefore, requires effort and perseverance in order to accomplish a gradual extension of the realm of the secondary process. It is not the aim of psychoanalysis, however, to achieve an ideally perfect psychological organization in which the Unconscious has become totally accessible and transformed. The defect in human psychological equipment to which Freud alluded on a number of occasions is not the existence of a repression barrier or of the defense mechanisms but their relative inadequacy. Analysis, therefore, strives to establish the dominance of the secondary process only in those segments of the psyche where the defenses have proved ineffectual. When anamnestic data from childhood or evidence obtained from dreams point toward repressed material that has been contained effectively by socially acceptable and satisfactory defensive activities, no attempt is made to stir up such dormant conflicts during an analysis. If a violently hostile attitude toward a father figure has been superseded by devotion to a life task of promoting social justice for the aged, for example, there is no indication for attempting to undermine this ego-syntonic system of values unless neurotic inhibitions (due to a threatened breakthrough of the original hostility) interfere with this segment of psychic adjustment. Any walled-off content for which the defense mechanisms are securely anchored is thus left untouched. A perfectionistic attitude about uncovering the repressed is, at best, the sign of the amateur; at worst, it may betray the fanatic who, hiding some secret from himself, must forever wrest secrets from others.

VANTAGE POINTS OF PSYCHOANALYTIC OBSERVATION; THE GENETIC POINT OF VIEW

The intricate system of psychoanalytic concepts and formulations (often referred to as metapsychology) becomes more easily understandable if we isolate the various interrelated lines of approach which the analyst follows in ordering the psychological data. These basic observational positions of the psychoanalyst are known as the dynamic, the economic, the topographic and structural, and the genetic points of view.

The fact that the analyst conceives of wishes, urges, and drives as expressions of psychological forces, and that he sees psychological conflicts as clashes between these forces, is designated as the psychodynamic point of view. In addition, the analyst acknowledges the fact that psychological forces have a certain strength: there are lukewarm wishes, for example, and there are burning desires. The fact that the analyst pays attention to the relative strength of the psychological forces which he observes is referred to as the psychoeconomic point of view.

The recognition of a more or less stable grouping of psychological forces led to the concept of areas of the mind and to their diagrammatic rendition in the psychoanalytic models of the mind. Freud's early diagram, the topographic model, divided the psyche into two areas: the Unconscious and the Preconscious. The conceptual mode of approach to the data of observation which is based on the topographic diagram is called the topographic point of view. A growing number of observations, however, could not be fitted into the classical topographic model. It had to be revised in order to be consistent with newly gained insights about mental functioning, and it had to be expanded in order to accommodate the newly discovered areas of the psyche. The revised and expanded psychoanalytic diagram is the structural model; the mode of approach that is based on it is the structural point of view. The topographic point of view has already been discussed at length; some aspects of the structural point of view will be reviewed later.

In the following we will discuss briefly the genetic point of view. This term refers to the fact that the analyst focuses his attention on the childhood of the individual whom he studies, with the expectation that he may discover a specific set of experiences that occurred at a specific time or during a specific period of childhood, following which a particular symptom, character trait, or behavioral tendency arose for the first time. Genetic explanations in therapeutic psychoanalysis refer, of course, most frequently to the origin of adult psychopathology and, thus, to those traumatic childhood situations in which a preceding non-pathologic arrangement of psychological forces was replaced permanently by a new, pathologic one. The potential discovery of the pathogenic experiences of childhood through the investigation of unconscious endopsychic material is a specific and characteristic objective of psychoanalysis. The modern offshoots of psychoanalysis (such as the various popular schools of dynamic psychiatry) restrict their investigations of endopsychic material to the comprehension of repetitive dynamic patterns which are then correlated with known historical data from childhood, such as the specific family constellation, the personalities of the parents, deaths of parents or siblings, and so forth. Their examination stops short of the ultimate goal of psychoanalysis: the therapeutic revival and recovery of the unconscious memories of traumatic experiences.

A brief clinical vignette may clarify the difference between the understanding of dynamic patterns and the penetration into genetic material.

A man described a recent job situation in which his work (which had been satisfactory previously) deteriorated after the appearance of a younger co-worker. It was found in the course of the analytic work that he had felt guilty about his jealousy towards the new worker, and that the slackening of his work had been motivated by a wish to withdraw from the competition. The same dynamic pattern could be established in relation to previous job situations. Similar conflicts had occurred in childhood with schoolmates and especially with his brothers. The pattern was repeated in his analysis. At first he did good work with a steady flow of free associations; then came a setback and resistance. His associations alluded hesitatingly one day to another patient whom he had seen in the waiting room. The same dynamic formulation as before was interpreted, and the analytic work flowed again. On a later occasion intense resistance set in, followed by the reluctant disclosure of fantasies that the other patient might be ill. Memories of illnesses in a sibling then emerged. Finally, after many phases of intense resistance, dream material made possible the reconstruction (later supported by relevant memories) that an infant brother had died during a phase of intense hostile jealousy during the patient's early childhood. The genetic elucidation of this pattern was now possible. Not only had he experienced a normal amount of hostility toward rivals prior to the fateful event (the sibling's death), but he had also gradually learned to recognize that there is a significant difference between (the psychologic reality of) angry thoughts and wishes, on the one hand, and (the external reality of) angry and hurtful actions, on the other. The death of the brother (aided by auxiliary factors, such as the parents' withdrawal from the patient during the traumatic period) had shattered the ego's barely acquired differentiation between impulse, fantasy and deed. Angry wishes and fantasies were regressively experienced as magically powerful, and the weak ego, traumatically flooded with anxiety, defended itself against the dangerous impulses by repression. Thereafter, hostile, jealous and competitive strivings were excluded from the realm of the ego, preventing their further differentiation and integration and precluding the acquisition of eventual conscious control over them.

THE STRUCTURAL MODEL OF THE MIND

As indicated before, new observational data and new insights made the classical topographic model inadequate, and necessitated (in the 1920s) the creation of a new diagram of the arrangement and interrelationships of psychological forces, the structural model of the mind. The new model contains a series of major revisions and expansions; best known among the innovations is undoubtedly the new nomenclature, the introduction of the terms id, ego, and superego, corresponding with a new division of psychic functions which conforms more accurately with the data of clinical observation than the simpler correlations of the topographic model. The very fact that Freud introduced a new terminology for the structural model bespeaks the magnitude of the conceptual changes, since Freud was usually disinclined to replace already established terms.

Later we will turn our attention to a notable expansion in the conceptual scope of the structural point of view, which permits the meaningful inclusion of a whole new range of psychological phenomena into the framework of psychoanalytic theory. First, however, we must review some of the major modifications and corrections which transformed the topographic into the structural model: the discovery of unconscious defense mechanisms, the recognition of the role of aggression, and the comprehension of the genetic and structural cohesion of the various constituents of endopsychic morality.

The investigation of new areas of psychopathology, particularly the obsessions and compulsions, led to the discovery that repression (i.e., the withdrawal of a fragile psyche, under the impact of trauma, from further participation in specific infantile wishes) was not the only mechanism by which the immature mental apparatus could maintain its organization under stress. Freud recognized that the psyche also employs other important means of keeping the dangerous archaic drives in check: chronic characterologic attitudes (the so-called reaction formations) serve to maintain and reinforce previously established repressions; magical modes of thought and action (the mechanism of undoing) are employed to ward off threats to a weakening repression; and ideas and affects are kept apart (the mechanism of isolation) by a superstitiously fearful psyche in order to render impulses harmless which might penetrate through the repressions.

The discovery that a variety of defense mechanisms exists in the psyche contributed to the depth and the subtlety of clinical understanding; of even greater importance, however, both clinically and theoretically, was the recognition that these various defense mechanisms directed against archaic infantile wishes and impulses, were themselves not only archaic (i.e., part of the primary process) but also inaccessible to Consciousness (i.e., belonging to the Unconscious). The revised conceptualization of the interrelationships of psychic forces, which takes these new discoveries into account, recognizes that the essential opposition is between an enclave of unmodified infantile strivings (the repressed id) and a system composed predominantly of mature, preconscious functions (the ego). The ego, however, applies archaic means (the unconscious defenses) to maintain the integrity of its territory of rationality. This particular structural relationship is analogous to the use of magical threats by parents, educators, and religious authorities in order to foster the creation of superstitious beliefs in children, in the service of drive control and of other rational aims.

The following diagram presents the new conceptualization of the relationship between ego, id, Preconscious, and Unconscious.

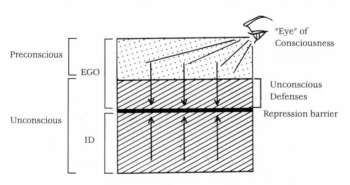

The area below the repression barrier is the id; the area above is the ego. The lined area is the Unconscious, the dotted area the Preconscious. The opposing arrows symbolize the structural conflict between repressed infantile drives and the defenses. Note that the main part of the defenses is unconscious.

Only brief mention need be made about the increasingly significant position which aggression began to occupy in psychoanalytic theory. The clinical importance of aggressive strivings had been obvious, of course, from the beginning; the Oedipus complex, for example, the foremost clinical discovery of psychoanalysis, which was presented as early as 1900, involves not only a libidinal but also an equally important aggressive component (cf. the little boy's death wishes toward his father). Unlike the later investigations of compulsion neurosis and depression, however, the early investigations of hysteria did not lead with equal clarity to the recognition that the vicissitudes of aggressive drives paralleled widely those of the libidinal drives. Like the libido, aggression is present in a repressed, unmodified, infantile form; its breakthrough is feared and defended against; it enters into transferences; and it lends itself to maturing influences and to useful integration into the higher functions of the psyche. It was on the basis of these new observations that the new dual-drive theory was incorporated into the structural model: the id was conceived of as containing not only infantile libidinal but also infantile aggressive tensions which strive for discharge and are kept repressed.

We turn now to the concept of the superego, the new conceptualization of endopsychic moral forces. The presence of endopsychic moral forces had been acknowledged from the early days of psychoanalysis, and it was recognized that they contributed decisively to the motivation for and the maintenance of repressions. The widening scope of clinical observations, however, led, step by step, to the discovery that the moral forces not only fulfill a variety of related functions but also that they constitute a cohesive genetic and functional unit which demanded their conceptualization as a distinct structure of the psyche, the superego. The study of hysteria already allowed the assumption that moral influences could be unconscious, like the drives; and this assumption became well-nigh a certainty when Freud discovered that an unconscious sense of guilt could induce people to commit crimes in order to provoke punishment. The decisive studies, however, were instigated by the discovery that, in certain depressions, the moral forces (although in a malignant state of regression) have gained a circumscribed position of tyrannical power over the rest of the personality and are in the process of subjugating and of destroying it. Freud extended and deepened his study of the various components of endopsychic morality (the censoring and punitive forces, the standards of the ego ideal, the approving and loving powers) and ultimately came to the conclusion that the essential cohesiveness of these variegated functions resulted from the fact that they had once been united, outside the personality, in the parental authority: that the parent-authority had been the embodiment of the censor and punisher who was feared by the child, the admired ideal and prototype who could make the child feel small and inferior, the source of love and approval when the commands had been obeyed, and the reservoir of shared pride and pleasure when the child lived up to the parental example. Because Freud recognized the functional and genetic cohesion of the various aspects of the internal moral forces, he conceived of them as a distinct psychological structure. Even the name which he chose, the superego, reflected the fact that approval and disapproval, and standards and ideals are experienced as if located above the ego: a residual from the time when the child was small and looked up to the approving or disapproving admired figures.

In addition to the fact that the structural point of view introduces a number of important changes into psychoanalytic theory (e.g., revision of the theory of repression, of the theory of drives, and of the theory of endopsychic morality), it also constitutes a significant expansion of the conceptual scope of psychoanalysis: it allows the integration of the dynamic-economic-genetic understanding of a variety of nonpathological functions with those essential, classical findings and formulations of psychoanalysis which had been derived from the study of dreams and of psychopathology.

This expansion in the scope of psychoanalytic theory finds its diagrammatic expression specifically in the fact that, in the structural model of the psyche, the barrier of defenses separates only a small part of the infantile psychological depth from the areas of mature psychic functioning, while the deep, unconscious activities in the remainder of the diagram are in broad uninterrupted contact with the preconscious layers of the surface. Kohut[6] has referred to the dichotomized segment of the psyche as the area of

---

6. See Kohut (1961).

transferences, and to the uninterrupted segment as the area of progressive neutralization.

The following diagram presents the two segments of the psyche in a schematic fashion. The actual relationships would be rendered more accurately if the barrier of defenses were made to shade into the nondichotomized segment of the psyche. This gradual merging of the defense barrier into the neutralizing matrix of the psyche is hinted at in the diagram but is not fully carried out. The right side of the diagram represents the area of transferences; here infantile impulses, which have met with frustration of traumatic intensity, exert their transference influence across the barrier of defenses and produce compromise formations (between primary and secondary processes) with the preconscious contents of the ego. The left side of the diagram represents the area of progressive neutralization, where the infantile impulses which have encountered optimal frustration are transformed gradually into neutralized mental activities.

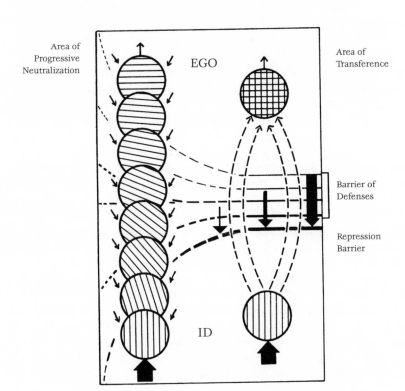

Although the area of transferences constitutes only a small portion of the structural diagram, its significance remains undiminished since it is there that we find those activities and phenomena that are the result of structural conflicts and transference: dream formation; the symptoms of the transference neuroses; such psychic formations as slips of the tongue, errors, and the like, which Freud referred to as psychopathology of everyday life; and especially the transferences to the analyst in the course of psychoanalytic treatment.

As we have seen, the structural model of the mind depicts the bulk of the psychological organization as a continuum from the depths to the surface. The neutralizing psychological structure which constitutes the nondichotomized portion of the psyche (the area of progressive neutralization) was formed by the internalization of innumerable experiences of optimal frustration. The barrier of defenses, on the other hand, which walls off an unmodified residue of infantile strivings, is the result of the internalization of frustrating experiences and prohibitions of traumatic intensity.

The differences between childhood experiences of traumatic and of optimal frustration are differences in degree. It is the difference between one mother's harsh "N-O!" and another mother's kindly "no." It is the difference between a frightening kind of prohibition, on the one hand, and an educational experience on the other. It is the difference between one father's handling a child's temper tantrum by an equally hostile counter-tantrum, and another father's picking up the child and calming him—firm but nonaggressive, and loving but not seductive. It is the difference between an uncompromising prohibition, which stresses only what the child must not have or cannot do, and the offering of acceptable substitutes for the forbidden object or activity.

Replicas of the experiences of traumatic frustration and of the experiences of optimal frustration (identifications) are established in the mind via the mechanism of introjection. The child incorporates permanently into his own psychic organization the restraining attitudes and behavior of the childhood objects who curbed his wishes, demands, needs and strivings. The child's drives are opposed originally by the prohibitions of the parents. If these prohibitions are of nontraumatic intensity, the child incorporates the parents' drive-restraining attitudes in the form of innumerable benign memory traces. In this way the matrix of the nondichotomized portion of the psychologic structure is created, which transforms the archaic, infantile drives into aim-inhibited activities. As a result of having introjected many experiences of optimal frustration in which his infantile drives were handled by a calming, soothing, loving attitude rather than by counter-aggression on the part of his parents, the child himself later acts in the same way toward the drive demands that arise in him. Optimally frustrating experiences lead, therefore, to the formation of a drive-restraining (neutralizing) structure which, itself, is composed of neutralized memory traces and works with the aid of neutralized endopsychic forces. Crude, infantile aggressive impulses, for example, can be transformed into non-hostile purposive activities through internalized drive-restraining attitudes which, themselves, have lost their aggressive or sexual quality.

Individuals undoubtedly differ in their constitutional potentialities for the development of optimally neutralizing, drive-restraining structures. The most important source of a well-functioning psychological structure, however, is the personality of the parents, specifically their ability to respond to the child's drive demands with non-hostile firmness and non-seductive affection. Psychoanalysis also takes into account the existence of constitutional variations in the readiness of the child's psyche to be traumatized and to ward off conflictual drive demands through the establishment of repressions and of massive defenses. Even the most mature parents cannot (and need not) prevent the establishment of repressions and of other defenses, which are, after all, economical means of dealing with tensions at a time when the more subtle steps toward psychological growth cannot yet be taken. If a child is exposed chronically to immature, hostile, or seductive parental reactions toward his demands, then the resulting intense anxiety or overstimulation leads to an impoverishment of the growing psyche, since too much of his drive-equipment is repressed and thus cannot participate in psychic development. In addition, the intensity of the unmodified infantile drives and the brittleness of the defenses are the antecedents of later psychological imbalance, and of the sudden breakthrough of repressed material which leads to neurotic illness.

The foregoing discussion has not taken up all of the major changes in psychoanalytic theory brought about by the structural point of view; and of those that were reviewed, only the highlights could be depicted. Completeness, however, is neither possible nor even desirable in a brief survey of a complex field. The aim of this presentation was, rather, to attempt to provide a better comprehension of the meaning of the theoretical formulations of psychoanalysis, a sense of the continual development and expansion of psychoanalytic theory, and an appreciation of the interrelatedness between theoretical formulation and (clinical) observation. Consideration of the structural point of view shows how earlier theoretic formulations were revised under the influence of new clinical findings; it also demonstrates with particular clarity the expansion in the scope of psychoanalytic theory, in particular its increasing ability to define and explain the most mature and highly developed psychic activities in genetic-dynamic-economic terms, and to integrate these new insights with the older formulations.

The formulations of the structural point of view exerted a considerable influence on the theoretic principles of child rearing practices. It hardly needs to be stressed that the structural point of view also modified the theory of psychoanalytic technique and the conduct of therapeutic psychoanalysis. The fact that during psychoanalysis one part of the patient's psyche observes and comprehends, while the other part permits regression and transferences (what Sterba later aptly called the "therapeutic split in the ego"), had probably been understood for a long time. The deeper comprehension, however, of the meaningful relationship of the observing part of the psyche with the analyst (i.e., of the patient's capacity to form and maintain a reliable relationship of cooperation which rests on the foundations of childhood experience yet is not transference) could only be attained through the formulations and insights of the structural point of view.

Recognition of the advances in theoretic understanding that are embodied in the structural diagram does not prevent the acknowledgment that it contains important areas that await further exploration and reformulation. What, for example, is the nature of the psychic contents of the id? Are its primitive wish-strivings attached to memories and fantasies; and, if so, is there, beneath the barrier of defenses, a further differential layering between id-contents of greater and lesser primitiveness? Are there formal distinctions between the archaic psychic processes in the unconscious part of the ego and those in the id? What are the differences between the early identifications in the deepest layers of the psyche and those that are deposited later, nearer the surface? These and other topics await detailed exploration, and there is little doubt that the structural diagram will be modified in due course as a result of further clinical research.

The development of psychoanalysis has, in fact, not ceased since the introduction of the structural model. The newer formulations seem to point toward an increasing preoccupation of analysts with the functions of the ego. Analysts (cf. H. Hartmann) now emphasize that ego functions mature in a predetermined fashion which is to some extent independent of environmental influences (primary autonomy), and also that ego functions may ultimately free themselves from the nexus of endopsychic conflicts and thus, again, become independent (secondary autonomy).

It is neither possible nor desirable to present an orderly survey of the most recently formulated theories of a developing science such as psychoanalysis. The modern theories have been mentioned primarily to prevent the possible misapprehension that psychoanalysts consider the theories of the structural point of view as the final word of wisdom. True, psychoanalysis, like any other science, does not discard well-established theories lightly; a degree of conservatism is necessary to prevent a theoretical and conceptual chaos. Yet, if we take a broad view we can safely say that while the theory of psychoanalysis influences the analyst's mode of observation and the evaluation of his data, it remains itself open to change by the impact of new experience.

Part III

Kohut's Method of Synthesizing Freudian Theory

Philip F. D. Rubovits-Seitz

Kohut's Method of Synthesizing Freudian Theory

Philip F. D. Rubovits-Seitz

Freudian theory is extensive, multifaceted, and complex. Like other theoretical systems in the human, social, and behavioral sciences, it is loosely "concatenated" rather than deductively hierarchical. The methodologist Abraham Kaplan (1964) explained that a concatenated theory is one in which the components constitute a network of relations that form an identifiable configuration or pattern. Theories of this kind are characterized by "tendency" statements, which depend on their joint application for closure. Facts are explained by such theories when their place in the overall pattern can be demonstrated. "The 'big bang' theory of cosmology, the theory of evolution, and the psychoanalytic theory of the neuroses may all be regarded as being of this type" (p. 298).

Because of their loosely organized character, concatenated theories are difficult to systematize and explicate. David Rapaport (1960), for example, was frustrated and dissatisfied with his determined effort to systematize psychoanalytic theory. A number of other writers have undertaken the task with varying degrees of success (e.g., Brill, 1913; Hitschmann, 1913; Hartmann, 1927; Nunberg, 1932; Menninger, 1937; Glover, 1939; Hendrick, 1939; Sterba, 1942; Fenichel, 1945; Jones, 1948; Kubie, 1950; Waelder, 1960; Brenner, 1961; Wyss, 1966, pp. 45–255; Fine, 1973; and others).

These writings provided some of the early textbooks of psychoanalysis. They organized the material in various ways, often employing a historical approach to the evolution of Freud's theories. Some resorted to oversimplified presentations of psychoanalytic theory—which seems to have displeased Freud, judging by his Foreword to Nunberg's (1932/1955) *Principles of Psychoanalysis*:

In this book Nunberg gives the most complete and accurate presentation we have at this time of a psychoanalytic theory of neurotic processes. Those who seek a simplification and glossing
over of the problems with which it deals will be disappointed in
this book. Those, however, who prefer scientific thinking, who
appreciate theoretical formulations which never abandon their
ties to experience, those who can savor the rich diversity of psychic events—those persons will value and eagerly study this work
[1955, p. xi].

On the basis of numerous conversations with Kohut regarding
his views on psychoanalytic theory and method, I got the impression that he did not set out to systematize Freudian theory. The
explication of Freud's theories that he presented in his lectures
on psychoanalytic psychology appeared to have grown out of his
own efforts to understand psychoanalytic theory and to help students comprehend it in a coherently organized way.

Kohut occasionally referred to a type of intellect that he called
an "organizing intelligence"—by which he meant not just an
organized mind, but one that is continually organizing the information it encounters. I believe that Kohut's intelligence was of
the organizing type and that he approached the complexities of
Freudian theory with an inherent talent and preference for
organizing it. In one of his writings, for example, he mentioned
his lifelong admiration of the capacity for synthesizing diverse
phenomena:

My intellectual development was strongly influenced by a histo-
rian, a high school teacher—I can still see him in front of me—
whose mode of thinking struck some kind of chord in me that
never stopped vibrating from the days I sat spellbound and listened to him. I remember vividly how he began to explain the
absolutist regime of the late Bourbons in France by talking about
the way the parks were laid out. I was impressed by his ability to
demonstrate the essential unitariness of seemingly diverse phenomena of a culture, a period in history. He didn't write, he did-
n't grade, he was not a feared professor, and he was a very low
man on the totem pole among the teachers I had. Yet, to me, he
remained an unforgotten inspiration [Kohut, 1975b, pp. 771–772].

In preparing the present volume I became increasingly interested in how Kohut dealt with the complexities of psychoanalytic
theory without oversimplifying its wide-ranging, multifaceted
subject matter. I reviewed in detail the compendium of his
"Lectures on Psychoanalytic Psychology" and the essay that we

coauthored on Freudian theory. I was surprised to find what appeared to be a pattern in the Freudian concepts that Kohut emphasized in both his lectures and the essay. He seemed to focus frequently on a particular type of concept that is prevalent in Freud's writings—namely, syncretistic (or syncretic) concepts, which combine conceptual entities that differ from or oppose each other in specific ways.

To illustrate, Freud frequently employed what might be called "continuum concepts," which are distinctly syncretic: for instance, the continuum between normal and pathological mental functioning. Freud postulated, for example, that normal phenomena such as the psychopathology of everyday life, dreams, and jokes share the same underlying structurodynamic mechanisms as psychoneurotic symptoms. Kohut selectively emphasized that Freudian concept in his very first lecture on psychoanalytic psychology. While outlining the contents of the course, he referred to Hartmann's (1939) concepts of primary and secondary autonomy, explaining that an activity such as orderliness can be a symptom of compulsion neurosis, on the one hand, but on the other hand can be primarily or secondarily autonomous and thus free of conflict or neurosis—illustrating the continuum between mental health and illness.

Kohut returned to this subject in his second lecture, pointing out that the reason Freud (1901) worked so hard on "The Psychopathology of Everyday Life" was because he was intent on developing a theory that encompassed both normal and pathological behavior. Emphasizing this Freudian continuum in both the first and second lectures of the course exemplifies Kohut's affinity for and explanatory emphasis on syncretistic concepts in Freud's writings.

As I restudied Kohut's lectures and essay, I was struck by the frequency and variety of instances in which he zeroed in on such concepts in Freud's writings, using them to organize and explicate Freudian theory. Whether Kohut was aware of doing so is a moot question, although I doubt that he set out consciously to identify and emphasize such concepts. In many discussions with him about Freud's conceptual style and method of reasoning, for example, Kohut never referred to the frequency or importance of syncretizing concepts in Freud's writings. It seems more likely that his recognition and extensive use of such concepts was a creative, preconscious act of perception and synthesis.

I do not mean to imply that Kohut's emphasis on syncretic concepts was the sole reason that his synthesis of Freudian theory was so successful—that is, so well-received and valued by his students. I suspect, however, that it was an important factor, because concepts of that type possess unusual synthesizing and explanatory power. The discussions that follow illustrate how frequently and extensively Kohut drew on and stressed syncretizing concepts in Freud's writings.

Additional "Continuum Concepts"

In Lecture 6, Kohut stated, "If one thinks of a continuum from Unconscious to Preconscious, one may then conceive of a gradual change from primary to secondary process, and from Pleasure Principle to Reality Principle." In this example Kohut starts with a single continuum, between Unconscious and Preconscious, which he then expands to encompass two additional theoretical entities: the relations of primary and secondary processes and of the Pleasure and Reality Principles. This move has the syncretizing effect of bringing several different theories together rather than their standing apart from or opposing each other. The explanatory power of the unified conceptual entity greatly exceeds that of the individual concepts.

In Lecture 13, Kohut raised the question: "Why in the greatest one hundred pages of Freud's entire writings [chapter 7 in "The Interpretation of Dreams"] does he introduce the subject with such a seemingly minor point, the forgetting of dreams? The answer is that by approaching the matter in this way his major discoveries do not seem like oddities but appear built into our everyday mental functioning. That is, the same forces that are operative in the 'strange' activity of dreaming during the sleep state also operate in our more familiar waking state." Here again Kohut focused on and emphasized Freud's syncretizing concept of a continuum between conscious and unconscious mental activities.

The Sequence of Freud's Interests and Investigations

In his first lecture, Kohut called attention to a "logical sequence in Freud's clinical interests and investigations: starting with hysteria, then going to compulsion neurosis, next to melancholia, and finally to paranoia and schizophrenia. He seems to have worked from the surface downward—from the less to the more severe forms of psychopathology." Aside from its tribute to Freud's prescience as an investigator, this concept suggests that the various kinds and degrees of pathology form a continuum in terms of regressive depth and clinical severity. A further connection is implied between Freud's starting with less severe forms of pathology and the technical principle of interpreting from the surface downward.

Freud's Ordering Principles

Freud's attitude toward "simplification and glossing over" of the "rich diversity of psychic events" was mentioned previously in connection with his Foreword to Nunberg's (1932/1955) treatise. Kohut identified strongly with Freud's inductivist, particularistic approach. He stressed the necessary complexity of psychoanalytic data and concepts, and he cautioned against overgeneralizing and oversimplification.

At the end of his second lecture, for example, Kohut referred to the "mass of psychological data" with which the psychoanalyst is confronted, and he explained that Freud developed a "simple set of 'ordering principles'" to cope with and classify the extensive clinical material. The ordering principles included the concept of "depth psychology," that is, levels of mental functioning; and the topographic, dynamic, psychoeconomic, and genetic viewpoints.

The syncretizing capability of these ordering principles rests on the fact that they deal with different but related aspects of clinical phenomena. By employing the entire set of perspectives, a more complete, holistic, and coherent understanding results. Kohut did not view these so-called metapsychological perspectives merely as abstract theories, but he considered and referred to them as "vantage points of clinical observation" (Kohut and Seitz, 1963, p. 130). The latter is a highly syncretizing concept, bringing the ordering principles into direct relation with clinical data.

Holt (1983) notes similarly that the more he studied Freud's case histories, "the more he realized that metapsychology was not only intertwined with the clinical theory but actually directed Freud's observations of his patients as well" (p. 696). Edelson (1975) also regarded the metapsychological perspectives as "what an interpreter should look for" (p. 51). Thus we listen to patients with only relatively unfocused attention. We listen attentively for undercurrents of conflict, for manifestations of defenses, for the relative strengths of interactive motives, for recurrent patterns of behavior, for childhood memories, and for the repetition of past experiences in the present—trends in clinical data that encompass the full range of metapsychologic vantage points.

In addition, from the outset of every analysis, the therapist urges the patient to pay selectively attuned attention to particular associations; compare, for example, Freud's (1913a) instructions to patients regarding the basic rule:

> As you relate things various thoughts will occur to you which you would like to put aside. . . . You will be tempted to say to yourself that this or that is irrelevant here, or is quite unimportant, or nonsensical, or that there is no need to say it. You must never give in to those criticisms, but must say it in spite of them—indeed, you must say it precisely *because* you feel an aversion to doing so [pp. 134–135].

Thus Freud enjoins the patient to pay particular attention to associations that he or she feels conflict about and resistance to revealing—a syncretizing concept that ties together a metapsychologic (structurodynamic) conception of pathogenesis and the clinical method of free association. Kohut's extensive use of Freud's syncretic ordering principles (see, e.g., Kohut, 1971, p. 177; 1972–1976, pp. 65, 183, 207; 1977b, p. 6, fn. 6, p. 225; 1981a, p. 532) helps to explain Ornstein's (1978c, p. 4) observation that Kohut's lectures moved naturally and effortlessly from the empirical to the theoretical, and from the theoretical to the empirical.

The Psychoeconomic Perspective

Following Freud's example, Kohut employed the economic vantage point syncretistically in a number of ways: for example, by positing continua (as well as distinctions) between primary and secondary processes; between traumatic experiences and experiences of "optimal frustration"; emphasizing the role of optimal frustration in the formation of neutralizing ego structure, which serves as the basis of nonrepressive drive-restraint; resurrecting the concepts of "actual neurosis" and "psychoeconomic imbalance," which Freud had posited as the core of both neurotic and psychotic symptom formation; and explaining concepts such as mourning, play, and working through.

In Lectures 5 through 7, Kohut emphasized that the difference between primary and secondary processes is largely an economic or quantitative one. He referred to the continuum (and distinction) between traumatic in contrast to optimally frustrating experiences as a psychoeconomic issue par excellence. Traumatic experiences are of such intensity that they can be dealt with only repressively, rather than undergoing progressive neutralization and integration into preconscious secondary process functioning. Experiences of optimal frustration, on the other hand, are of sufficiently low to moderate intensity that they can be transformed gradually from primary to secondary process, from Pleasure Principle to Reality Principle. The latter changes lead to learning as well as to the formation of neutralized (and functionally neutralizing) ego structure, which is capable of restraining drives without resort to repressive defenses.

In Lecture 9, Kohut emphasized the psychoeconomic aspects of "actual neurosis," which involves a damming-up of and consequent increase in drive pressure. For example, the regression involved in both psychoneurotic and psychotic symptom formation results in a reactivation of undischarged infantile drives that threaten to produce an "actual neurosis." Freud considered the intrapsychic state of "psychoeconomic imbalance" the "actual neurotic core" of psychoneurotic and psychotic pathology. All of the foregoing concepts, and others, are tied together in a nonreductive way by the syncretizing vantage point of psychoeconomics.

Gediman (1989, pp. 295–296, 298–300) notes that Kohut revived Freud's psychoeconomic concepts of traumatic and actual neuroses as the traumatic core of all psychopathology; and in recent studies of psychoeconomics, Meissner (1995a,b,c) concludes that "psychoanalysis cannot do without a principle of economics" (1995c, p. 287).

Use of "Bridging" Concepts

Kohut also coopted Freud's frequent use of "bridging" concepts. An example appears in Lecture 5, where Kohut cited Freud's concept of daydreams as a realm of mental functioning that serves as a bridge between primary process–Pleasure Principle activity and secondary process–Reality Principle thinking. In daydreams, Kohut explained, the wish and its fulfillment are one and the same: "The pleasure in primary process hallucinations, therefore, is not really given up entirely, but to some extent is merely trans-ferred to omnipotence fantasies about one's secondary process thinking."

Another example of a bridging concept occurs in Lecture 3, regarding the relation of Consciousness to the Unconscious. Kohut stated that

> One of Freud's greatest strokes of genius was that, whereas most people tended to think either of neurological activity or of con-scious mental functioning, Freud could conceive of a psychologi-cal life consisting of wishes, fantasies, dreams, and so on, which exist in the same sense that the external world exists. We assume that the external world exists whether we are looking at it or not. Freud was able to conceive of the same being true of the psycho-logical life.

Kohut pointed out that Freud constructed a bridge between Consciousness and the Unconscious by conceiving of Conscious-ness as an inner sensory organ. Consciousness of the psychologi-cal thus becomes a directing of attention to the psychological, which goes on whether paid attention to and perceived by Con-sciousness or not.

The concept of "parental passage," discussed in Lectures 27 and 28, is another example of a bridging concept. The posited projection of the child's drives to the parents, where ideally they undergo neutralization, and their subsequent reintrojection in modified form bring together syncretistically intrapsychic devel-opmental processes in the child, the vicissitudes of parental behavior, and interpersonal relations between child and parents.

Still another example of a "bridging" concept appears in Lecture 26. Asked by a student what is internalized in the process of introjection, an object or an experience, Kohut replied suc-cinctly and syncretically: "The object as it is experienced."

Syncretizing Concepts Based on Parallels and Contrasts

Kohut explained the relations of conscious and unconscious men-tal functioning still further by describing how Freud inferred the characteristics of the Unconscious. He noted that Freud's con-cepts regarding the nature of unconscious processes were derived largely from study of similarities and contrasts between precon-scious and unconscious mental activities (Kohut and Seitz, 1963, p. 191); that is, by indicating either how the Unconscious differs from or how it is similar to consciously experienced mental contents. Certain qualities of the primary process (for example its form, intensity, and speed) came to be conceptualized and described by pointing out how they differ from (familiar) qualities of the secondary process. The characteristic wish-fulfilling nature of unconscious strivings, on the other hand, came to be described largely as a result of recognizing similarities with consciously observable phenomena such as wish-fulfilling daydreams [pp. 123–124].

Another example of a syncretizing concept based on parallels appears in Lecture 21. Kohut cited Freud's reference (in section E of chapter 7) to two parallels between sensory perceptions during sleep and day residues: Both are located in the Preconscious, and both contribute to dream formation.

In Lectures 14 and 19, Kohut called attention to a significant parallel between dreaming and the analytic situation—namely, regression in the service of the ego for an adaptive purpose:

One of the reasons Freud worked so hard to develop the model of sleep was because it provided a model for psychoanalytic therapy. That is, the analyst takes over the function of protective-supportive wakefulness, while the patient lies down as if asleep and undergoes a controlled ego regression. The parallel between sleeping and the therapeutic situation in psychoanalysis was worked out further by Lewin (1954).

An example of a syncretizing concept based on contrast appears in Lecture 25, in which Kohut noted that Freud's development of the structural theory introduced a change in the model of mind: In contrast to the transference side of the model, Freud now counterposed a nontransference side consisting of neutralized structure derived from experiences of optimal rather than traumatic frustration.

Some examples of syncretic concepts are based on both parallels and contrasts. In Lecture 27, for example, Kohut described not only the differences between the sexual and aggressive drives, but also their similarities: namely, their urgency, intensity, being directed at objects, producing conflicts, and being defended against.

Another example involving both parallels and contrasts is discussed in Lectures 9 and 12, in which Kohut compared Freud's concepts of psychoneurotic and psychotic symptom formation. With the exception of regression, which is deeper and to an object-less state in the psychoses, the processes of symptom formation in the neuroses and psychoses are similar. Another difference between the two, in addition to regression, is that "oedipal phobias" (as in the case of Little Hans) are the nucleus of transference neuroses, whereas "preoedipal phobias" constitute the nucleus of narcissistic regressions. Comparisons of this kind, based on parallels and contrasts, have a distinctly syncretizing effect in bringing together multiple clinical phenomena and complexly interrelated theoretical issues.

SYNCRETIC CONCEPTS THAT POSTULATE PSYCHOLOGICALLY EQUIVALENT PROCESSES

In Lecture 4 (see also Kohut and Seitz, 1963, pp. 191–192), Kohut explained the reasoning behind Freud's syncretizing postulate that unconscious mental processes, infantile sexual experiences, and a specific aspect of adult sexual experience are related by a "meaningful equivalence":

> We must keep in mind that "infantile sexuality" is not exactly the same as sexuality in the adult sense. The closest that adult mental life (e.g., adult experience) comes to the intensity of infantile sexuality may be something like the height of orgasm which, significantly, is associated with a different kind of Consciousness—a Consciousness of primary process, of which orgasm may be our only remaining example as adults.

Kohut pointed out further that Freud was reluctant to change the term *sexuality* for these infantile experiences, because he had chosen the term *a potiori*; that is, he chose a term that refers to the best known of various experiences of similar kind. When a baby sucks, for example, the intensity of its pleasure is comparable with that of sexual experiences. Freud proposed that every activity was originally highly "sexualized" in this way: walking, looking, talking, and others—all began as "sexually" experienced movements.

SYNCRETIZING "GENERIC CONCEPTS"

In Lectures 3 and 4 (see also Kohut and Seitz, 1963, pp. 119–120), Kohut emphasized and explained a highly significant aspect of

Freud's thinking that is often overlooked: that is, Freud's concept that human beings are inherently predisposed to intrapsychic conflict.

> Freud conceived of the mind as a dynamic system with an inherent tendency toward an inner organization of forces which oppose and balance each other. Even external frustrations (of inner drives) could be viewed as having a counterpart within the mental apparatus itself, that is, an inner readiness to take a stand of opposition to the drives.

This syncretizing "generic concept" of a built-in tendency toward internal conflicts applies to and helps explain the prevalence of conflict in normal persons, in psychopathology, and in clinical work.

Another example of a syncretizing generic concept appears in Lecture 4 (see also Kohut and Seitz, 1963, pp. 183–184). Kohut emphasized Freud's (1900) concept that "the influence of the primary process on the secondary process (the penetration of unconscious psychic contents and forces into preconscious thoughts, feelings, or wishes) was originally designated by the term 'transference'" and "it is important to note that transference, in the original meaning of the term, referred essentially to an endopsychic, not an interpersonal process" (Kohut and Seitz, 1963, p. 183).

Freud's discovery of transference to the analyst, or so-called technical transference, came only after he had recognized that dreams, slips, and psychoneurotic symptoms result from such intrapsychic transferences. Technical transference to the analyst, therefore, is but another instance of Freud's "generic concept" of transference. This is one of the most original, syncretizing, and useful refinements of Freudian theory that Kohut proposed during his earlier (pre–self psychological) theorizing.

HOLISTIC CONCEPTS AND SYNCRETISM

In Lecture 31, Kohut proposed a highly syncretic, holistic definition of mental health. He noted the temptation to define mental health simplistically in terms of of the autonomous ego functions, which would characterize the normal or healthy personality as a smoothly functioning, problem-solving machine.

But while specific functions can be evaluated in that way, the total personality cannot. Mental health, normalcy, successful relationship to tasks and especially to the human environment, require not only cognitive functions but also access to all areas and aspects of the mind. There are times when we need access to the forces of the id, when survival or success depends more on our capacity to respond passionately and less on the refinement of dispassionate cognitive functions. There are even times when the ego must make use of transference intrusions, either as an incentive for adaptive behavior or in the service of interpersonal communication in situations that call for a response or an appeal to irrational motivations in the human environment.

This argument of Kohut's rests on a syncretizing, holistic conception of mind.

Summary

Close study of Kohut's lectures on psychoanalytic psychology and our essay on psychoanalytic concepts suggests that Kohut's method of explicating Freudian theory drew frequently on syncretizing concepts, which Freud employed extensively in his writings. Use of such concepts appears to have enhanced the integration and coherence of Freudian theory, which, like other theories in the human, social, and behavioral sciences, is by nature highly complex and loosely concatenated rather than hierarchically organized.

Kohut employed a wide variety of syncretistic concepts drawn from Freud's writings, including concepts based on various types of continua; on sequences and analogies; Freud's metapsychologic ordering principles or vantage points, including psychoeconomic concepts; bridging concepts; concepts derived from parallels and contrasts; concepts positing psychological equivalences; "generic" concepts; holistic concepts; and others.

Kohut's explication of Freudian theory was neither overgeneralized nor oversimplified, but consistently combined particularistic and holistic approaches—another noteworthy example of syncretism (cf. also Kohut, 1978a). His use of such concepts contributed to an unusually effective, nonreductive synthesis of Freudian theory, much of which is still relevant to present-day psychoanalytic theory, practice, and research.

Part IV

Kohut's Concepts of Narcissism and Self Psychology: Continuities with Freudian Theory

---

Philip F. D. Rubovits-Seitz

Kohut's Concepts of Narcissism and Self Psychology: Continuities with Freudian Theory

Philip F. D. Rubovits-Seitz

During the final fifteen years of his life, from 1966 to 1981, Kohut proposed some major additions to and revisions of psychoanalytic theory and therapy—changes dealing with the subjects of narcissism and the psychology of the self. Some writers (e.g., Ornstein, 1978c, p. 105) have referred to Kohut's concepts as a "new paradigm" for psychoanalysis, but Kohut (1980b) disliked the term *paradigm* and took the position that self psychology represents "an unbroken continuum with traditional psychoanalytic theory" (1978b, p. 937; see also Kohut, 1980b, pp. 501, 505, 514–515, 520; and Ferguson, 1981). He wrote in his 1971 monograph:

> This book is a continuation and expansion of a series of studies, published in 1959, 1963 (with Seitz), 1966, 1968. The case material and the conclusions drawn from it, and the conceptualizations contained in these papers, have been used freely throughout the ensuing pages. This monograph constitutes the rounding out and completion of the investigation of the libidinal aspects of narcissism which had been initiated in these earlier essays [pp. xv–xvi].

This statement seems to imply that Kohut intended a fundamental, not merely an incidental, continuity between his earlier synthesis of Freudian theories and the new directions that he was exploring. In another connection he referred to his methods and concepts as a continuation of Edward Glover's (1939, 1947) contributions to psychoanalysis (Kohut, 1980a, pp. 487–488).

In the final period of his writings (e.g., 1977b, 1984) Kohut's formulations began to sound considerably less like traditional psychoanalysis. This chapter presents detailed material from his later writings, however, which suggests that he did not abandon his Freudian traditions but viewed his concepts of narcissism and the psychology of the self as continuations of and additions to Freudian theory. Near the end of his final volume, for example, Kohut (1984) stated, as he had many times previously, that he did not consider self psychology "a deviation from traditional theory but an expansion of analytic understanding," and also that "self psychology does not advocate a change in the essence of analytic technique" (p. 208).

Kohut (1984, p. 221, n.1) reminded readers that his psychoanalytic background and experience were almost exclusively classical and thus an adequate understanding of his work is not possible without a thorough knowledge of traditional psychoanalysis. He also expressed his continuing respect for classical analysis, especially ego psychology, and added that his long-standing commitment to the traditional approach had not ceased. Similarly, in his last public address, Kohut (1981a) objected to attempts by some analysts to reinterpret Freud's views in order to make them sound more like self psychology. Kohut stated forcefully that Freud was a genius, and that bypassing him was no way to treat a genius: "Freud has to be respected for what he gave us" (p. 529). See also in this connection Siegel's (1996) book on Kohut, about which Golden (1998) notes "the fair and balanced presentation of classical theory that always illuminated Kohut's writing and his abiding respect for that theory even after his own views could no longer be contained within it" (p. 205).

This is not to say that there are no differences between traditional psychoanalysis and self psychology. The present chapter suggests, however, that at the level of basic methods and concepts the continuities between self psychology and traditional psychoanalysis are as significant as their differences. Michael Basch (1984a), one of Kohut's original followers, pointed out, for example, that Kohut's work was fundamentally Freudian—part of a continuum based on the methodologic underpinnings defining psychoanalysis. Basch (1984a) added that

> Kohut would never let himself be provoked or seduced into leaving the main body of psychoanalysis; he knew very well that that is where his work belonged. Thanks to his persistence and willingness to suffer what he had to in order to maintain those ties,

the once evident pressure to separate from the parent body is pretty much a thing of the past [p. 15].

In a subsequent report Basch (1989) maintained that "it is a mistake to think of comparing Freud's and Kohut's work as if they represented fundamentally different positions," for Kohut "always thought he was a contributor to Freudian psychoanalysis" (p. 20). Kohut (1980b) himself stressed that "self psychology adds something to traditional analysis; it does not substitute for it" (p. 505).

This chapter suggests further that the same syncretic tendency that appeared to characterize Kohut's earlier formulation of Freudian theory seems to have been operative also in the continuities that he constructed between traditional psychoanalysis, his later concepts of narcissism, and his development of self psychology. An incident that occurred during one of his *Chicago Institute Lectures* (1972–1976) illustrates how extensively Kohut employed, and also enjoyed, his syncretizing ability. He usually started his lectures by asking whether there were any questions about topics discussed previously, or were there other subjects that anyone wished to bring up? On that particular occasion several students had questions for him: One requested a shift in emphasis from theory to technique; another wished to hear more about termination; and a third asked about the process of trial internalizations. Kohut responded:

> Good. As you know I like to collect a few suggestions, because then I try to combine them and see whether there are some general trends. So far the only common denominator I can see in what you've asked today is that they all start with "t": technique, termination, and trial internalization. So let's talk about "t" then. Certainly technique and termination are to some extent one topic, and then there is the question of trial internalization. I gather you're particularly interested in how this works out in the course of an analysis [p. 366].

When confronted with differences between his own concepts and those of traditional psychoanalysis, Kohut appears to have favored combining, integrating, or synthesizing them in some way. If he was unable to find some method of uniting disparate concepts, as a last resort he would consider replacing an older concept with a newer one; even then he seemed to prefer a syncretic solution to the problem of theory change. A good example appears in one of his *Chicago Institute Lectures* (1972–1976, pp. 389–390, 393–394), in which he acknowledged that he had found it necessary to formulate two very different psychologies of the self, but then his postulated syncretic tendency asserted itself: He brought the two self psychologies together by proposing a "complementarity" between them (for an informative study of complementarity in Kohut's work, see Sucharov, 1992).

Kohut (1972–1976, pp. 385–386) emphasized similarly that, depending on the type of pathology with which one is dealing, both conflict and self psychologies are valid approaches. He insisted repeatedly that we need

> both approaches: man as mental apparatus with forces in conflict with each other, and yet man who has formed a self that has become an independent body moving in a certain track, trying to unroll its destiny. These two together, it seems to me, are our principle of complementarity that explains the psychological phenomena as we know them. And one does not rule out the other [pp. 393–394].

Still another example is Kohut's (1977a, p. 935) response to Ornstein's (1978c) historical review of self psychology. Kohut described the conflict he had felt about recognizing the need for greater emphasis on the self in psychoanalytic theory. Rather than replacing traditional psychoanalytic concepts with his theory of the self, however, he found a way to combine the two: "The solution I found was in harmony with my three demands. It preserved the continuity with the past, it acknowledged the adequacy of classical tenets within a limited field, and, by stressing the relativity of all theorizing, did not impose undue restrictions on future creative developments" (Kohut, 1977a, p. 937; see also Kohut, 1972–1976, pp. 74–75; 1977b, pp. xv, 223).

Before discussing the numerous continuities that Kohut constructed between his own concepts and those of traditional psychoanalysis, a word should be said about the standpoint from which the present study addresses this issue. This study does not concern itself with the validity of Kohut's concepts, but attempts to situate his contributions historically and epistemologically in relation to Freud's theoretical system. A basic assumption underlying the study is that psychoanalysis—even "traditional" psychoanalysis—is not a static or completely coherent theory, but from its inception has been a complex, dynamic, and continuously developing set of ideas, assumptions, and practices. Freud, for example, ceaselessly modified his concepts and theories.

The behavioral science methodologist Abraham Kaplan (1964) pointed out that psychoanalysis differs from the hierarchical theories of the physical sciences. He classified psychoanalysis as a loosely "concatenated" theory, like the "big bang" theory of cosmology and the theory of evolution, whose component parts form a "network of relations that constitute an identifiable configuration or pattern" (p. 298). Thus the present study has assumed that the relation of Kohut's work to traditional psychoanalysis must be understood in the context of the complex, developing, and in some respects contradictory set of concatenated concepts and theories that comprise the discipline of psychoanalysis.

Kohut's concepts appear to be part of a gradual movement within the history of psychoanalysis, starting with the original, largely endopsychic model of drive psychology, which then evolved into an ego psychological model in which the psyche mediates between drives and the external world and is shaped to a considerable extent by its interaction with the environment; and, more recently, the development of more distinctly interactive models, including self psychology, in which the psyche is conceptualized largely in terms of internalizations of the external environment. The present study assumes further, therefore, that understanding Kohut's work and its relations to traditional psychoanalysis necessitates placing his concepts within the context of this continuing, long-term historical trend in psychoanalysis.

An additional assumption underlying the present study is that Kohut's operational definition of psychoanalysis is yet another key to understanding his concepts, theories, and clinical methods. Kohut (1959) took seriously the notion that what we see is determined by how we see it—which led to his conclusion that psychoanalysis is defined operationally by the systematic application of the introspective–empathic method in the analytic situation. A corollary of that definition emphasized that introspection and empathy necessarily focus on and can only comprehend *experiences*—a methodologic stance that led Kohut to develop and emphasize the concept of an "experiencing self."

Defining psychoanalysis operationally is not a departure from the "classical" model, but represents a particular way of conceptualizing psychoanalysis as science—a definition that has been widely held, although not clearly articulated, by many analysts. In addition, the emphasis on experience, which is logically connected with Kohut's operational definition and constitutes the basis of self psychology, is central to the way many analysts understand their patients.

The preceding assumptions regarding the loosely concatenated nature of psychoanalytic theories, their complex and still evolving history, and Kohut's operational definition of how psychoanalytic knowledge is acquired have been included in the present study to understand how Kohut both extended psychoanalytic traditions and at the same time constructed numerous and diverse continuities between his concepts and Freud's.

Turning now to Kohut's writings on narcissism and self psychology, his contributions to these subjects can be divided into
three distinct periods:

1. *The Initial Period:* His writings from 1966 through 1971—
   from "Forms and Transformations of Narcissism" (1966) to
   The Analysis of the Self (1971). During this period Kohut's
   concepts were still informed significantly by ego psychology and drive theory.
2. *The Period of Transition:* From *The Analysis of the Self* (1971)
   to *The Restoration of the Self* (1977b)—including especially
   his *Chicago Institute Lectures* (1972–1976). Kohut introduced
   the concept of a bipolar self and began to articulate his concept of a supraordinate self, in *The Restoration of the Self*
   (1977b).
3. *The Period of Consolidation:* His writings from *The Restoration
   of the Self* (1977b) to his final volume, *How Does Analysis
   Cure?* (1984). These writings include his most fully developed concepts of self psychology.

If one were to consider only Kohut's initial writings on these
subjects (1966–1971), there would be no question that Freudian
traditions continued to guide his clinical and theoretical work.
Systematic comparisons of Kohut's and Freud's views appear to
suggest, however, that even in the transitional and final periods
of Kohut's work (1971–1977 and 1977–1981), his earlier synthesis
of Freudian concepts and theories continued to illuminate his
later investigations, conceptualizations, and conclusions.

Some major areas of continuity between Kohut's concepts and
traditional psychoanalysis will be discussed in terms of the following clinical, theoretical, and methodological categories:

1. Definitions of psychoanalysis and self psychology.
2. The defining concepts of transference and resistance.
3. Narcissism.
4. Basic methodologic concepts.
5. Metapsychologic vantage points.
   a. Psychodynamics: drives and conflict; hostility and rage; danger situations and anxiety; repression and other defenses
   b. Psychoeconomics: drive and emotional intensities; optimal *vs.* traumatic frustration and/or deficit

     c. Psychogenetics: maturational and developmental stages, including the oedipal period; and the concept of a complemental series between innate and environmental factors

     d. Structural theory

6. Clinical method.

7. Clinical interpretation and reconstruction.

8. The process of therapeutic change.

9. The benefits of treatment.

Material from all three periods of Kohut's later writings (1966–1984) are included to illustrate the posited continuities in each category. There are too many examples to present all of them in detail, however, so for each category only one or two illustrations are discussed in detail, additional examples being included only briefly or as reference citations.

Continuity in the Definitions of Psychoanalysis and Self Psychology

Kohut's definition of what constitutes the scientific domain of psychoanalysis (including self psychology) coincided closely with Freud's views. Kohut (1980b, p. 515) stated that it is not specific theories that define our science, but the field of investigation that we study, that is, the inner life of man and how we study it:

> It is the basic psychoanalytic situation, in other words, the situation of someone reporting his inner life, while another empathically listens to the report in order to be able to explain it, that defines analysis and not the particular theory or ordering principle that the listener employs [p. 516; see also Kohut, 1977b, pp. 298–312].

Freud expressed similar views in several of his writings. In "On Narcissism" (1914c), for example, he emphasized that the foundation of science is not its theories but its methods of observation: "One dislikes the thought of abandoning observation for barren theoretical controversy," because the latter "are not the bottom but the top of the whole structure, and they can be replaced and discarded without damaging it" (p. 77). Freud (1915a) expanded on this view in the opening passage of "Instincts and Their Vicissitudes":

> We have often heard it maintained that sciences should be built up on clear and sharply defined basic concepts. In actual fact no science, not even the most exact, begins with such definitions. The true beginning of scientific activity consists rather in describing phenomena and then in proceeding to group, classify and correlate them [p. 117].

Both Freud and Kohut thus emphasized the central role of subject matter and observational methods, not theoretical preferences, in their respective definitions of psychoanalysis and self psychology. Self psychology's field of study is coextensive with that of psychoanalysis, and for the most part self psychology employs the vocabulary of clinical psychoanalysis (Moore and Fine, 1990, p. 175). Kohut (1977b) stated in this connection:

> There are a number of what I consider important reasons for retaining the classical terminology. First, I believe that we should do our best to ensure the continuity of psychoanalysis and should therefore whenever possible retain the established terms, even though their meaning may gradually change. Second, the direct confrontation between the new and the old meanings of the established terms allows us, indeed forces us, to be explicit with regard to the redefinitions and reformulations we feel obligated to introduce. Third, and most important, significant connections do indeed exist between the substance of the classical findings from which the old terms were derived and the substance of the findings we are dealing with now [p. 172n.].

The Defining Concepts of Transference and Resistance

In his essay, "On the History of the Psycho-Analytic Movement," Freud (1914b) insisted that "no one can know better than I do what psychoanalysis is, how it differs from other ways of investigating the life of the mind, and precisely what should be called psychoanalysis and what would better be described by some other name" (p. 7). He continued:

> The theory of psycho-analysis is an attempt to account for two striking and unexpected facts of observation which emerge whenever an attempt is made to trace the symptoms of a neurotic back

to their sources in his past life: the facts of transference and of resistance. Any line of investigation which recognizes these two facts and takes them as the starting-point of its work has a right to call itself psycho-analysis, even though it arrives at results other than my own [p. 16].

Kohut both retained and extended Freud's concepts of transference and resistance. In the Epilogue of *The Restoration of the Self*, Kohut (1977b) wrote: "I am not able to imagine how analysis could at this time do away with two concepts—transference and resistance" (p. 308). He retained the psychoanalytic theory of object-differentiated transferences in the classical neuroses and extended the concept of transference to include narcissistic varieties in which the analyst is experienced as part of the patient's self. With respect to the concept of transference neurosis, Miller (1987) notes that "self psychology enlarges and enriches the concept of transference neurosis, and reaffirms its importance to psychoanalysis" (p. 535).

In his *Chicago Institute Lectures* (1972–1976), Kohut indicated that the concepts of transference and resistance apply also to the analysis of the self:

I think that much of psychoanalytic work in analyzing the self is, again, a mode of making aspects of the self conscious that formerly were not conscious. And the whole idea of transference and resistance that Freud speaks about in terms of drive psychology and ego psychology is also to be applied to the self [p. 237].

In his 1971 monograph (pp. 242–243), Kohut looked more deeply into the question of whether the phenomena that he had conceptualized as narcissistic transferences were actually transferences in the metapsychological sense described by Freud (1900, p. 562). The answer to this question depends on whether pathological narcissistic structures undergo repression, whether they are retained in the unconscious, and whether they can return from repression later in the form of transferences, as Freud (1915b) had proposed for the object-differentiated transferences of the neuroses. Kohut (1971) answered the question by presenting a clinical vignette, demonstrating

the existence of unconscious narcissistic structures, i.e., of specific repressed ideas and fantasies concerning the self which are cathected with narcissistic energies. The existence of unconscious structures alone, however, is not transference but only a precondition for it; we must, in addition, ascertain that the old self representation (in its activated state) exerts its influence on thought contents which relate to present-day reality and, conversely, that it, too, is responsive to current factors (i.e., that it is reactivated in response to current events which act as psychological triggers). In our clinical example we can indeed discern these two relationships between the therapeutically activated past and the present [p. 244].

Freud had recognized and referred briefly to examples of both extraclinical and clinical narcissistic transferences, but he did not emphasize or elaborate on these phenomena (see, e.g., 1914a; 1914c, pp. 88; 1923, p. 50n.). He also described a type of patient who tends to choose

a sexual ideal after the narcissistic type which possesses the excellences to which he cannot attain. This is the cure by love, which he generally prefers to cure by analysis. Indeed, he cannot believe in any other mechanism of cure; he usually brings expectations of this sort with him to the treatment and directs them towards the person of the physician [1914c, p. 101].

Freud observed further that such a patient often "withdraws from further treatment in order to choose a love-object, leaving his cure to be continued by a life with someone he loves" (p. 101). He added that, "We might be satisfied with this result if it did not bring with it all the dangers of a crippling dependence upon his helper in need" (p. 101).

In Kohut's terminology the patient's "helper in need" would be called a "selfobject." Kohut (1984) later referred to narcissistic transferences as "selfobject" transferences; he considered his explication of such transferences his most important contribution to psychoanalysis (p. 104). Kohut's (1971, p. xiv) concept of selfobjects has some parallels also with Freud's (1914c, p. 90) observation that narcissistic love may involve someone who was once part of oneself, and with Freud's (1914c, pp. 93–94, 101–102) theory of ego ideal formation in which narcissism is displaced onto an external ideal that, when the ideal is fulfilled, produces narcissistic satisfaction (p. 100). Freud referred also to the fear of losing the parents' love and observed that "later the parents are replaced by an indefinite number of fellow-men" (p. 102; see also 1914a, p. 244)—"selfobjects" in Kohut's terminology.

It is important to note in this connection that Kohut considered the infant's experience of the selfobject an intrapsychic phenomenon (Kohut, 1972–1976, p. 352; cf. also Goldberg's [1988, p. xiv; 1990, p. 126; 1998, p. 245] arguments that self psychology is a one-person psychology). The latter conclusion, and the endopsychic nature of the infant's selfobject experiences, suggest still further parallels with traditional psychoanalytic concepts—in this case with the representational world.

From the standpoint of Kohut's posited syncretizing propensity, one would expect him to include both selfobjects and differentiated (nonself) objects in his concepts. He (1984) wrote, as expected:

> It is fruitful to look upon the "I's" experience of the "You" within two separate frames of reference: (1) with regard to the role the "You" plays in supporting the cohesion, strength, and harmony of the self, that is, to the experience of the "You" as a "selfobject"; and (2) with regard to the "You" (a) as the target of our desire and love and (b) as the target of our anger and aggression when it blocks the way to the object we desire and love, i.e., to the experience of the "You" as "object" [p. 52].

Kohut (1984) then continued:

> Echoing Freud (1914a, 1955, 13:241–44) I have emphasized (Kohut [1972/Ornstein, 1978b], 2:618–24) that object love strengthens the self, just as any other intense experience, even that provided by vigorous physical exercise, strengthens the self. Furthermore, it is well known that a strong self enables us to experience love and desire more intensely [p. 53].

With respect to *resistance*, Kohut (1972–76) asserted that it is

> nothing but the internal defensive activities of the patient being transferred to the analytic situation itself, where it belongs. Resistance must be part and parcel of every analysis. An analysis proceeds either by analysis of the resistances or defenses, or by explanations of the resistances as defenses, which is probably the best way of putting it [p. 98; see also pp. 202–203].

Kohut's views of resistance included the concept of resistance as a necessary, if archaic, defense against retraumatization by the environment. M. Shane (1985a, pp. 77–79) notes an important similarity, however, with Freud's concept of defense: Both imply a protective function against psychically painful experiences. Both traditional and self psychological approaches emphasize the analysis of resistances, and both attempt to show why the resistances once made sense (e.g., were phase appropriate) and were necessary. Kohut gave credit to Freud (1917a) for recognizing that

each individual brings in some generalized narcissistic resistances against the analytic procedure: not to be passive, not to
reveal everything about oneself, not to feel that someone else
understands the implications of what one is talking about before
one understands it oneself, and so on. Freud described this in his
beautiful paper called "A Difficulty in the Path of Psychoanalysis"
[Kohut, 1972–1976, p. 324].

Like Freud, Kohut (1970, 1977b, p. 136) emphasized the ubiquity
of narcissistic resistances against all interpretations of unconscious or ego-alien contents (cf. Gediman, 1989, p. 296). Kohut
also recognized the importance of other types of defenses and
resistances in the classical transference neuroses (discussed
further in the sections Basic Methodologic Concepts and Psychodynamics: Repression and Other Defenses). His continued references to the concept of resistance persisted throughout the
transitional and final periods of his work (see, e.g., Shane, 1985a,b).
In the *Chicago Institute Lectures* (1972–1976) he made the
point that

narcissistic defenses, which in the broader, technical sense are
quite appropriately referred to as resistances, are not the same
thing, even phenomenologically or symptomatically, as primary
narcissistic disturbances, that is, disturbances of the self-organiza-
tion. Avoidance, the wish not to expose oneself to narcissistic
injuries, *may* be a defense against an underlying disease of the
self but not necessarily so. It may also defend against structural
conflicts [p. 327].

Kohut (1972–1976) observed further that whereas self psychologists do not look on patients as bundles of resistances against
unacceptable drive wishes, people with narcissistic personality
disturbances "have resistances against analysis just as strong as
do people with well-organized oedipal structural neuroses"
(pp. 370–371). He emphasized that the treatment of such patients
includes the analysis of those resistances.

Narcissism

The subject of narcissism was a key conceptual issue and theoretical turning point for both Freud and Kohut. In the Editor's Note
to Freud's (1914c) essay "On Narcissism," Strachey pointed out
that this paper is among the most important of Freud's writings

and represents a pivot in the evolution of his views (p. 70; see also Smith, 1985; Baranger, 1991). Studies of narcissism were pivotal also in Kohut's contributions, and he readily acknowledged Freud's influence in the development of his own concepts. He wrote, "Although in certain areas I arrived at conclusions that go beyond the outlines indicated by Freud, the general pattern of my own thought has also been determined by them" (1966, p. 245). Kohut (1966, pp. 245–247, 256n.4; 1971, p. 106) explained that Freud's (1915a, p. 136) postulated stage of a "purified pleasure ego," during which the infant attempts to deal with disturbances in its primary narcissism by attributing everything pleasurable to itself and everything unpleasant to the "outside," corresponds roughly with his own concept, the "narcissistic (grandiose) self." He stated further that Freud's (1914c, pp. 94, 96, 100; 1921, pp. 110, 112–113) theory that the infant also attempts to regain a state of narcissistic balance by attributing perfection and power to the parent and then staying closely attached to the idealized object corresponds with his own concept of the "idealized parent imago" (Kohut, 1966, p. 246, 246n.5). Kohut differed from Freud, however, in the much greater emphasis that he placed on the environment's response to these narcissistic developments in the child.

Kohut's concepts of narcissism and the self were influenced also by August Aichorn, who had been Kohut's personal analyst in Vienna (Corbett and Kugler, 1989, p. 191). Aichorn (1936) described the development of "narcissistic transferences" in young delinquent patients and the transformation of their infantile narcissism into an ego ideal. Kohut's concept that the self develops from empathic mirroring and idealizing activities of parents and parent-figures also appears to have been influenced by Aichorn (Havens, 1986, pp. 364–365; see also Kohut, 1971, pp. 163–164).

The Tolpins (1996) note that the principal themes of Kohut's (1972–1976) *Chicago Institute Lectures* are "the normal development of narcissism and the self—its maintenance and restoration and the laying down of its structures, its dangers and defensive measures, and its transferences and resumed structural growth" (p. xi). This scheme of studying and explicating narcissism is very similar to Freud's approach in its overall structure and categories of investigation. The Tolpins (p. xii) point out further that during this transitional stage of Kohut's theorizing (1972–1976), his concepts of narcissism retained a conceptual and terminologic bridge to drive theory. Later he formulated such problems within the framework of the self—its development, disturbances, fragmentation, and reintegration.

Kohut (1972–1976) credited the "genius of Freud" (1914c, p. 77) with the recognition that something must be added to autoerotism to bring about narcissism—a conclusion that contributed to Kohut's (1972–1976) concept that narcissism develops when earlier experiences "become united by becoming constituents of a cohesive self" (p. 74):

> I thought I had been able to extract a more explicit meaning from Freud's rather cryptic remark that "there must be something *added* to auto-erotism—a new psychical action—in order to bring about narcissism." The new "action" of which Freud speaks is, I believe, nothing else but the birth of the nuclear self [1975a, pp. 740–741].

This particular example of Kohut's syncretizing ability is noteworthy because in it he attributed a similar syncretic proclivity to Freud: He commented that Freud's brief statement that something must be added to autoerotism to bring about narcissism "was derived from a host of preconsciously synthesized empirical impressions" (p. 741).

Kohut (1966, pp. 247, 270; 1970) did not view narcissism merely as a defense against or simply as a precursor of object love, but proposed that narcissism also has its own development and vicissitudes. During this early period of Kohut's (1966) expanded concepts of narcissism, however, he did not rule out the possibility that narcissism might be, at least in part, a precursor of object love. He wrote that "there are various forms of narcissism which must be considered *not only* as forerunners of object love but also as independent psychological constellations" (1966, pp. 269–270, italics added; see also 1971, p. 106). In addition, he referred to the idealized parent imago as "a partial step toward object love" (1966, p. 250).

Conversely, although Freud usually theorized that narcissism is a stage in the development of object love, at various points in his writings (e.g., 1914c; 1921, p. 102) he referred to narcissism and object love as two separate and sometimes competing motivations. He noted, for example, that the attachment and narcissistic types of object choice exist "side by side" (1914c, pp. 87–88; see also 1921, p. 102). The view that attachment and narcissistic types of object choice exist "side by side" appears also in Kohut's (1972–1976, p. 72) statement that study of complex experiences always reveals, "side by side," both object-libidinal and narcissistic investments—that there is no experience of any substance that does not involve a mixture of the two object choices. He insisted, for example, that to subsume the idealized object imago under the heading of narcissism alone would tell only half the story (1966), because the narcissistic cathexis of the idealized object is amalgamated with features of true object love: "The idealized parent imago is partly invested with object-libidinal cathexes; and the idealized qualities are loved as a source of gratifications to which the child clings tenaciously" (p. 247; see also 1972, p. 363; 1972–1976, pp. 33–34, 72). Thus Kohut wrote in 1972:

> We must, without prejudice, study all analytic data—oedipal and preoedipal, object-instinctual and narcissistic—and determine their developmental and genetic significance. We shall therefore do well to refrain from setting up a choice between theoretical opposites concerning the question of the genetic importance of the young child's experiences in the narcissistic and in the object-instinctual realm [p. 367].

The following are additional examples of what appear to be continuities between Kohut's and Freud's concepts of narcissism:

1. Kohut's (1966, p. 270; 1972–1976, p. 235) agreement with Freud (1914c, 1917a) regarding the ego's "taming" of narcissism and transforming it into higher aims.
2. Kohut's (1966, p. 273; 1971, p. 299; 1972–1976, p. 375) agreement with Freud's (1900, p. 398n.; 1917b, p. 156) concept that a man who has been the undisputed favorite of his mother retains the feeling of a conqueror, which often contributes to real success.
3. Kohut's (1971, pp. 25–26; 1972, p. 379) use of Freud's (1921, p. 91) *a potiori* form of argument regarding pregenital sexuality to posit a genetic and dynamic unity for diverse narcissistic phenomena. This example is noteworthy because it illustrates not only Freud's and Kohut's shared proclivity for syncretism, but also their use of the same syncretic device for similar purposes.
4. Kohut's (1971, p. 108) agreement with Freud (1914c, p. 98) regarding the dependence of self-esteem on narcissism.
5. Kohut's (1972, pp. 372–373) agreement with Freud's (1933, p. 66) formulation of the genetic basis of Emperor Wilhelm II's lifelong reaction of shame to his withered arm—namely, his narcissistic mother's rejection of her imperfect child.

6. Kohut's (1972–1976, p. 33) agreement with Freud regarding the narcissistic injury produced by slips of the tongue.
7. Kohut's (1972–1976, p. 94) agreement with Freud that the difference between normalcy and pathology (including healthy and pathological narcissism) is a quantitative one.
8. Kohut's (1972–1976, pp. 1–4, 284) agreement with Freud's (1905a, pp. 231–243) views about the relations of sexual development to the pathogenesis of perversions. He added (syncretistically), however, that the intensity of the urge in perversions and addictions results from the convergence of both sexual pleasure-gain and the filling-in of a structural defect.
9. Kohut's (1972–1976, p. 40) agreement with Freud that narcissism and homosexuality are closely related; he added in this case that the function of homosexuality in paranoia includes an attempt to prevent further regression and disintegration of the self (1972–1976, p. 285).
10. Kohut's (1972–1976, pp. 132, 134, 138) comparison of his additions to psychoanalysis with Freud's introduction of the structural model, both providing broadened theoretical frameworks for psychoanalysis. With respect to his own contributions, he added:

> As important as I believe these changes of outlook are, I think they are completely in line with the spirit of the psychoanalytic tradition. The shift I am advocating does not throw away anything, rather it adds something. It does not do away with the important, and still valuable, explanatory conceptualizations of the original, relatively simple theory, the classical libido theory. Those formulations were the first great steps in a new science; and even though we may recognize now that they cannot do justice to *all* the phenomena we observe, they must be acknowledged as the indispensable foundation of our continuously developing science [1972–1976, p. 189].

BASIC METHODOLOGIC CONCEPTS

According to Rapaport (1944), the basic methodologic (core) concepts of Freud's theoretical system include the concept of an unconscious mind, continuity, determinism, overdetermination, instinctual drives, conflict, defense, transference, and the importance of childhood experiences. Unlike specific clinical theories that tend to generate single rather than alternative interpretive hypotheses, the broad general background assumptions or methodologic core concepts of a science do not force interpretations into preconceived conclusions; thus new, unique interpretations of clinical data are possible within the basic methodologic concepts of psychoanalysis (De Groot, 1969, pp. 35, 56; Rubovits-Seitz, 1998, p. 59). The following discussions illustrate that Kohut employed all of the basic methodologic (core) concepts that underlie Freud's theoretical system.

The concept of an unconscious mind: Kohut applied this basic methodologic concept throughout his investigations of narcissism and the self—for example: "I think that much of psychoanalytic work in analyzing the self is, again, a mode of making aspects of the self conscious that formerly were not conscious" (1972–1976, p. 237). Elsewhere in the same lectures he stated:

> The self, like any other psychological content, is in essence unconscious. In other words, we would say that while we learn about it through experiencing it, there ought to be other ways of formulating its power and its effect, apart from whether we see it or not or whether we are aware of it or not. And from that I would draw an immediate conclusion about ourselves: following Freud's thinking about consciousness–unconsciousness, I would say that most of the time we are not at all conscious of our selves [p. 233].

As indicated previously, Kohut differed somewhat from Freud regarding the reason for such unconsciousness. Freud emphasized the avoidance of wishes that are disturbing to the psyche itself, an intrapsychic tension. Kohut stressed the dynamic of avoiding retraumatization by the environment. The two views have in common the factor of avoiding psychic pain.

Continuity: Discussing possible bases for an enduring sense of self, Kohut (1972–1976) concluded that it cannot be due simply to the various contents of the self because they tend to be changeable; but "beyond specific, circumscribed contents and functional centers, there is a peculiarly unique, *habitual relationship* among them that remains constant" (p. 338). The latter concept appears to rest on and exemplify the basic methodologic concept of continuity. Freud (1915–1916) viewed continuity among mental processes and contents as ubiquitous: "Everything is related to everything, including small things to great" (p. 27). Kohut (1972–1976) also drew on the continuity principle to explain a technical procedure in the treatment of patients with insecure self-cohesion:

> I think a skillful therapist will employ a kind of unifying "histori-cal" help by talking about the patient's past and about his future — not to find the genesis of his disturbance, but to help him by functioning as a self-object who supplies a sense of the *continuity* of his existence, which the patient can no longer maintain on his own [p. 339; italics added].

In psychoanalysis generally, interpretive work provides conti-nuity by emphasizing relations and patterns in clinical data and among the various parts of the patient's life and self (or psyche).

Determinism: Discussing the nature and development of the self, Kohut (1972–1976) employed the basic methodologic con-cept of determinism in the following way:

> No doubt many of the narcissistic strivings of people are rooted in early zonal pleasures. But there is a central sector in the human personality — the specific tension gradient between cer-tain basic ambitions, certain talents and skills, and certain ideal-ized goals — we experience as one's self, a central sector of the personality that, once it has been programmed, cannot be repro-grammed by anyone. You can say that there is a *deterministic* background in the formation of the self [p. 192; italics added].

Kohut's conceptualization of the firmly formed self as like a "coiled spring" or "wound clock" that must live out its destiny, express its own pattern, has some similarity to the traditional psychoanalytic concepts of "personal fate" and "fate neurosis," which unfold "according to an unchanging scenario, and consti-tute a sequence of events which may imply a lengthy temporal evolution" (Laplanche and Pontalis, 1973, p. 161; see also Freud, 1916, 1920, 1924; Deutsch, 1930, 1959; Fenichel, 1945, pp. 506–507; Kaplan, 1984).

In both traditional psychoanalysis and self psychology the concept of determinism proceeds from the assumption that things had to turn out as they did, given the constitutional and environmental contexts of the individual, past and present. In both approaches, the task of the analyst is to understand and explain why things turned out as they did — indeed, had to turn out that way.

Overdetermination: In one of his *Chicago Institute Lectures,* Kohut (1972–1976) applied the overdetermination principle to symptoms of addiction and perversion:

In an addiction or a perversion the intensity of the urge is accounted for neither by the structural defect alone nor by the pregenital fixation and regression alone but by the convergence of both. It is the convergence of the sexual pleasure-gain of the pregenital part-instinct, added to the irresistible quality of the need to fill a structural defect, that makes the urge so intense and irresistible [p. 4].

In a lecture titled "What Are Patients Angry About?" Kohut (1972–1976) suggested a technical application of the overdetermination principle—namely, when a patient attacks the therapist, pointing out his flaws, the therapist should not be too quick to admit that the patient is right. Kohut would say to the patient:

"You know, you may very well see certain things about me but the fact is that I've always been the same person and there was a time you didn't feel that way about me. There must be, in addition, something that's going on now. And also I have very little doubt that something from the past is in there, too." In other words, you begin to show it from all sides [p. 17].

Instinctual drives: Kohut (1972–1976) stressed that when we speak about the formation of the self, we remain largely within the framework of classical theory:

We say that the self has to be cathected with libido, that a person must be capable, as it were, of loving himself, that self-confidence is the capacity of cathecting the self. And we also say—and this is a critical point—that these psychic acts of cathecting the self are not in contrast to, are not diminished or abolished by, a person's intense love for another person [p. 183].

Elsewhere in the same lectures, Kohut (1972–1976) stated forcefully: "By no means do I see drives as disintegration products *only*. That statement would be true only under certain special circumstances, which I have very specifically spelled out" (p. 260). And as late in his writings as the year before his death, Kohut (1980b) referred to himself as "much more of a drive psychologist than some of the critics of self psychology. Self psychology does not replace drive psychology any more than quantum physics replaces the physics of Newton. We are dealing with different vantage points, shifts in outlook, complementarity of perspectives"; he then added that the self, after all, is "pushed toward others by sexual and aggressive drives" (p. 501; for further examples of Kohut's views on drives, see the later section titled Metapsychology, Psychodynamics).

The fact that Kohut accepted the existence and role of drives in human psychology does not imply, however, that he was an advocate of drive theory or drive psychology. Kohut understood the psyche as a self, as an experiential rather than a biological construct. The posited self must deal with the body's biological urges, but in the same way that it deals with the phenomena that it experiences from the outer world. The instincts are thus another part of the environment that the self experiences and processes. Kohut viewed psychoanalysis as psychology rather than as psychobiology—as the explanation in depth of experience rather than an objective, biologically based system.

Conflict: Although Kohut came to believe that unconscious conflict has become less prevalent as a basis of psychopathology than it was in Freud's time, he did not abandon the concept completely, especially in relation to the classical transference neuroses. In fact, he attempted to show how self psychology (in the narrower sense) enriches conflict psychology. By "self psychology in the narrow sense" Kohut (1972–1976) meant a psychology in which the self is a content of the mind in a theoretical system that "has stood us in such good stead about conflict psychology" (p. 389):

> In everyday conflict psychology the self is not thought about, but sort of taken for granted; it is implicit. When we talk about a drive versus a defense, we are really talking about a driven self versus a defending or defensive self. This is self psychology in the narrow sense, and it can do a great deal to improve and enrich traditional mental apparaus psychology. And, as such, it is a useful, important psychology insofar as man is concerned with conflicts within himself [pp. 389–390].

Defense: Kohut (1972–1976) applied the concept of repression to the psychology of the self: "The libidinal cathexis of the object can be suppressed, it can be repressed, and it can be made conscious again. And the same is true of aspects of the self" (p. 237). In his 1971 monograph, Kohut presented a clinical vignette illustrating the operation of repression in relation to narcissistic configurations and the self (pp. 242–244). In a lecture on the "vertical split" (1972–1976), he referred to several defense mechanisms: rationalization (p. 50), denial (p. 51), resistances (p. 53), and the repression barrier or "horizontal split" (p. 55). In discussing the concept of "vertical split," Kohut (1972–1976) pointed out that "this is not a concept that I developed; it is a concept that Freud [1927; 1940a, pp. 202–204; 1940b] developed. He spoke about a split of the ego in terms of fetishism" (pp. 50–51; see also 1971, p. 79, n.1, and pp. 176–178).

In a discussion of narcissistic defenses, Kohut (1972–1976, p. 327) referred to "avoidance" as a defensive wish not to expose oneself to narcissistic injuries. As indicated previously, Kohut's difference from Freud regarding avoidance was not the defense itself but the motive behind the defense—that is, an attempt to avoid retraumatization. He added that avoidance may defend against an underlying disorder of the self but also may serve as a defense against structural conflicts. He observed further that grandiosity is usually found to be defensive (1972–1976, p. 371).

In his essay on narcissistic rage, Kohut (1972) drew on Freud's (1920, p. 16) postulated defense of "turning a passive experience into an active one" and a defense mechanism described by Anna Freud (1936) of "identification with the aggressor," to explain "the sadistic tensions retained in individuals who as children had been treated sadistically by their parents" (Kohut, 1972, p. 381). Kohut added, "These factors help to explain the readiness of the shame-prone individual to respond to a potentially shame-provoking situation by the employment of a simple remedy: the active (often anticipatory) inflicting on others of those narcissistic injuries which he is most afraid of suffering himself" (p. 381; for further examples of the basic methodologic concept of defense in Kohut's work, see Kohut, 1971, pp. 242–243; Shane, 1985a,b; Leider, 1996, pp. 147–148; and the later section Metapsychology, Psychodynamics).

Transference: Kohut's retention and extensions of the basic methodologic concept of transference have been discussed in the previous section, The Defining Concepts of Transference and Resistance. In his 1971 monograph, Kohut observed about this core concept that

> the meaning of the term transference has gradually shifted since Freud's structuro-dynamic definition of 1900 and now has a broad clinical acceptation. The concept to which it refers has thus tended to lose some of its early metapsychological precision. As asserted elsewhere (Kohut, 1959), however, Freud's early conceptualization of the transference has by no means lost its basic, direction-setting significance [pp. 242–243].

Like analysts generally, Kohut employed the concept of transference to include transferences to the environment—that is, to objects. A selfobject, for example, is a transference object.

Importance of childhood experiences: Freud (1905b) noted that "it is not easy to estimate the relative efficacy of the constitutional and accidental factors. In theory one is always inclined to overestimate the former; therapeutic practice emphasizes the importance of the latter" (p. 239). He then added: "We shall be in even closer harmony with psychoanalytic research if we give *a place of preference* among the accidental factors to the experiences of early childhood" (p. 240; italics added).

Kohut consistently emphasized the role of childhood experiences in the development of psychopathology and of health. He considered the basic personalities of the parent-figures to be the most important factor in childhood experiences (1971, pp. 78–86; 1972–1976, pp. 132, 298). His emphasis on the role of parent-child interactions applied to both self disorders and to structural neuroses. He postulated that in the former a lack of responsiveness in the self-object matrix contributes to self pathology, whereas overinvolvement with children may lead to oedipal pathology. Kohut stressed the needs of children for optimal closeness to, but also optimal distance from, parents (1972–1976, pp. 344–345; see also Tolpin and Tolpin, 1996, p. xix).

Summing up the preceding discussions, significant continuities appear to exist between Kohut's contributions and all of the basic methodologic concepts that Rapaport (1944) delineated in Freud's theoretical system (see also Kohut, 1979b,c). These continuities support Kohut's judgment that his concepts of narcissism and self psychology are integral to psychoanalytic theory, methodology, and practice, rather than representing a separate scientific domain.

METAPSYCHOLOGIC VANTAGE POINTS: PSYCHODYNAMICS

Like Freud, Kohut employed both "experience near" and "experience distant" concepts. With respect to the latter, he made extensive use of Freud's metapsychologic vantage points. In his *Chicago Institute Lectures* (1972–1976), for example, he stated: "I want to be sure you understand my perception of metapsychology. Unless you take in the totality of a situation, a single definition becomes meaningless. Each definition has to be understood within the totality of a psychological experience" (p. 65). Later in the same lectures he added that when speaking about the formation of the self, "on the whole we remain within the framework of classical theory; that is, we apply the dynamic, genetic, and structural points of view" (p. 183). In his 1971 monograph he wrote that, "The nature of the analyst's interventions is decisively influenced by his grasp of the metapsychological basis of the psychopathology which he analyzes" (p. 177); and in 1981a he commented that "in analysis an interpretation means an explanation of what is going [on] in genetic, dynamic, and psychoeconomic terms" (p. 532; see also 1972–1976, p. 207; 1977b, p. 36, fn.6, p. 225). This section includes examples of continuities between Kohut's and Freud's *psychodynamic* concepts—that is, concepts dealing with drives, conflicts, defenses, danger situations, and anxiety.

Some of Kohut's views about *drives* have just been reviewed in the preceding section, Basic Methodologic Concepts, for example, his forceful statements that "by no means do I see drives as disintegration products *only*" and that the self is "pushed toward others by sexual and aggressive drives" (1980b, p. 501). In his final volume, Kohut (1984) attempted to correct the widespread misconception that self psychology neglects aggression: "In fact," he insisted, "nothing could be further from the truth" (p. 137). Discussing varieties of aggression, he referred to "a biological and psychobiological readiness to express oneself aggressively. It is this readiness that I consider to be directly related to the conception of aggression as a drive" (1972–1976, p. 67). He indicated also that he considered aggression both a reactive phenomenon and a drive: "These are two theories on two different levels, but they are not in opposition to each other" (p. 212; see also pp. 334–335).

With respect to *conflict*, Kohut considered it less important in psychopathology, particularly in the narcissistic personality disorders, than traditional analysts do (see, e.g., Kohut, 1972–1976, p. 40). At the same time, however, he did not neglect or discard the concept, and he analyzed conflict when it presented itself in the transference (1984, p. 115). He indicated also that in the development of the self "it isn't only breaches in empathy that contribute to the establishment of the self but, in addition, there are conflicts that occur that do not involve breaches in empathy"; and "the conflict itself is part of what contributes to the establishment of the self. The conflict, in fact, is not only inescapable but it may even be a necessary phenomenon in regard to the establishment of the self" (1972–1976, pp. 222–223).

Kohut viewed conflicts as an integral part of life and considered the strength or weakness of the self (i.e., the experience of oneself as a cohesive personality) as a major factor in determining how successfully or unsuccessfully one deals with such problems.

Kohut sometimes used other terms for what traditional analysts would call conflicts. In an essay called "How Kohut Actually Worked," for example, Miller (1985, p. 23) described a patient's dream to Kohut who felt that it expressed the patient's growing identification or merger with the analyst and a "secondary fear" of losing his self–selfobject relationship with the analyst. Traditional analysts would probably refer to that psychological configuration as a conflict between the merger fantasies and fear of possible consequences from merging with the analyst.

Some self psychologists (e.g., Brandchaft, 1985, p. 85; Stolorow, 1985) maintain that latent conflict is not confined to the traditional transference neuroses, but occurs also in narcissistic disorders. Kohut (1977b) commented in this connection that the difference between the transference neuroses and the narcissistic personality disorders is "not very great: in the former, we are dealing with a conflict between psychological structures; in the latter, with a conflict between an archaic self and an archaic environment—a precursor of psychological structure (cf. Kohut, 1971, pp. 19 and 50–53)—that is experienced as part of the self" (1977b, pp. 136–137; see also Gediman, 1989, pp. 295, 302).

Turning to specifically *oedipal conflicts*, Kohut (1972–1976) summed up his remarks on continuities between self psychology and oedipal conflict by pointing out that "this is clearly not an issue of superseding drive psychology or oedipal psychology, or of replacing or substituting it with another kind of psychology. I am suggesting an expanded framework in which the old conflict and the classical conflict psychology continues to play a very important role" (p. 266). For example, in addition to patients with narcissistic disorders who dramatize romantic conflicts of the oedipal period because it gives them a sense of being alive, Kohut (1972–1976) emphasized that "there are indeed cases in which oedipal pathology and narcissistic pathology are both present" (p. 117). He (1984) expanded further on this theme in his final volume:

> For long times during the analysis of an oedipal transference, for example—that is, for long times during the analysis of an Oedipus conflict that has been remobilized in the transference— the analyst will properly function as the analysand's selfobject only if he focuses his interpretations on the latter's incestuous desires and death-wishes and on the well-known conflicts of ambivalence that accompany those drive-fed impulses. Should the analyst attempt to bypass the Oedipus complex and push the patient prematurely toward the failures of the oedipal selfobjects of childhood which led to the Oedipus complex, the analysand

will feel misunderstood and retreat, whether by open resistance or protest or—one of the strongest resistances encountered—via external compliance [pp. 67–68; see also 1972–1976, pp. 260–263, 330–331, 344–345].

In his reinterpretation of and distinction between the oedipal phase and Oedipus complex, Kohut (1984, pp. 14–27) shifted the emphasis once again from a biologically determined intrapsychic perspective to a psyche (or self) that is in constant interaction with its environments (internal and external) and is shaped ultimately by that interaction. He emphasized that how a child experiences the oedipal phase of development depends on how the parents function as oedipal selfobjects: "the healthy child of healthy parents enters the oedipal phase joyfully" and "a boy who is exposed to the responses of psychologically healthy parents does not experience a significant degree of castration anxiety during the oedipal phase" (p. 14). By contrast, Kohut described "the specific parental psychopathology which, as I see it, leads to the relacement of the normal oedipal stage by the pathology I now refer to as the Oedipus complex" (p. 23; see also 1977b, pp. 223–248, 269–273).

Kohut employed the concept of *defense* extensively; although his view of defense and resistance differed somewhat from that of traditional psychoanalysis, there is nevertheless an important similarity: Both his and Freud's concepts of defense imply a protective function against psychically painful experiences (M. Shane, 1985a, pp. 77–79). Kohut also retained the concept of a repression barrier. For example, he described a common type of personality split that occurs in a male child who is intensely tied to his mother. The mother overstimulates his grandiosity, but only on condition that he remain tied to her. The result is both vertical and horizontal splits in the child. Kohut (1972–1976) explained:

> In the horizontal split the deprivation leads to low self-esteem and underneath that is some small core of male initiative by self-cathexis. But, you see, this was not responded to and, therefore, he could not get by this repression barrier and did not form those ego structures that make sense out of this originally fixated part [p. 55].

Kohut (1972–1976) noted also that in the presence of unbridled aggressions or libidinal wishes, "we can see various primitive defenses that have established themselves against such primitive drives, as, for example, turning against the self" (pp. 215–216). In another lecture, Kohut (1972–1976) referred to intellectual defenses that

> can be a protection against disorders of self-cohesion, which the rigorous, cohesive intellectual systems help to overcome; however, such defensive modes can also be nonspecifically used against either oedipal neuroses or narcissistic personality disturbances that are not subject to serious or protracted disorganizations of a very fragile self [p. 329; see also pp. 42–43].

With respect to *danger situations* and *anxiety*, Kohut distinguished between the signal anxiety experienced by a person with a relatively cohesive self when confronted by one of the danger situations described by Freud (1926a) and "disintegration anxiety" experienced by a patient whose nuclear self is threatened with loss of cohesion. However, comparison of Kohut's and Freud's views of severe anxiety in relation to the relative strength or weakness of ego and self reveals significant similarities. During the later, ego psychological phase of his theorizing, Freud (1926b) wrote that "the nodal point and pivot of the whole situation is the relative strength of the ego organization"; he added that "the relative feebleness of the ego is the decisive factor for the genesis of a neurosis" (p. 242; see also pp. 202–203; 1926a, pp. 81, 168). Kohut (1977b) stated similarly that "the intensity of the drive is not the cause of the central pathology (precariousness of self-cohesion), but its result." Thus, "the core of disintegration anxiety is the anticipation of the breakup of the self" (p. 104).

Kohut (1984, p. 213, n.5) acknowledged that all of the forms of anxiety ennumerated by Freud contain admixtures of disintegration anxiety. Fenichel (1945) wrote, for example, that "in the last analysis, all anxiety is a fear of experiencing a traumatic state, the possibility that the organization of the ego [cf. self or psyche] may be overwhelmed" (p. 133). Gediman (1989) writes similarly that "the anticipation of traumatic intensity of excessive stimulation and the corresponding feeling of psychic helplessness as a narcissistic catastrophe underlies all the danger situations" (p. 298; cf. Kohut, 1984, p. 16; Baker and Baker, 1987, p. 5).

Kohut's concept of disintegration anxiety is also very similar, descriptively, to Freud's theory of "traumatic" (in contrast to signal) anxiety. Freud described such anxiety as a panicky dread of losing ego organization and control, which would repeat the infantile traumatic state of helplessness. In addition, both traditional analysts (e.g., Freud, 1915c; Fenichel, 1945, pp. 415–452) and Kohut (1977b, pp. 106–108) have noted that states of severe (traumatic or disintegration) anxiety are often associated with acute, incipient, prepsychotic states.

Psychoeconomics

Kohut's views of normal and pathological development, structure formation, and therapeutic change all rest on the psychoeconomic concepts of traumatic *versus* optimal frustration, psychoeconomic imbalance, traumatic (actual) neurosis, and the development of tension regulating structure through internalization. Kohut had employed these same concepts in his pre–self-psychological synthesis of Freudian theory (see chapters 5, 25–28 in his "Lectures on Psychoanalytic Psychology" and the sections Optimal Frustration and The Structural Model in our 1963 essay), which he carried over to his theories of narcissism and self psychology (see also Kohut, 1984, p. 109, where he referred specifically to these sources of his psychoeconomic formulations).

Leider (1989, p. xv) notes that the concept of optimal frustration and its relation to the development of tension regulating structure through internalization is based on mechanisms described by Freud (1917c, pp. 237–238) in "Mourning and Melancholia." Gediman (1989, pp. 294–295, 298–300) points out that Kohut revived Freud's psychoeconomic concepts of traumatic and actual neuroses as the traumatic core of all psychopathology; Cooper (1993, p. 45) observes that various writers including Stolorow, Brandchaft, and Atwood (1987) and Leider (1989) have commented on the similarity between the concept of optimal frustration and Freud's (1923, p. 25) view that ego development is promoted by frustrating experiences with the external world. Kohut (1972–1976, p. 59) also employed Freud's (1915c) metapsychologic theory of psychosis, but modified the psychoeconomic process of decathexis, viewing it as a loss of cathexis of the self rather than, as Freud described it, a decathexis of unconscious ties to objects.

For additional references to his extensive use of psychoeconomic concepts, see Kohut (1971, pp. 47–50; 1972–1976, pp. 54, 63, 117, 223, 344–345; 1977b, pp. 86–88, 188; 1980b, p. 518).

Psychogenetics

Kohut (1984, p. 132) indicated that his approach was in harmony with the *complemental series* of genetic factors (innate and environmental) proposed by Freud (1916–1917, pp. 346–347). Kohut suspected, however, that after Freud had been fooled initially by the seduction stories of his hysterical patients, he tended to concentrate more on innate factors; Kohut added:

> When I refer to the formulations of traditional psychoanalysis in order to contrast them with those of self psychology, I do not have in mind Freud's general statements about neurosogenesis in childhood—here he did indeed stress from early on the influence of environmental factors and acknowledged their influence [1984, p. 217, n.2; cf. Freud's (1905b, p. 240) having suggested "a place of preference" in the complemental series for the experiences of early childhood; and see also Kohut, 1972–1976, p. 307; 1972, p. 362; M. Shane, 1985a, pp. 75–76].

Like Freud, who was at pains to demonstrate the continuities between normal and pathological behavior, Kohut argued similarly for continuities between normal and pathological narcissism and between the normal self and self pathology. He was "intent on showing that naive grandiosity and idealization are the nucleus of positive childhood development and should not be mistaken for pathological narcissism when it is revived in transferences" (Tolpin and Tolpin, 1996, pp. xi–xii).

Kohut (1972–1976) drew also on Freud's concept that originally all of the infant's and small child's activities are "sexual": "Early needs, early desires, are always closer to sexual experience because the younger the child is, the closer he is to the intensities of the pleasure experience, to what later on one calls libidinal or sexual" (p. 8). Discussing the phallic phase of devlopment, Kohut (1972) emphasized that the genitals during that period "are not only the instruments of intense (fantasied) *object-libidinal* interactions, they also carry enormous *narcissistic* cathexes" (p. 374).

With respect to the oedipal period and phase of development, Kohut (1972–1976, pp. 344–345) presented a continuity between the traditional concept of oedipal pathology and the self psychological concept regarding the importance of empathic experiences in childhood. Rather than a lack of responsiveness on the part of parents, which one sees frequently in the narcissistic disorders, patients with oedipal pathology have often been overstimulated by parents' "unempathic overcloseness" to the child, in contrast to the "optimal distance" that the child needs—"what the early hysterics experienced and described as seduction experiences of early life" (p. 344).

Structure

The editors of Kohut's (1972–1976) *Chicago Institute Lectures,* Paul and Marian Tolpin, point out that Kohut conceptualized the self in structural terms, a vicissitude and product of narcissistic development that consists of the grandiose exhibitionistic self substructure and the idealized parent imago substructure. Thus, "narcissistic patients' disorders do not, in fact, reflect 'too much' untamed narcissism, libido, or aggression. On the contrary, the primary disorder is the result of 'too little' development of narcissistic (self) structures" (p. xi). In this connection, Kohut (1966) called attention to an important continuity between his concepts of narcissistic structures and "the ego's capacity to harness the narcissistic energies and to transform the narcissistic constellations into more highly differentiated, new psychological configurations" (p. 257).

Leider (1996) observes that Kohut's later-proposed tripolar self "is, in form, analogous to the earlier models of Freud's topographic and structural theories and that it was constructed for the same purpose: to represent the phenomena and structures (groups of functions) central to the theory" (p. 139; see also Meissner, 1986; Fast, 1990). Both Leider (1996, p. 146, n.21) and Markson (1992) note that Kohut emphasized the role of internalization in structure formation, and that "Kohut's view of internalization is rather similar to classical theory, which also sees frustration and disappointement as the impetus for development" (Markson, 1992, p. 211).

Another important structural concept in Kohut's approach is that of *compensatory structures,* which he distinguished from defensive structures by their function of compensating for rather than merely covering over defects in the self (1977b, p. 3). He emphasized that compensatory structure is strong and flexible and that only when a compensatory structure is endangered do symptoms develop. Basch (1992) pointed out that "patients work with us mainly at the level of the damaged compensatory structure, not at the basic infantile trauma which is too sensitive to reopen" (p. 19). Kohut (1977b) wrote, for example, that "the cure is not achieved through a complete filling in of the primary defect, but through the rehabilitation of compensatory structures" (p. 134; see also, however, Gedo, 1989, p. 416).

Kohut's distinction between compensatory and defensive structures is similar to Freud's (1939) descriptions of the positive and negative effects of trauma. The positive effects "may be taken up into what passes as a normal ego and, as permanent trends in it, may lend it unalterable character-traits, although, or rather precisely because, their true basis and historical origin are forgotten" (p. 75; see also Freud, 1916–1917, p. 318 regarding the constructive aspects of compensatory character structures). The negative reactions to trauma, Freud (1939) wrote, "follow the opposite aim: that nothing of the forgotten traumas shall be remembered and nothing repeated. We can summarize them as 'defense reactions.' Their principal expressions are what are called 'avoidances'" (p. 76).

Freud's (1937a) remarks on the treatment of character problems also suggest continuities with Kohut's focus on compensatory structures:

> Our aim will not be to rub off every peculiarity of human character for the sake of a schematic "normality," nor yet to demand that the person who has been "thoroughly analyzed" shall feel no passions and develop no internal conflicts. The business of the analysis is to secure the best possible psychological conditions for the functions of the ego; with that it has discharged its task [p. 250; cf. Kohut's (1977b) remarks regarding "the kind of incompleteness that would be acceptable as a realistic compromise," p. 183].

Summing up the posited metapsychologic continuities between Kohut's and Freud's approaches, it appears that Kohut employed all of the vantage points of Freud's metapsychology, and he did so freely and effectively. It is worth noting in this connection that metapsychology is more than a highly abstract theory of mind; it is an integral part of clinical methodology, contributing in a quiet but crucial way to both clinical observation and interpretation. To illustrate: Because of metapsychology we listen to patients with only relatively unfocused attention; we listen attentively for undercurrents of conflicts, manifestations of defenses, the relative strengths of interacting motives, recurrent patterns of response, childhood memories, and the repetition of past experiences in the present—trends in clinical data that encompass the full range of metapsychologic catetgories. "In every interpretation that is given, a metapsychologic statement is implicit" (Eissler, 1968, p. 168).

CLINICAL METHOD

The continuities between Kohut's and Freud's views are so numerous in the category of clinical method that it is impossible to describe them fully in a single chapter. To illustrate their range and depth, however, a list of the continuities is presented, including relevant references. As the following examples suggest, virtually every aspect of Kohut's clinical method has roots in Freud's therapeutic approach, which led the editors of Kohut's (1972–1976) *Chicago Institute Lectures* to comment that the lectures show "how difficult it is to clearly formulate a really new psychoanalytic idea that significantly advances treatment" (p. xxi; see also Kohut and Wolf, 1978; Basch, 1989, p. 3).

1. Kohut compared his clinical approach with Freud's repeatedly: for example, their shared emphasis on empiricism (1975a, p. 749); the role of introspection (1976 [in Ornstein, 1978, p. 794]; p. 794); their "using the same tools," that is, "interpretation followed by working through in an atmosphere of abstinence" (1984, p. 75); and his conclusion that in principle both employed the same approach (1984, p. 81). Kohut's view of the clinical parallels between self psychology and traditional psychoanalysis appears to contradict the claims of some post-Kohutian self psychologists—for example, Chessick's (1990) assertion regarding "the vast differences in approach between self psychologists and traditional psychoanalysts" (p. 350).

2. With respect to the analyst's stance, Kohut wrote that "the analyst's proper attitude as given by Freud also applies to the analysis of narcissistic personality disturbances" and that "the basic attitude which Freud recommends is as valid here as it is in the transference neuroses" (1971, p. 88; see also 1971, p. 207; 1972–1976, pp. 94–96).

3. Like Freud, Kohut (1972–1976) maintained that "much of analytic work is, again, a mode of making aspects of the self conscious that formerly were not conscious" (p. 237; see also pp. 204, 241, 369). In the same vein, Kohut (1972–1976)

stated: "It is the art of analysis, both in the transference neuroses and in the narcissistic disturbances, to recognize, to acknowledge, to point out—and by so doing to free—a formerly repressed aspiration, whether it be a murderous wish or a wish to fly" (p. 241).

4. Discussing the difficulty of determining whether a patient's feelings toward the analyst belong mainly to the present or include a repetition of something from the past, Kohut (1972–1976) concluded that "the old rule that one begins from the surface is, of course, quite correct" (p. 16). In another lecture (1972–1976) he suggested, in the spirit of traditional psychoanalysis, that "the way to deal with defenses is to make the investigation of their meaning a cooperative enterprise between the patient and the analyst" (pp. 324–325). And in a discussion of transference sequences, he (1984) employed the basic psychoanalytic assumption that "the process of analysis generally leads from the surface to the depth, and correspondingly, that transference sequences generally repeat developmental sequences *in the reverse order*" (p. 22).

5. In his chapter on self psychology in Nersessian and Kopff's *Textbook of Psychoanalysis*, Leider (1996) writes that

    self psychological and classical psychoanalytic theory and practice are comparable. Both share the essential elements of psychoanalysis: belief in a *dynamic unconscious* and recognition of the phenomena of *transference*. Formulations regarding the mechanisms of unconscious mental processes, of dream work, of transference phenomena, and of symptom formation are identical, as is the interpretive method [p. 160; see also Basch, 1989, p. 3].

6. In addition to the two major essays in which Kohut (1959, 1981b) presented and explicated his view that the method of introspection and empathy defines psychoanalysis, in his 1966 essay he drew a parallel between his own method of introspection and empathy for prolonged periods and the psychoanalyst's "customary observational attitude ('evenly suspended attention'; avoidance of note taking; curtailment of realistic interaction; concentration on the purpose of achieving understanding rather than the wish to cure or help)" (p. 263). Kohut noted that these traditional methods of clinical listening encourage empathic comprehension. In a later essay subtitled "Reflections on the Self-Analysis of

Freud," Kohut (1976) referred to a direct continuity between Freud's use of an introspective approach in a systematic way and the fact that "psychoanalysis has continued to employ the introspective–empathic approach in the same fashion" (p. 794, fn.1; see also Basch, 1983). In his final volume Kohut (1984, p. 172) acknowledged that the empathy employed by self psychologists is essentially no different than that employed by traditional analysts.

7. Elaborating on the method of freely hovering attention, Kohut (1977b) characterized it as "the analyst's active empathic response to the analysand's free associations, a response in which the deepest layers of the analyst's unconscious from the [conflict-free] area of progressive neutralization (Kohut, 1961; Kohut and Seitz, 1963) participate" (1977b, p. 251; see also 1972–1976, p. 367). He felt that these statements were "in full harmony with the basic principles of analysis; and the attitude they advocate is one that furthers the analyst's recognition of the emerging unconscious material" (p. 252).

8. Kohut (1972–1976) also described the processes of free association and freely hovering attention in structurodynamic and economic terms: "We are trying to increase the area of progresive neutralization and to decrease the area of repression, or, clinically, we are trying to increase the ability to organize progressive neutralizations and to decrease the necessity for transferences. This is the area in which analytic work is done" (p. 369).

9. Kohut (1971, p. 164) agreed with Freud's (1923, p. 50n.) caveat regarding the temptation to play the role of prophet or savior to the patient by encouraging him to put the analyst in place of his ego ideal. Kohut (1972–1976, p. 373) emphasized, as Freud had, that "play-acting" is contraindicated in analysis:

> The active encouragement of an idealization of the analyst leads to the establishment of a tenacious transference bondage (analogous to the attachments which are fostered by organized religions), bringing about a cover of massive identification and hampering the gradual therapeutic alteration of the existing narcissistic structures [Kohut, 1971, p. 164].

10. Asked repeatedly by students how to distinguish clinically between the pathology of structural conflict and narcissistic personality disturbances, Kohut drew on Freud's concept of

waiting for the transference to reveal the underlying pathology. Freud (1913a) had said that "so long as the patient's communications and ideas run on without any obstruction, the theme of transference should be left untouched" (p. 139). Kohut (1972–1976) explained similarly that "there isn't anything so special about this particular differentiation"—that, "as always, there is only one foolproof way of going about making decisions. That is to leave the patient alone, to watch the transference and see how it gradually unfolds, and to see whether it veers toward self pathology or toward structural conflict" (p. 334).

11. In his essay "How Kohut Actually Worked," Miller (1985) concludes that, "In general, Kohut was a 'classicist' in that he tended to focus first on the transference relationship and, later, when the material seemed propitious, to link this up with genetic material in an increasingly broad and explanatory manner" (p. 28). In his final book, Kohut (1984, p. 210) asserted unequivocally that self psychology is at one with traditional psychoanalysis in accepting the technical principle that interpretation, particularly of transferences, is the major instrument of therapeutic psychoanalysis.

12. Discussing the significance of early material in an analysis, Kohut (1972–1976) applied a traditional psychoanalytic concept to the treatment of narcissistic personality disorders:

We have often heard, and it is quite true, that very early communications to the analyst—earliest symptomatic actions in the course of the first analytic session, the first encounter with the analyst, the first dreams—that in these firsts, there is a unique balance of forces that allows the emergence of deep material in a comparatively clear way that will never again be as clear. These are very telling moments that one can learn a great deal from. Such moments give you a story about the major defense mechanisms or the major traumas that a person suffered early in life, and things of that type (compare, Freud, 1917b). When you are able to observe such material, be alert to the expression of the goals of the nuclear self that a person wants to achieve; they may be revealed in early symptomatic acts, in early lies, for instance [p. 60].

13. Discussing the concept of working through, Kohut (1972–1976) pointed out in essentially traditional psychoanalytic terms, "An analysis is kept in motion by keeping pathogenic conflicts optimally activated. That's really all you

need to do. You don't cure the patient. The patient cures himself. All you need to do is point out again the sequence of events that have happened" (p. 204). He added:

> The really important thing is only to repeat the essential conflicts over and over again, to make them conscious, and to explain them in their broad context. And in working them through, over and over again, in the dynamic transference situation, in making the genetic content connections with the past, new structure is developed. An increased, expanded mastery is achieved [p. 204].

And in agreement with the traditional caution regarding patient compliance, Kohut commented, "We must not forget that patients tend to comply. If you overwhelm a patient with your sense of conviction, then he will agree with you" (p. 207).

14. Kohut (1972–1976) said he found it more fruitful in clinical work to reconstruct the total experiential significance that an event had for a child, rather than focusing on the specific event itself. He compared this approach with Freud:

> When Freud wrote about the impact of the birth of a sibling in "Constructions in Analysis" (1937b), for example, he did not have in mind that the birth of the sibling, in and of itself, causes some particular simple reaction. Rather, he reconstructed the total experiential significance that the event had for the child at that particular time [Kohut, 1972–1976, pp. 353–354].

15. Basch (1992, pp. 18–19) called attention to Kohut's (1977b, p. 3) emphasis on the importance of compensatory structures in his clinical method. Compare in this connection Freud's (1937a, p. 250) previously mentioned comments on the treatment of character problems, and see the previous section Methodologic Vantage Points, Structure for a related discussion of this continuity.

16. To sum up and highlight the discussion of continuities between Kohut's and Freud's clinical methods, the following vignette from Miller's (1985) essay "How Kohut Actually Worked" is presented to illustrate how thoroughly Kohut had integrated his self psychological approach with that of traditional psychoanalysis.

The patient was a highly successful man in his 30s, married with several children, who complained of diffuse, restless anxiety;

contentless depression; and disturbing homosexual feelings and fantasies. Miller was the treating analyst and Kohut the supervisor. Both agreed on the diagnosis of a narcissistic personality disorder and that the predominant transference in the analysis was an idealizing one. The following clinical material is a paraphrase of an appointment during the last two years of the patient's successful five-year analysis:

> The analyst had cancelled the previous appointment. The patient came in saying he was exhausted and depressed, which he connected (intellectually) with the missed appointment. He described an exciting sexual experience with his wife in which she was on top of him, moving about and masturbating while fully clothed. That night he dreamed that the rear end of their small station wagon burst into flames, which the patient extinguished with a garden hose. Then he was supposed to insert his penis in a certain-shaped can held by a woman. He was reminded of a previous dream in which he was supposed to insert his penis into a disposal. He mentioned being hungry several times and recalled a movie of a young man eating prodigious amounts of food. He said he was hungry enough to eat a horse, which the analyst connected with the missed appointment. Later he said he was hungry enough to eat the picture on the analyst's wall and that he could almost eat the couch. The analyst commented that the patient's eating fantasies were getting closer to him. At that point the patient reported fantasies of sucking ferociously, then more passively, on someone's penis, then someone's breast. He recalled the breast pump his father used to obtain milk from his mother's breast for the patient's hospitalized infant brother. At that point he said he felt less fatigued, more energized [pp. 16–17].

Kohut noted that the session contained a consistent sequence of "classical material." That is, after missing the appointment, the patient came in with a dream of sexual excitement which was probably homosexual, indicated by the "rear end" of the car in flames. Then a reference to castration fear in the associated dream of putting his penis in a disposal. And finally the orality, which could have been toward the analyst's penis or may have involved oral incorporation of the analyst. Kohut suggested that the material could have been interpreted in essentially classical terms: "A classical interpretation of this kind can be made when the material is this clear in the analysis of a narcissistic personality disorder or, for that matter, in the analysis of any other type of condition, assuming that the other indicators of appropriateness of interpretation are favorable" (p. 17).

Kohut also felt, however, that the most central aspect of this session was the patient's idealizing transference to Miller, in which he reacted to the analyst as the good father he did not have while growing up. The analyst's cancelling the previous appointment and not being available over the weekend constituted a narcissistic injury that produced some fragmentation of the patient's self. By the time he returned for the present appointment, however, the breach had healed. In a complete interpretation, Kohut concluded, one would include the narcissistic injury and the break in the self–selfobject relationship; but, he added, one could also interpret the patient's response to the interruption of the selfobject relationship "in an essentially classical manner" (p. 18).

Clinical Interpretation

As in the previous section, Clinical Method, the number of continuities between Kohut's and Freud's concepts in the category of clinical interpretation is too extensive to permit detailed discussions of the numerous parallels. Instead, a variety of examples is presented with brief descriptions of some major continuities.

1. Kohut's (1984) agreement with traditional psychoanalysis regarding the importance of interpretation is illustrated by his statement that "self psychology is at one with the technical principle that interpretation in general, and the interpretation of transferences in particular, is the major instrumentality of therapeutic psychoanalysis" (p. 110; see also p. 75; and Goldberg, 1978, pp. 9, 446–448).
2. Kohut's clinical approach was distinctly interpretive. He was not a very active analyst, but "practiced a traditional form of 'expectant' analysis'" (Miller, 1985, p. 30).
3. Kohut's concepts regarding the functions of interpretation were congruent, for the most part, with those of traditional psychoanalysis: for example, his division of the interpretive process into two phases, understanding and explanation. Kohut (1981a) maintained that analysis cures by giving explanations in genetic, dynamic, and psychoeconomic terms (pp. 532–534; see also 1972–1976, p. 9). He proposed another function of interpretations that may add something to traditional psychoanalytic theory—namely, that correct interpretations have an optimally frustrating effect that

contributes to healthy new structure formation in both classical transference neuroses and disorders of the self (1984, pp. 102–107; see also the later section, The Process of Therapeutic Change).

4. Kohut (1977b, pp. 143, n.2; 306n.) noted that his view of empathy in depth psychology was in harmony with Freud's (1921, p. 110, n.2) observation that empathy makes possible "any attitude at all towards another mental life" (see also Freud, 1905a, pp. 186, 196–197, 201, 226; 1907, p. 45; Basch, 1983, 1984b, p. 168; Leider, 1989, p. xii, fn.1). Freud (1921) wrote also that empathy "plays the largest part in our understanding of what is inherently foreign to our ego in other people" (p. 108). According to Goldberg (1998, p. 243), Kohut felt that empathy is the basis of all depth psychology but has no particular tie or special affinity to self psychology. Kohut (1984, p. 172) stated clearly, for example, that the self psychologist's empathy is not esentially different than that of the traditional psychoanalyst and that self psychology does not achieve cure by a novel kind of empathy.

5. Although at times Kohut stressed the uniqueness and centrality of empathy in depth psychological understanding (e.g., 1972–1976, pp. 228–229; 1984, p. 32), at other times he was more circumspect about its role in clinical interpretation. Kohut (1971) wrote, for example, that "if empathy, instead of limiting its role to that of a data-collecting process, begins to replace the explanatory phase of psychoanalysis . . . then we are witnessing a deterioration of scientific standards and a sentimentalizing to subjectivity" (pp. 300–301). Kohut's own description of the empathic method, its operations, limitations, and the need for alternative constructions coincides closely with the traditional psychoanalytic approach—for example, "We think ourselves into another person by various cues that we get from him, then we reconstruct his inner life as if we were that other person. In other words, we trust the resonance of the essential likeness of ourselves and the observed other" (1972–1976, p. 228). Kohut readily acknowledged, however, that "even with like experiences there are many possible errors" (p. 228). These days, in agreement with traditional psychoanalysis, an increasing number of self psychologists appears to believe that "information obtained through external observational methods should be recognized, correlated, and integrated

integrated with empathically derived theories" (Leider, 1989, p. xiv; see also Lichtenberg, 1981; Basch, 1984a,b, 1986; Goldberg, 1988; Galatzer-Levy, 1991; Shane and Shane, 1993).

6. In keeping with the best traditions of depth-psychological interpretive methodology, Kohut (1984) emphasized that "as analysts we must have the capacity to postpone closures and to apply closures tentatively, observing the analysand's reactions to our tentative interpretations, and to consider as many explanations as possible" (p. 199). Kohut (1977b, p. 168) referred to the use of "trial empathy" as a way of obtaining alternative hypotheses. He recommended that the clinical interpreter "consider the greatest possible number of explanatory configurations. The more the better" (1972–1976, p. 110). "In other words, the skill of the intuitive psychoanalytic observer is not automatically to fall into the groove of 'that's it' "; for, "the sense that you have all the evidence to sustain one conclusion should not close your mind to searching for other conclusions. You should keep in mind that despite the seeming cohesion and fit, it might yet be something else" (p. 111; see also pp. 206–207; 384–385).

7. Some examples were presented in the earlier section, Clinical Method, of Kohut's agreement with Freud's (1913a, p. 140) concept of interpreting from the surface downward. Kohut (1971) also stressed in this connection that the analyst "always addresses himself to the reality ego" (p. 178). And in his consultations with Miller (1985) he suggested that "one should take analytic material first in a 'straight' manner, as if it means what it seems to mean. If this does not prove productive, then one can consider inverting it or manipulating it in various other ways" (p. 15; see also p. 20; and Kohut, 1984, pp. 93–94).

8. Among the various cues from patients that Kohut employed in order to "think his way into another person" (1972–1976, p. 228), he mentioned a traditional psychoanalytic practice of searching for precipitating factors and events. He would ask himself and the patient, "When did this begin? What kind of material were we just transacting before this began?" (p. 98). Leider (1996, p. 157) notes in this connection that interpretive activity in self psychology focuses primarily on disruptions in the self–selfobject transference, which the analyst attempts to recognize and then interprets

to the patient in terms of the events that precipitated the disruption. Later, the preceding sequence is explained in dynamic and genetic terms.

9. With repect to the interpretation of dreams, Kohut (1980b) wrote that for "the majority of dreams, we have at no time voiced any doubt that they can indeed be deciphered only if the associative material to each of the dream elements is pursued in the traditional way" (p. 510). Kohut (1977b, p. 109) also proposed another type of dream, so-called self-state dreams, which he considered similar to the dreams of children as described by Freud (1900), the dreams of traumatic neuroses (Freud, 1920), and hallucinatory dreams that occur in toxic states or high fever. Rather than relying on the patient's associations, which are not helpful in understanding this type of dream, Kohut based his interpretation on the dream's manifest content and on the analyst's knowledge of the patient's vulnerabilities, including his knowledge of the particular situation that had stimulated the dream (Kohut, 1977b, p. 109).

   Kohut (1980b) indicated clearly that his concept of self-state dreams applied only to "a specific, circumscribed, identifiable group of phenomena," not to dreams generally (p. 510). A significant continuity between Kohut's concept of self-state dreams and Freud's views can be seen in the latter's writings (1900, pp. 503–506, 523–524; 1914a, p. 97) on Herbert Silberer's (1909, 1912, 1919) studies of "functional phenomena" and anagogic imagery—which Freud (1914a) referred to as "one of the few indisputably valuable additions to the theory of dreams" (p. 97; cf. also Seitz, 1963a,b, 1967, 1969). A further continuity between Kohut and Freud along these lines is that both recognized and described mixed forms of the two types of dreams (see Freud, 1900, p. 505; Kohut, 1977b, pp. 110–111).

10. Kohut (1984) expressed a significant continuity with traditional psychoanalysis (cf. Freud, 1940a, p. 128) in the following discussion of interpretive accuracy and its importance in the process of therapeutic change. Referring to the analysis of oedipal conflicts, Kohut observed that during such periods

    the analyst will properly function as the analysand's selfobject only if he focuses his interpretations on the latter's incestuous desires and death-wishes and on the well-known conflicts of ambivalence that accompany these drive-fed impulses. Should the analyst attempt to bypass the Oedipus complex and push the patient prematurely toward the failures of the oedipal self-objects of childhood which led to the Oedipus complex, the analysand will feel misunderstood and retreat [pp. 67–68].

11. Kohut's emphasis on the need for alternative interpretations, his acknowledgment of empathy's limitations, and his caveat regarding the "many possible errors" in interpretive work point to yet another continuity with traditional psychoanalysis—namely, recognition that clinical interpretations are highly fallible. He argued that because there is a host of possible errors, analysts must learn "not to be naive in thinking that one automatically knows" (1972–1976, p. 384). He pointed out that attempting to understand latent contents "is all very relative." Kohut noted also that theory can interfere with understanding (1971, p. 288; 1979a, pp. 408, 414–415; see also Basch, 1984b, pp. 23, 38; Schwaber, 1987, pp. 746–748). For example, the following statement by Kohut is congruent with Freud's (1912, pp. 114–115) view that one should forget about theory until the treatment is finished: "If one sticks to the conviction that what one is seeing is organized in a certain way, that certain established concepts *must* be used to order the data of observation," then, "in fact, it is like the old joke: heads I win, tails you lose. We have loaded the dice; it doesn't work" (Kohut, 1972–1976, p. 209; see also pp. 127–129).

12. Kohut's (1975a) recognition of the need for methods of justifying interpretations is congruent also with scientific psychoanalysis. He insisted that empathy must be carefully checked: "Here, correctness of the results of our efforts can never be established with certainty; we can only strive to increase the probability that our claims are valid by supporting them through empirical data and by examining them" (p. 754). But he envisioned more definitive methods of justification: "The future might bring a quantifying approach in which the increasing conviction of the empathic investigator is [tested] by means of a quantifying methodology that determines the number of data or counts the number of details that form meaningful configurations when seen from a particular point of view" (1977b, p. 145, fn.3; see also Rubovits-Seitz, 1998, pp. 211–248).

13. Finally, with respect to the technique of interpretation, that is, whether, what, when, and how to convey depth-psychological information to patients, Kohut cited Freud's (1937b, p. 261) advice regarding the style and form of communicating interpretations and reconstructions—namely, in a tone of "accepting explanatory objectivity." Kohut (1971) considered Freud's technique "an especially apt example" of the tone that should be employed also in interpreting narcissistic structures to patients (pp. 224–225).

Summing up the continuities between Kohut and traditional psychoanalysis in the category of clinical interpretation, parallels have been posited and illustrated regarding numerous aspects of interpretive methods, problems, and techniques. As far as technique is concerned, Kohut appears to have seen little or no distinction between self psychology and traditional psychoanalysis.

The Process of Therapeutic Change

Kohut (1984) stated in his final volume that, "with respect to the issue of cure, the continuity between ego psychology and self psychology is most palpable. This continuity lends weight to our assertion that self psychology, although at the present time still unassimilated by the majority of analysts, is placed squarely in the center of the analytic tradition" (p. 95). Leider (1989, p. xvii) notes that Kohut addressed the problem of therapeutic change many times in his writings. His final position was that empathy does not cure but, rather, that the change process involves, first, a phase of understanding, followed by a phase of explanation—a view, Leider observes, that corresponds closely with Freud's concepts.

Examining Kohut's concepts of therapeutic change more closely, one finds that its continuities with traditional psychoanalysis apply mainly to the first two of three steps that Kohut (1984) described in the process of cure (pp. 65–66). The first two steps—defense analysis and the development of transferences—involve readily recognizable parallels with traditional psychoanalytic concepts of therapeutic change. The third step, which Kohut considered "the essential one because it defines the aim and the result of cure" (pp. 65–66), differs in some respects, although not completely, from traditional concepts of the mutative process.

Kohut proposed that the disruptions of empathy that inevitably occur during analysis, and their repair through understanding and interpretation, are essential to the curative process. Disruptions of this kind and their repair constitute a form of optimal (nontraumatic) frustration, through which the patient acquires new psychological structure and functions by internalizing the manner in which the therapist deals with such disruptions. These concepts, which Kohut had enunciated in his pre–self-psychological "Lectures on Psychoanalytic Psychology" (see, e.g., Lectures 5, 25–28) and in our 1963 chapter, seem at least partially consonant with certain traditional concepts of therapeutic change. Leider (1989, p. xv) observes, for example, that Kohut's concepts of optimal frustration and its relation to the acquisition of tension regulating structure through internalization is based on mechanisms described by Freud in "Mourning and Melancholia" (1917c, pp. 237–238). Leider notes further that these concepts are central not only to Kohut's theory of therapeutic change, but also to his concepts of normal and pathological development, and to structure formation generally (see also Terman, 1989).

Kohut (1984) commented in this connection that his reason for proposing the preceding concepts was not to argue that self psychological analysis is different from traditional psychoanalytic therapy. "On the contrary, my intention was to demonstrate that it is in principle exactly the same"; for "self psychology does not differ from traditional psychoanalysis in its characterization of what is going on between analyst and patient that eventuates in a cure" (pp. 103–104)

Kohut (1984) stated emphatically that "self psychology relies on the same tools as traditional analysis (interpretation followed by working through in an atmosphere of abstinence" (p. 75). With respect to the role of abstinence, Kohut added that "it is not enough for the analyst to be 'nice' to his patients, to be 'understanding,' warmhearted, endowed with the human touch"; for all of the evidence now available indicates that these attributes cure "neither the classical neuroses nor the analyzable disturbances of the self" (p. 95).

Goldberg (1978) asserts similarly that "a correct or ideal emotional position on the part of the analyst is insufficient by itself; interpretations must carry the brunt of the analytic process" (pp. 8–9). He pointed out further that,

> The analyst does not actively soothe; he interprets the analysand's yearning to be soothed. The analyst does not actively mirror; he

interprets the need for confirming responses. The analyst does not actively admire or approve grandiose expectations; he explains their role in the psychic economy. The analyst does not fall into passive silence; he explains why his interventions are felt to be intrusive. Of course, the analyst's mere presence, or the fact that he talks, or, especially, the fact that he understands, all have soothing and self-confirming effects on the patient, *and they are so interpreted.* Thus the analytic ambience that makes analytic work possible becomes itself an object for analytic interpretation. The whole analytic process in this way blocks exploitation for mere gratification [pp. 447–448].

As mentioned previously, Kohut (1972–1976, p. 237) concluded that much of the therapeutic work in analyzing the self involves making aspects of the self conscious that formerly were not conscious. This suggests that he considered the process of derepression a significant factor in therapeutic change, which coheres with traditional psychoanalysis. At the same time, he wrote that the role of insight is not as important now as it was during the early years of psychoanalysis when the dominance of the topographic model led to an emphasis on knowledge-accretion (1977b, p. 135). The latter concept seems congruent with the views of some contemporary mainstream psychoanalysts (cf. Wallerstein, 1985, p. 395).

Kohut (1971, p. 164) agreed with Freud's (1923, p. 50, fn.) reservations regarding "active" methods of analysis such as attempts to induce an idealizing transference, but he also stressed that spontaneously occurring selfobject transferences should not be interferred with in any way. (For an interesting example of Freud's having used actively supportive measures in his treatment of a narcissistic patient, see Kris, 1994; and cf. also Hughes, 1992, p. 266.)

For the role and importance of "compensatory structures" in Kohut's concepts regarding the process of cure, and their posited continuities with traditional psychoanalytic concepts of therapeutic change, see an earlier discussion in the section Metapsychologic Vantage Points: Structure.

The Benefits of Treatment

One of the most suggestive continuities between Kohut's and Freud's concepts regarding the benefits of treatment is the patient's development of "freedom to choose." For example, Kohut (1972–1976) referred to Freud's (1923) "famous footnote always quoted from 'The Ego and the Id,' that all that therapy can do is to get the patient the freedom to decide this way or that" (p. 300):

> He was arguing against becoming a messiah for the patient; he was saying that one mustn't attempt to effect one's therapeutic goals by messianically persuading the patient to follow the analyst's health ideals. In principle, of course, this is unassailable. The question is whether it applies to disturbances of the self; I believe that to a very large extent it does. It applies particularly to those disturbances of the self in which the essential task is to free an already existing nuclear self that has been kept in repression [p. 301].

Another likely continuity in this category concerns the limits of what can be achieved by analysis. Freud (1937a) had written that "our aim will not be to rub off every peculiarity of human character for the sake of a schematic 'normality'; and that "the business of analysis is to secure the best possible psychological conditions for the functions of the ego" (p. 250). Kohut (1972–1976) stated similarly:

> As far as the nuclear self is concerned, our therapeutic task has its limits: if the nuclear self is weak, I think it is our task to help it to become stronger; if it is vulnerable and tends to fragment, I think it is our task to help it congeal more firmly; if it is hidden and does not dare to expose itself, it is our task to help the person to be able to make the choice toward self-expression. Again, only the choice. But I don't think it is part of our legitimate therapeutic task to interfere in any way with the nature of a patient's nuclear self. It is an extremely interesting task to understand how the many, many variants of human personalities come about, but that is not a therapeutic task; it is a research task [p. 295].

Compare also in this connection Kohut's concept (1977b, pp. 58–62; see also Basch, 1992, p. 19) that self psychologists work with patients mainly on the level of compensatory structures and that when successful the analyst helps the patient to restore, expand, or otherwise improve his faltering compensatory structure for coping with the world and with his own subjective needs (see also, however, Gedo, 1989, p. 416).

Kohut (1984) also agreed with traditional psychoanalysts (e.g., Kramer, 1959; Schlessinger and Robbins, 1974, 1975, 1983) that the development of a self-analytic function suggests that the treatment has reached a successful conclusion:

> Clearly we are not in search of perfection, neither as an outcome of normal development nor as an outcome of that belated developmental move that occurs during analysis. It is therefore appropriate to consider an analysis to have terminated with a thoroughly satisfactory result if it has led to a reliably maintained life of well-being, creativeness, and inner balance, but one in which the former patient supports himself during times of stress by activating the self-analytic function [p. 154].

Summary and Conclusions

The principal argument of this chapter is that Kohut's Freudian traditions continued to illuminate his later investigations and concepts of narcissism and self psychology. In support of that view I have presented numerous examples from Kohut's writings regarding his definitions of psychoanalysis and self psychology, his concepts of transference and resistance, narcissism, basic methodologic concepts, metapsychologic vantage points, clinical method, clinical interpretation, the process of therapeutic change, and the benefits of treatment. In all of these categories, the cited material suggests that even in his final, most original writings, such as *The Restoration of the Self* (1977b) and *How Does Analysis Cure?* (1984), Kohut did not abandon his Freudian foundations but continued to draw on them in formulating his evolving clinical and theoretical concepts.

To appreciate the extent and depth of Kohut's continuing commitment to Freudian theory and therapy, it is helpful to review his pre–self-psychological "Lectures on Psychoanalytic Psychology" (1958–1960) and related essay on "Concepts and Theories of Psychoanalysis" (1963). Some of the most important concepts in those earlier works were carried over to his later conceptualizations regarding narcissism and self psychology (see also Ornstein, 1978a, p. 38).

A related theme of the present chapter concerns Kohut's posited syncretizing proclivity, which appears to have contributed significantly both to his earlier synthesis of Freudian theory and also to the subsequent integration of his new concepts with those of traditional psychoanalysis. Some suggestive evidence has been presented in this and the preceding chapter that

Kohut shared with Freud an unusually well developed capacity for syncretic reasoning.

The differences between Kohut's concepts and Freud's deal mainly with Kohut's revisions of and additions to traditional psychoanalysis—especially his concepts regarding the psychology of the self. These differences do not appear to be irreconcilable, however, as Kohut himself was the first to point out. Another source of differences between Kohut's and Freud's concepts concerns the predominant type of pathology that each investigated—classical neuroses in the case of Freud, in contrast to narcissistic personality disturbances studied and treated by Kohut. The latter differences are partially reconcilable but require some extensions and revisions of traditional psychoanalytic theory and technique, which Kohut attempted to develop.

Some writers have compared Kohut's concepts of narcissism and self psychology with the viewpoints of various other psychoanalytic schools and with the ideas of thinkers in other fields (see, e.g., the volume edited by Detrick and Detrick, 1989; cf. also Toulmin, 1986). With the exception of a few writers, however (e.g., Treurniet, 1980, 1983, 1989; Basch, 1981, 1984a,b,c, 1986, 1991; Wallerstein, 1983, 1985; Shane, 1985a,b; Shane and Shane, 1988, 1993; Stolorow, 1988; Gediman, 1989; Leider, 1989, 1996; Siegel, 1996), surprisingly little attention has been paid to the most obvious source of continuities with Kohut's work—the source that Kohut himself pointed to repeatedly—namely, Freud's theoretical system and clinical approach.

Despite the care that Kohut took to acknowledge and to spell out the continuities between his concepts and Freud's, a widespread misconception has persisted that his contributions were not Freudian but a deviation from traditional psychoanalysis. The misconception has been promulgated by both opponents and proponents of Kohut's concepts. Opponents have been intent on guarding Freudian theory from any possible apostasy—in spite of Freud's (1914b) assertion that any line of investigation that takes the phenomena of transference and resistance as its starting point is psychoanalytic, "even though it arrives at results other than my own" (p. 16). Some of Kohut's proponents, on the other hand, have attempted to parlay Kohut's extensions and revisions of Freudian theory into a "new paradigm" of depth psychology, despite Kohut's clear and forceful statements that self psychology represents an "unbroken continuum" with traditional psychoanalysis, that it adds something to psychoanalytic theory but does not replace it (e.g., 1980b, p. 505).

In a recent overview of self psychology since Kohut, Goldberg (1998) describes the development of three main branches within self psychology that compete for influence in the field: the traditional, intersubjective, and relational groups. What is most surprising in Goldberg's review is how little emphasis is given to Kohut's concepts, even among the traditional group of self psychologists. Goldberg observes, for example, that self psychology began with Kohut's writings and continues with "several of his ideas and concepts" (p. 240). Only several? The present chapter illustrates that self psychology is replete with Freudian concepts. With respect to the traditional group of self psychologists, Goldberg refers to only two contributions by Kohut: the concepts of selfobjects and of selfobject transferences. One is left to wonder, What happened to the psychology of the self? Goldberg appears to answer that question in his further statement that self psychology "is working itself free from an absolute allegiance to Kohut" (p. 242) and that "Kohut's original aim for self psychology to have an established place within organized psychoanalysis has given way to the rather surprising emergence embodied in a solid group of clinicians and investigators outside of the psychoanalysis that Kohut knew" (p. 240).

Kohut's Freudian vision may have become a sticking point for some self psychologists, preventing their accepting, perpetuating, and building on Kohut's concepts. In an attempt to establish its group self as an "independent center of initiative," self psychology may be trying to emancipate itself from both of its progenitors, Freud and Kohut. But as the philosopher Toulmin (1990) reminds us:

> The belief that, by cutting ourselves off from the inherited ideas of our cultures, we can 'clean the slate' and make a fresh start, is as illusory as the hope for a comprehensive system of theory that is capable of giving us timeless certainty and coherence [p. 178].

Kohut knew this well and thus did not hesitate to acknowledge the "unbroken continuum" between his concepts and Freud's views.

In conclusion, this chapter has not concerned itself with the validity of Kohut's concepts but has attempted to situate his contributions clinically and epistemologically in relation to Freud's theoretical system. Kohut's concepts of narcissism and the psychology of the self grew out of Freud's theories, and thus they include numerous continuities with and innovative extensions of Freud's views.

References

Aichorn, A. (1936), The narcissistic transference of the "juvenile impostor."
In *Delinquency and Child Guidance,* ed. O. Fleischmann, P. Kramer & H.
Ross. New York: International Universities Press, 1964, pp. 174–191.

Alexander, F. (1950), *Psychosomatic Medicine: Its Principles and Practices.* New
York: Norton.

Baker, H. & Baker, M. (1987), Heinz Kohut's self psychology: An overview.
Amer. J. Psychiatr., 149:1–9.

Baranger, W. (1991), Narcissism in Freud. In *Freud's "On Narcissism: An
Introduction,"* ed. J. Sandler, E. Person & P. Fonagy. New Haven, CT: Yale
University Press, pp. 108–130.

Basch, M. (1981), Selfobject disorders and psychoanalytic theory: A historical
perspective. *J. Amer. Psychoanal. Assn.,* 29:337–352.

———— (1983), Empathic understanding: A review of the concept and some
theoretical considerations. *J. Amer. Psychoanal. Assn.,* 31:101–126.

———— (1984a), The selfobject theory of motivation and the history of psychoanalysis. In *Kohut's Legacy: Contributions to Self Psychology,* ed.
P. Stepansky & A. Goldberg. Hillsdale, NJ: The Analytic Press, pp. 3–17.

———— (1984b), Selfobjects and selfobject transference: Theoretical implications. In *Kohut's Legacy: Contributions to Self Psychology,* ed. P. Stepansky &
A. Goldberg. Hillsdale, NJ: The Analytic Press, pp. 21–41.

———— (1984c), Selfobjects, development, and psychotherapy. In *Kohut's
Legacy: Contributions to Self Psychology,* ed. P. Stepansky & A. Goldberg.
Hillsdale, NJ: The Analytic Press, pp. 157–169.

———— (1986), Clinical theory and metapsychology: Incompatible or complementary? *Psychoanal. Rev.,* 73:261–271.

———— (1989), A comparison of Freud and Kohut: Apostasy or synergy? In
Self Psychology: Comparisons and Contrasts, ed. D. Detrick & S. Detrick.
Hillsdale, NJ: The Analytic Press, pp. 3–22.

——— (1991), Are selfobjects the only objects? Implications for psychoanalytic technique. In *The Evolution of Self Psychology: Progress in Self Psychology, Vol. 7*, ed. A. Goldberg. Hillsdale, NJ: The Analytic Press, pp. 3–15.

——— (1992), Self psychology and the transference. In *New Therapeutic Visions: Progress in Self Psychology, Vol. 8*, ed. A. Goldberg. Hillsdale, NJ: The Analytic Press, pp. 17–20.

Brandchaft, B. (1985), Resistance and defense: An intersubjective view. In *Progress in Self Psychology, Vol. 1*, ed. A. Goldberg. New York: Guilford, pp. 88–96.

Brenner, C. (1961), *An Elementary Textbook of Psychoanalysis*. New York: International Universities Press.

Breuer, J. & Freud, S. (1893–1895), Studies on hysteria. *Standard Edition*, 2:3–395. London: Hogarth Press, 1955.

Brill, A. (1913), *Psychoanalysis: Its Theories and Practical Application*. Philadelphia: Saunders.

Chessick, R. (1990), Review of *Learning from Kohut: Progress in Self Psychology, Vol. 4*, ed. A. Goldberg [Hillsdale, NJ: The Analytic Press, 1988]. *Psychoanal. Bks.*, 1:349–352.

Cooper, S. (1993), The self construct in psychoanalytic theory: A comparative view. In *The Self in Emotional Distress*, ed. Z. Segal & S. Blatt. New York: Guilford, pp. 41–67.

Corbett, L. & Kugler, P. (1989), The self in Jung and Kohut. In *Dimensions of Self Experience: Progress in Self Psychology, Vol. 5*, ed. A. Goldberg. Hillsdale, NJ: The Analytic Press, pp. 189–208.

De Groot, A. (1969), *Methodology: Foundations of Inference and Research in the Behavioral Sciences*. The Hague: Mouton.

Detrick, D. & Detrick, S., eds. (1989), *Self Psychology: Comparisons and Contrasts*. Hillsdale, NJ: The Analytic Press.

Deutsch, H. (1930), Hysterical fate neurosis. In *Neuroses and Character Types—Clinical Psychoanalytic Studies*. New York: International Universities Press, 1965, pp. 14–28.

——— (1959), Psychoanalytic therapy in the light of followup. *J. Amer. Psychoanal. Assn.*, 7:445–458.

Edelson, M. (1975), *Language and Interpretation in Psychoanalysis*. Chicago: University of Chicago Press.

Eissler, K. (1968), The relation of explaining and understanding in psychoanalysis—demonstrated by one aspect of Freud's approach to literature. *The Psychoanalytic Study of the Child*, 23:141–177. New York: International Universities Press.

Fast, I. (1990), Self and ego: A framework for their integration. *Psychoanal. Inq.*, 10:141–162.

Fenichel, O. (1945), *The Psychoanalytic Theory of Neurosis*. New York: Norton.

Ferenczi, S. (1913), Stages in the development of the sense of reality. In *Sex in Psychoanalysis*. New York: Basic Books, 1950, pp. 213–239.

Ferguson, M. (1981), Progress and theory change: The two analyses of Mr. Z. *The Annual of Psychoanalysis*, 9:133–160. New York: International Universities Press.

Fine, R. (1973), *The Development of Freud's Thought*. New York: Aronson.

Fisher, C. (1954), Dreams and perception: The role of preconscious and primary modes of perception in dream formation. *J. Amer. Psychoanal. Assn.*, 2:389–445.

—— & Paul, I. (1959), The effects of subliminal visual stimulation on images and dream: A validation study. *J. Amer. Psychoanal. Assn.*, 7:35–83.

Freud, A. (1936), *The Ego and the Mechanisms of Defense*. New York: International Universities Press, 1966.

Freud, S. (1894), The neuro-psychoses of defence. *Standard Edition*, 3:45–61. London: Hogarth Press, 1962.

—— (1895), Project for a scientific psychology. *Standard Edition*, 1:283–397. London: Hogarth Press, 1966.

—— (1900), The interpretation of dreams. *Standard Edition*, 4, 5:1–750. London: Hogarth Press, 1953.

—— (1901), The psychopathology of everyday life. *Standard Edition*, 6:1–290. London: Hogarth Press, 1960.

—— (1905a), Three essays on the theory of sexuality. *Standard Edition*, 7:130–243. London: Hogarth Press, 1958.

—— (1905b), Jokes and their relation to the unconscious. *Standard Edition*, 8:9–243. London: Hogarth Press, 1960.

—— (1907), Delusions and dreams in Jensen's "Gradiva." *Standard Edition*, 9:7–95. London: Hogarth Press, 1959.

—— (1909a), Analysis of a phobia in a five-year-old boy. *Standard Edition*, 10:5–149. London: Hogarth Press, 1955.

—— (1909b), Notes upon a case of obsessional neurosis. *Standard Edition*, 10:155–318. London: Hogarth Press, 1955.

—— (1910), The psycho-analytic view of psychogenic disturbance of vision. *Standard Edition*, 11:211–218. London: Hogarth Press, 1957.

—— (1911a), Psycho-analytic notes on an autobiographical account of a case of paranoia (dementia paranoides). *Standard Edition*, 12:9–82. London: Hogarth Press, 1958.

—— (1911b), Formulations on the two principles of mental functioning. *Standard Edition*, 12:218–226. London: Hogarth Press, 1958.

—— (1912), Recommendations to physicians practicing psycho-analysis. *Standard Edition*, 12:109–120. London: Hogarth Press, 1958.

—— (1913a), On beginning the treatment (Further recommendations on the technique of psycho-analysis I). *Standard Edition*, 12:123–144. London: Hogarth Press, 1958.

—— (1913b), Totem and taboo. *Standard Edition*, 13:1–161. London: Hogarth Press, 1955.

—— (1914a), Some reflections on schoolboy psychology. *Standard Edition*, 13:241–244. London: Hogarth Press, 1955.

—— (1914b), On the history of the psycho-analytic movement. *Standard Edition*, 14:7–66. London: Hogarth Press, 1957.

—— (1914c), On narcissism: An introduction. *Standard Edition*, 14:73–102. London: Hogarth Press, 1957.

———— (1915a), Instincts and their vicissitudes. *Standard Edition,* 14:117–140. London: Hogarth Press, 1957.

———— (1915b), Repression. *Standard Edition,* 14:146–158. London: Hogarth Press, 1957.

———— (1915c), The unconscious. *Standard Edition,* 14:166–215. London: Hogarth Press, 1957.

———— (1915-1916), Introductory lectures on psycho-analysis (Parts I and II). *Standard Edition,* 15:9–239. London: Hogarth Press, 1963.

———— (1916-1917). Introductory lectures on psycho-analysis (Part III). *Standard Edition,* 16:243–463. London: Hogarth Press, 1963.

———— (1916), Some character types met with in psycho-analytic work, II. Those wrecked by success. *Standard Edition,* 14:316–331. London: Hogarth Press, 1957.

———— (1917a), A difficulty in the path of psycho-analysis. *Standard Edition,* 17:135–144. London: Hogarth Press, 1955.

———— (1917b), A childhood recollection from "Dichtung und Wahrheit." *Standard Edition,* 17:145–156. London: Hogarth Press, 1955.

———— (1917c), Mourning and melancholia. *Standard Edition,* 14:243–258. London: Hogarth Press, 1957.

———— (1918), From the history of an infantile neurosis. *Standard Edition,* 17:7–122. London: Hogarth Press, 1955.

———— (1920), Beyond the pleasure principle. *Standard Edition,* 18:7–64. London: Hogarth Press, 1955.

———— (1921), Group psychology and the analysis of the ego. *Standard Edition,* 18:69–143. London: Hogarth Press, 1955.

———— (1923), The ego and the id. *Standard Edition,* 19:12–66. London: Hogarth Press, 1961.

———— (1924), The economic problem of masochism. *Standard Edition,* 19:159–170. London: Hogarth Press, 1961.

———— (1925), Negation. *Standard Edition,* 19:235–239. London: Hogarth Press, 1961.

———— (1926a), Inhibitions, symptoms and anxiety. *Standard Edition,* 20:87–172. London: Hogarth Press, 1959.

———— (1926b), The question of lay analysis. *Standard Edition,* 20:183–258. London: Hogarth Press, 1959.

———— (1927), Fetishism. *Standard Edition,* 21:152–157. London: Hogarth Press, 1961.

———— (1932), The acquisition and control of fire. *Standard Edition,* 22:187–193. London: Hogarth Press, 1964.

———— (1933), New introductory lectures on psychoanalysis. *Standard Edition,* 22:5–182. London: Hogarth Press, 1964.

———— (1937a), Analysis terminable and interminable. *Standard Edition,* 23:216–253. London: Hogarth Press, 1964.

———— (1937b), Constructions in analysis. *Standard Edition,* 23:255–269. London: Hogarth Press, 1964.

———— (1939), Moses and monotheism. *Standard Edition,* 23:3–140. London: Hogarth Press, 1964.

———— (1940a), An outline of psycho-analysis. *Standard Edition,* 23:144–207. London: Hogarth Press, 1958.

———— (1940b), Splitting of the ego in the process of defence. *Standard Edition,* 23:275–278. London: Hogarth Press, 1964.

Galatzer-Levy, R. (1991), Introduction: Self psychology searches for its self. In *The Evolution of Self Psychology: Progress in Self Psychology, Vol. 7,* ed. A. Goldberg. Hillsdale, NJ: The Analytic Press, pp. xi–xviii.

Gediman, H. (1989), Conflict and deficit models of psychopathology: A unificatory point of view. In *Self Psychology: Comparisons and Contrasts,* ed. D. Detrick & S. Detrick. Hillsdale, NJ: The Analytic Press, pp. 293–309.

Gedo, J. (1989), Self-psychology: A post-Kohutian view. In *Self Psychology: Comparisons and Contrasts,* ed. D. Detrick & S. Detrick. Hillsdale, NJ: The Analytic Press, pp. 415–428.

Glover, E. (1939), *Psychoanalysis.* London: John Bale.

———— (1947), Basic mental concepts: Their clinical and theoretical value. *Psychoanal. Quart.,* 16:482–506.

Goldberg, A., ed. (1978), *The Psychology of the Self: A Casebook.* New York: International Universities Press.

———— (1988), *A Fresh Look at Psychoanalysis: The View from Self Psychology.* Hillsdale, NJ: The Analytic Press.

———— (1990), *The Prisonhouse of Psychoanalysis.* Hillsdale, NJ: The Analytic Press.

———— (1998), Self psychology since Kohut. *Psychoanal. Quart.,* 67:240–255.

Golden, H. (1998), Review of *Heinz Kohut and the Psychology of the Self,* by A. Siegel (1996). *Psychoanal. Bks.,* 9:204–207.

Hartmann, H. (1927), *Die Grundlagen der Psychoanalyse.* Leipzig: Thieme.

———— (1939), *Ego Psychology and the Problem of Adaptation,* trans. D. Rapaport. New York: International Universities Press, 1958.

———— & Kris, E. (1945), The genetic approach in psychoanalysis. *The Psychoanalytic Study of the Child,* 1:11–30. New York: International Universities Press.

———— ———— & Lowenstein, R. (1946), Comments on the formation of psychic structure. *The Psychoanalytic Study of the Child,* 2:11–38. New York: International Universities Press.

Havens, L. (1986), A theoretical basis for the concepts of self and authentic self. *J. Amer. Psychoanal. Assn.,* 34: 363–378.

Hendrick, I. (1939), *Facts and Theories of Psychoanalysis.* New York: Knopf.

Hitschmann, E. (1913), *Freud's Theories of the Neuroses.* London: Kegan Paul.

Holt, R. (1983), On the meanings and antecedents of metapsychology. In Panel, Metapsychology: Its Cultural and Scientific Roots, rep. L. Chattah. *J. Amer. Psychoanal. Assn.,* 31:689–698.

Hughes, A. (1992), Letters from Sigmund Freud to Joan Riviere (1921–1939). *Internat. Rev. Psychoanal.,* 19:265–284.

Jones, E. (1948), *What Is Psychoanalysis?* New York: International Universities Press.

Kaplan, A. (1964), *The Conduct of Inquiry: Methodology for Behavioral Science.* New York: Harper & Row.

Kaplan, D. (1984), Reflections on the idea of personal fate and its psychopathology: Helene Deutsch's "hysterical fate neurosis" revisited. *Psychoanal. Quart.*, 53:240–266.

Kleitman, N. (1963), *Sleep and Wakefulness,* 2nd ed. Chicago: University of Chicago Press.

Kohut, H. (1959), Introspection, empathy, and psychoanalysis—An examination of the relationship between mode of observation and theory. *J. Amer. Psychoanal. Assn.,* 7:459–483. Also in *The Search for the Self, Vol. 1,* ed. P. Ornstein. New York: International Universities Press, 1978, pp. 205–232.

———— (1961), Discussion of D. Beres's paper, "The Unconscious Fantasy." Presented to the Chicago Psychoanalytic Society, Sept. 26. Abstract, *Bull. Phila. Assn. Psychoanal.,* 11:194–195, 1961.

———— (1966), Forms and transformations of narcissism. *J. Amer. Psychoanal. Assn.,* 14:243–272. Also in *The Search for the Self, Vol. 1,* ed. P. Ornstein. New York: International Universities Press, 1978, pp. 427–460.

———— (1968), The psychoanalytic treatment of narcissistic personality disorders: Outline of a systematic approach. *The Psychoanalytic Study of the Child,* 23:86–113. New York: International Universities Press. Also in *The Search for the Self, Vol. 1,* ed. P. Ornstein. New York: International Universities Press, 1978, pp. 477–509.

———— (1970), Narcissism as a resistance and as a driving force in psychoanalysis. Presented to the German Psychoanalytic Association, Berlin, October 10. In *The Search for the Self, Vol. 1,* ed. P. Ornstein. New York: International Universities Press, 1978, pp. 547– 561.

———— (1971), *The Analysis of the Self.* New York: International Universities Press (Monograph 4 of *The Psychoanalytic Study of the Child*).

———— (1972), Thoughts on narcissism and narcissistic rage. *The Psychoanalytic Study of the Child,* 27:350–400. New York: Quadrangle. Also in *The Search for the Self, Vol. 2,* ed. P. Ornstein. New York: International Universities Press, 1978, pp. 615–658.

———— (1972–1976), *Heinz Kohut: The Chicago Institute Lectures,* ed. P. Tolpin & M. Tolpin. Hillsdale, NJ: The Analytic Press, 1996.

———— (1975a), Remarks about the formation of the self. Presented to the Research Seminar, Chicago Institute for Psychoanalysis, January. In *The Search for the Self, Vol. 2,* ed. P. Ornstein. New York: International Universities Press, 1978, pp. 737–770.

———— (1975b), The self in history. *Newsletter of the Group for the Use of Psychology in History,* 3:3–10. Also in *The Search for the Self, Vol. 2,* ed. P. Ornstein. New York: International Universities Press, 1978, pp. 771–782.

———— (1976), Creativeness, charisma, group psychology: Reflections on the self-analysis of Freud. In *The Fusion of Science and the Humanities,* ed. J. Gedo & G. Pollack. *Psychological Issues,* Monograph 34/35. New York: International Universities Press, pp. 379–425. Also in *The Search for the Self, Vol. 2,* ed. P. Ornstein. New York: International Universities Press, 1978, pp. 793–843.

———— (1977a), Conclusion: The search for the analyst's self. In *The Search for the Self, Vol. 2,* ed. P. Ornstein. New York: International Universities Press, 1978, pp. 931–938.

———— (1977b), *The Restoration of the Self.* New York: International Universities Press.

———— (1978a), Self psychology and the sciences of man. In *The Search for the Self, Vol. 3,* ed. P. Ornstein. New York: International Universities Press, 1991, pp. 235–260.

———— (1978b), The search for the analyst's self. In *The Search for the Self, Vol. 2,* ed. P. Ornstein. New York: International Universities Press, 1978, pp. 931–938.

———— (1979a), The two analyses of Mr. Z. *Internat. J. Psychoanal.,* 60:3–27. Also in *The Search for the Self, Vol. 4,* ed. P. Ornstein. New York: International Universities Press, 1991, pp. 395–446.

———— (1979b), Four basic concepts in self psychology. In *The Search for the Self, Vol. 4,* ed. P. Ornstein. New York: International Universities Press, 1991, pp. 447–490.

———— (1979c), Remarks on the panel on "The Bipolar Self." *J. Amer. Psychoanal. Assn.,* 29:143–159, 1981 (rep. S. Meyers). Also in *The Search for the Self, Vol. 4,* ed. P. Ornstein. New York: International Universities Press, 1991, pp. 475–481.

———— (1980a), Greetings. Presented to the Third Annual Conference on the Psychology of the Self, Boston, October 31–November 2. In *The Search for the Self, Vol. 4,* ed. P. Ornstein. New York: International Universities Press, 1991, pp. 483–488.

———— (1980b), Selected problems in self psychological theory. In *The Search for the Self, Vol. 4,* ed. P. Ornstein. Madison, CT: International Universities Press, 1991, pp. 489–523.

———— (1981a), On empathy. Presented to the Fifth Conference on Self Psychology, Berkeley, CA, October. In *The Search for the Self, Vol. 4,* ed. P. Ornstein. New York: International Universities Press, 1991, pp. 525–535.

———— (1981b), Introspection, empathy, and the semicircle of mental health. *Internat. J. Psychoanal.,* 63:395–407, 1982. Also in *The Search for the Self, Vol. 4,* ed. P. Ornstein. New York: International Universities Press, 1991, pp. 537–567.

———— (1984), *How Does Analysis Cure?* ed. P. Stepansky & A. Goldberg. Chicago: University of Chicago Press.

———— & Levarie, S. (1950), On the enjoyment of listening to music. *Psychoanal. Quart.,* 19:64–87. Also in *The Search for the Self, Vol. 1,* ed. P. Ornstein. New York: International Universities Press, 1978, pp. 135–158.

———— & Seitz, P. (1963), Concepts and theories of psychoanalysis. In *Concepts of Personality,* ed. J. Wepman & R. Heine. Chicago: Aldine, pp. 113–141. Also in *The Search for the Self, Vol. 1,* ed. P. Ornstein. New York: International Universities Press, 1978, pp. 337– 374.

———— & Wolf, E. (1978), The disorders of the self and their treatment: An outline. *Internat. J. Psychoanal.,* 59:413–425.

Kramer, M. (1959), On the continuation of the analytic process after psychoanalysis: A self observation. *Internat. J. Psychoanal.*, 40:17–25.

Kris, A. (1994), Freud's treatment of a narcissistic patient. *Internat. J. Psychoanal.*, 75:649–664.

Kris, E. (1952), *Psychoanalytic Explorations in Art*. New York: International Universities Press.

Kubie, L. (1950), *Practical and Theoretical Aspects of Psychoanalysis*. New York: International Universities Press.

Laplanche, J. & Pontalis, J.-B. (1973), *The Language of Psycho-analysis*. New York: Norton.

Leider, R. (1989), Introduction. In *Dimensions of Self Experience: Progress in Self Psychology, Vol. 5*, ed. A. Goldberg. Hillsdale, NJ: The Analytic Press, pp. xi–xxvii.

———— (1996), The psychology of the self (self psychology). In *Textbook of Psychoanalysis*, ed. E. Nersessian & R. Kopff. Washington, DC: American Psychiatric Press, pp. 127–164.

Lewin, B. (1954), Sleep, narcissistic neurosis, and the analytic situation. *Psychoanal. Quart.*, 23:487–510.

Lichtenberg, J. (1981), The empathic mode of perception and alternative vantage points for psychoanalytic work. *Psychoanal. Inq.*, 1:329–355.

Markson, E. (1992), Transference and structure formation. In *New Therapeutic Visions: Progress in Self Psychology, Vol. 8*, ed. A. Goldberg. Hillsdale, NJ: The Analytic Press, pp. 199–211.

Meissner, W. (1986), Some notes on Hartmann's ego psychology and the psychology of the self. *Psychoanal. Inq.*, 6:499–521.

———— (1995a), The economic principle in psychoanalysis: I. Economics and energetics. *Psychoanal. Contemp. Thought*, 18:197–226.

———— (1995b), The economic principle in psychoanalysis: II. Regulatory principles. *Psychoanal. Contemp. Thought*, 18:227–260.

———— (1995c), The economic principle in psychoanalysis: III. Motivational principles. *Psychoanal. Contemp. Thought*, 18:261–292.

Menninger, K. (1937), *The Human Mind*. New York: Knopf.

Miller, J. (1985), How Kohut actually worked. In *Progress in Self Psychology, Vol. 1*, ed. A. Goldberg. New York: Guilford, pp. 13–30.

———— (1987), The transference neurosis from the standpoint of self psychology. *Psychoanal. Inq.*, 7:535–550.

Moore, B. & Fine, B., eds. (1990), *Psychoanalytic Terms and Concepts*. New Haven, CT: Yale University Press.

Nunberg, H. (1932), *Principles of Psychoanalysis: Their Application to the Neuroses*. New York: International Universities Press, 1955.

Ornstein, P., ed. (1978a), *The Search for the Self: Selected Writings of Heinz Kohut: 1950–1978, Vol. 1*. New York: International Universities Press, pp. 1–509.

———— (1978b), *The Search for the Self, 1950–1978, Vol. 2*. New York: International Universities Press, pp. 511–969.

———— (1978c), Introduction: The evolution of Heinz Kohut's psychoanalytic psychology of the self. In *The Search for the Self, Vol. 1,* ed. P. Ornstein. New York: International Universities Press, pp. 1–106.

—— (1991a), *The Search for the Self, 1978–1981, Vol. 3,* ed. P. Ornstein. Madison, CT: International Universities Press, pp. 1–393.

—— (1991b), *The Search for the Self, 1978–1981, Vol. 4,* ed. P. Ornstein. Madison, CT: International Universities Press, pp. 395–848.

Poetzl, O. (1917), Experimentell erregte Traumgilder in ihren Bezieungen zum indirekten Sehen. *Zeitschr. Neurol. Psychiat.,* 37:278–349.

Rado, S. (1925), The economic principle in psychoanalytic technique. *Internat. J. Psychoanal.,* 6:35–44.

Rapaport, D. (1944), The scientific methodology of psychoanalysis. In *Collected Papers of David Rapaport,* ed. M. Gill. New York: Basic Books, 1967, pp. 165–220.

—— (1960), *The Structure of Psychoanalytic Theory: A Systematizing Attempt.* New York: International Universities Press.

Rubovits-Seitz, P. (1998), *Depth-Psychological Understanding: The Methodologic Grounding of Clinical Interpretations.* Hillsdale, NJ: The Analytic Press.

Schlessinger, N. & Robbins, F. (1974), Assessment and follow-up in psycho-analysis. *J. Amer. Psychoanal. Assn.,* 22:542–547.

—— & —— (1975), The psychoanalytic process: Recurrent patterns of con-flict and change in ego functions. *J. Amer. Psychoanal. Assn.,* 23:761–782.

—— & —— (1983), *A Developmental View of the Psychoanalytic Process: Follow-up Studies and Their Consequences.* New York: International Uni-versities Press.

Schwaber, E. (1987), Review of *Kohut's Legacy: Contributions to Self Psy-chology,* ed. P. Stepansky & A. Goldberg (1984). *J. Amer. Psychoanal. Assn.,* 35:743–750.

Seitz, P. (1963a), Representations of structures in the concrete imagery of dreams: A clinical method for investigating the structural theory. Presented to the Chicago Psychoanalytic Society, January 22. Abstract, *Bull. Phila. Assn. Psychoanal.,* 13:89–94, 1963.

—— (1963b), Representations of repression in the concrete imagery of dreams: Implications for the theory of repression. Presented to the American Psychoanalytic Association, St. Louis, May 3.

—— (1967), Representations of adaptive and defense mechanisms in the concrete imagery of dreams. Presented to the Chicago Psychoanalytic Society, January 24. Abstract, *Bull. Phila. Assn. Psychoanal.,* 18:91–95, 1968.

—— (1969), Freud's theory of dreams: Reevaluation and revisions. Presented to the Chicago Psychoanalytic Society, November 25. Abstract, *Bull. Phila. Assn. Psychoanal.,* 20:334–337, 1970.

—— & Molholm, H. (1947), The relation of mental imagery to hallucina-tions. *Arch. Neurol. Psychiatr.,* 57:469–480.

Shane, M. (1985a), Summary of Kohut's "The Self Psychological Approach to Defense and Resistance." In *Progress in Self Psychology, Vol. 1,* ed. A. Goldberg. New York: Guilford, pp. 69–79.

—— (1985b), Self psychology's additions to mainstream concepts of defense and resistance. In *Progress in Self Psychology, Vol. 1,* ed. A. Goldberg. New York: Guilford, pp. 80–82.

—— & Shane, E. (1988), Pathways to integration: Adding to the self psychology model. In *Learning from Kohut: Progress in Self Psychology, Vol. 4,* ed. A. Goldberg. New York: Guilford, pp. 71–78.

—— & —— (1993), Self psychology after Kohut: One theory or many? *J. Amer. Psychoanal. Assn.,* 41:777–797.

Siegel, A. (1996), *Heinz Kohut and the Psychology of the Self.* London: Routledge.

Silberer, H. (1909), Report on a method of eliciting and observing certain symbolic hallucination-phenomena. In *Organization and Pathology of Thought,* ed. D. Rapaport. New York: Columbia University Press, 1951, pp. 195–207.

—— (1912), On symbol-formation. In *Organization and Pathology of Thought,* ed. D. Rapaport. New York: Columbia University Press, 1951, pp. 208–233.

—— (1919), The dream: Introduction to the psychology of dreams, (trans. J. Blevner). *Psychoanal. Rev.,* 42:36, 1955.

Smith, D. (1985), Freud's developmental approach to narcissism: A concise review. *Internat. J. Psychoanal.,* 66:489–497.

Sterba, R. (1934), The fate of the ego in analytic therapy. *Internat. J. Psychoanal.,* 15:117–126.

—— (1942), *Introduction to the Psychoanalytic Theory of the Libido.* New York: Nervous & Mental Disease.

Stolorow, R. (1985), Toward a pure psychology of inner conflict. In *Progress in Self Psychology, Vol. 1,* ed. A. Goldberg. New York: Guilford, pp. 193–201.

—— (1988), Integrating self psychology and classical psychoanalysis: An experience-near approach. In *Learning from Kohut, Progress in Self Psychology, Vol. 4,* ed. A. Goldberg. New York: Guilford, pp. 63–70.

—— Brandchaft, B. & Atwood, G. (1987), *Psychoanalytic Treatment: An Intersubjective Approach.* Hillsdale, NJ: The Analytic Press.

Sucharov, M. (1992), Quantum physics and self psychology: toward a new epistemology. In *New Therapeutic Visions: Progress in Self Psychology, Vol. 8,* ed. A. Goldberg. Hillsdale, NJ: The Analytic Press, pp. 199–211.

Tausk, V. (1933), On the origin of the "influencing machine" in schizophrenia. *Psychoanal. Quart.,* 2:519–556.

Terman, D. (1989), Therapeutic change: Perspectives of self psychology. *Psychoanal. Inq.,* 9:88–100.

Tolpin, P. & Tolpin, M. (1996), Preface. In *Heinz Kohut: The Chicago Institute Lectures,* ed. P. Tolpin & M. Tolpin. Hillsdale, NJ: The Analytic Press, pp. ix–xxii.

Toulmin, S. (1986), Self psychology as a "postmodern" science. *Psychoanal. Inq.,* 6:459–477.

—— (1990), *Cosmopolis: The Hidden Agenda of Modernity.* Chicago: University of Chicago Press.

Treurniet, N. (1980), On the relation between concepts of self and ego in Kohut's psychology of the self. *Internat. J. Psychoanal.,* 61:325–333.

——— (1983), Psychoanalysis and self psychology: A metapsychological essay with a clinical illustration. *J. Amer. Psychoanal. Assn.,* 31:59–100.

——— (1989), On having and giving value. In *The Psychoanalytic Core,* ed. H. Blum, E. Weinshel & F. Rodman. Madison, CT: International Universities Press, pp. 394–420.

Waelder, R. (1960), *Basic Theory of Psychoanalysis.* New York: International Universities Press.

Wallerstein, R. (1983), Self psychology and "classical" psychoanalytic psychology—the nature of their relationship: A review and overview. In *Reflections on Self Psychology,* ed. J. Lichtenberg & S. Kaplan. Hillsdale, NJ: The Analytic Press, pp. 313–338.

——— (1985), How does self psychology differ in practice? *Internat. J. Psychoanal.,* 66:391–404.

Wepman, J. & Heine, R. (eds.) (1963), *Concepts of Personality.* Chicago: Aldine.

Wyss, D. (1966), *Depth Psychology: A Critical History—Development, Problems, Crises.* New York: Norton.

Zeigarnik, B. (1927), Das Behalten erledigter und underledigter Handlungen. *Psychol. Forschr.,* 9:1–85.

Index